Don J. Hibbard Ph.D., is an architectural historian.
He has taught a number of university courses on rock
music.

Carol Kaleialoha supervises and directs projects in
the fields of industrial sociology and psychology.

THE ROLE OF
ROCK

DON J. HIBBARD
with
CAROL KALEIALOHA

Discography by JAY JUNKER

A SPECTRUM BOOK

Prentice-Hall, Inc., Englewood Cliffs, N.J. 07632

Library of Congress Cataloging in Publication Data

Hibbard, Don
   The role of rock.

   "A Spectrum Book."
   Bibliography: p.
   Discography: p.
   Includes index.
   1. Rock music—History and criticism.   2. Music and
society.   I. Kaleialoha, Carol.   II. Title.
ML3634.H5   1983   784.5′4′009   83-4511
ISBN 0-13-782458-0
ISBN 0-13-782331-6 (pbk.)

This book is available at a special discount when ordered in
bulk quantities. Contact Prentice-Hall, Inc., General
Publishing Division, Special Sales, Englewood Cliffs, N.J. 07632.

10 9 8 7 6 5 4 3 2 1

ISBN 0-13-782441-6 {PBK.}

ISBN 0-13-782458-0

Editorial/Production supervision by Alberta Boddy
Manufacturing buyer: Doreen Cavello

Prentice-Hall International, Inc., *London*
Prentice-Hall of Australia Pty. Limited, *Sydney*
Prentice-Hall Canada Inc., *Toronto*
Prentice-Hall of India Private Limited, *New Delhi*
Prentice-Hall of Japan, Inc., *Tokyo*
Prentice-Hall of Southeast Asia Pte, Ltd., *Singapore*
Whitehall Books Limited, Wellington, *New Zealand*
Editoria Prentice-Hall do Brasil Ltda., *Rio de Janeiro*

We all remember that time. It was no different for me than for others. Yet we all do tell each other over and over again the particularities of the events we shared, and the repetition, the listening, is as if we are saying, "It was like that for you, too? Then that confirms it, yes, it was so, it must have been, I wasn't imagining things."

Doris Lessing
The Memoirs of a Survivor

Contents

Preface

This book has been in the brain nine years and essentially it has evolved as an attempt to come to grips with the powerful musical experience of the late 1960s. Its goal is to decipher the role rock has played in the lives of its audience, and to trace rock's development over time, from the inception of rock 'n' roll in the 1950s through the arrival of New Wave music in the 1980s. Primarily concerned with the influence of rock music on the lives of its listeners, this book will not attempt to record all the performers or all the musical moments that have made rock a major commercial and artistic force. Other books have performed this task well enough already, including those by Charlie Gillett, Jerry Hopkins, Arnold Shaw, and Nik Cohn. Also, reference works such as Lillian Roxon's *Rock Encyclopedia*, Norman N. Nite's *Rock On*, Charlie Gillett's *Rock Almanac*, and Joel Whitburn's *Record Research* series have already compiled much of the minutiae of the music.

Rather than define rock in terms of its personalities, this book will discuss the music in terms of its social function. It will focus on the motivations behind the music, its impact on its audience, and its relationship to society. In short, this book will attempt to unveil rock's connection to life and its symbols. Thus, it will view the music in the light of its associations, images, and myths. It will speak of rock as a social phenomenon.

By considering rock within its social context, this book casts various performers in larger-than-life roles; but this can only be expected, because these people were indeed the heroes of their age and age group. Their status was greatly magnified within the youth culture, and we have portrayed these people on this scale in an attempt to accurately capture their impact on the imagination of their audience.

In contrast to our approach, a number of people have claimed that rock must be viewed first and foremost as a musical form, or a pop/media experience, or a commercial product. Such viewpoints provide valuable analytical insights into rock and are considered within the text. However, these aspects of the music did not catapult rock to national prominence. These were not the factors that made rock important. Although these viewpoints throw some light on the music, they are more illuminated by the rock experience than it is by them. They do not confer significance upon the sound, but instead acquire their viability from the music's social vitality, its spirit and soul.

In creating this book, Carol and I have received invaluable assistance from many quarters. First and foremost, we must thank Joe Murray, Prentice-Hall's representative in Hawaii, whose unflagging confidence in this project over the past eight years finally led to a contract. Without his faith there would be no book. Joe, mahalo.

Next, Seth Markov and J.W., "Manu" Junker (that's pronounced Yunker), need special mention. We are totally indebted to them for patiently explaining what musically literate people perceive music to be, and translating rock into these terms. They also reviewed the manuscript and generously shared all sorts of information on rock with us. Again, Seth and Manu, mahalo for your time, energy, and support.

Other people also scrutinized and commented on the manuscript or segments of it. Their critical insights have greatly enhanced the final results. Thank you, Ken Ames, Reuel Denney, Alan Gowans, Hugo Keesing, Jim McCutcheon, and J.M. Neil. Your assistance was invaluable, and as the Beatles told Jude, you've taken a sad song and made it better. Further appreciation is extended to J.M. Neil for gathering certain bits of information unavailable to us in Honolulu.

A number of other persons have also provided input and support over the years. Although too numerous to mention all of them, special thanks go out to Paul Sherman, Gary Tasaka, Charlie Hodell, Greg Crawford, Joe Seldin, Floyd Matson, Owen Gan, Daniel Warner, Nathan Napoka, Richard Simmons, Jim Singer, Gail Vidunas, Steve Rice, Susan Murray, John Couture, Richard Rubin, Karson Mathers, Gerry Johnson, Frank Oreste, Merle Wells, Larry Jones, Ward Wakeland, Austin Kelly, Carl Schumaker, Ralston Nagata, Ralph Brande, Betty Neville, Alberta Boddy, Norma Ledbetter, Lynne Lumsden, and the reference librarians at the Hawaii State Library's main branch. Mahalo, one and all.

Finally, an undertaking of this sort must depend upon much information generated and published by others. We have tried to acknowledge these important sources in the footnotes and recommended further reading. Also, we employed a number of lyrical quotations to enhance and support our arguments. We would have liked to use more, but the cost made this impossible. However, a select circle of publishers very graciously allowed us free use of their materials. We extend our thanks to Alkatraz Corner Music, representatives for County Joe McDonald; ATM Music, representatives for the Blues Image; Interworld Music Group, representatives for Jimi Hendrix; Ice Nine Publishing Company, representatives for the Grateful Dead; Fleetwood Mac & Welsh Witch Music, representatives for Stevie Nicks; Island Music, representatives for Cat Stevens; Icebag Corporation, representatives for the Jefferson Airplane; and Gold Hill Music, Inc., representatives for Stephen Stills. We greatly appreciate your cooperation and understanding in this matter.

Don J. Hibbard

1

Rock in Theory

"Museums are cemeteries. . . . Great paintings should be where people hang out. The only thing where it's happening is on the radio and records, that's where people hang out. . . . Music is the only thing that's in tune with what's happening."

Bob Dylan

One of the most significant art forms to rise out of recent American culture is rock music. A generation grew up with it; danced and loved to it; dug on it; smoked, tripped, and rapped with it; and eventually united behind it. Rock, like they, was a product of, and a reaction to, a prosperous, urban, bureaucratic/computerized corporate state, whose heritage stressed, "life, liberty, and the pursuit of happiness." Although a spawn of modern America, rock differed from almost all the new products of 1950s civilization by reacting against the accepted style of life. The music defied the traditional middle-class standards of taste, was associated with antisocial values, and with time it came to embody a way of confronting the "system" on a day-to-day basis. With its maturity in the middle 1960s, it became the major art form of a nascent counterculture and a vehicle for the articulate expression of a growing discontent with the American way of "earning a living."

More than an expression of youthful rebellion, rock performed a critical role in defining and materializing a new world view; a vision based upon the images slipping through the minds of the generation coming of age. The late 1960s proved to be a rare instance when the fabric of the social order tore apart, revealing extraordinary options and creating new social forms. Rock, the medium

1

through which the nascent cosmos flowed, captured and encapsulated the "rush" of the period.

That time has passed. Energy levels subside, possible impossibilities fade. Within a decade an alternate approach to life has all but disappeared, absorbed into that greater whole, America. However, the memory that something happened remains. What happened? What did it mean? More importantly, what does it mean today? These are the guiding questions behind this retrospective.

ROCK AS ART

As a nonplastic, nongraphic product of the McLuhanistic age of electronics, rock fulfills the traditional functions associated with art: those of "substitute imagery," "illustration," and "conviction and persuasion."[1] Rock's achievement of these ends on an audio-visceral level well explains the nature of the medium, its appeal, and its effectiveness as a molder of perception. Throughout this book the concept of rock as an art form that articulates, reflects, and reinforces its audience-engendered reality will be developed and analyzed.

In the past, when the appearance of something needed to be preserved, art made pictures, which served as substitute images. Although rock music can not preserve appearances, it may act as an art of substitute imagery, as in the songs of the late 1960s, for example, which depicted drug experiences. Their intense musical and emotional shifts, intersticed with fragmentary lyrical thoughts and images, corresponded with the actual experience. The songs encapsulated, glorified, and preserved a drug-induced trip.[2]

Illustrative arts produce images which are used in whole or part to tell stories or record events. Rock neither tells stories nor records events in a traditional manner. Marshall McLuhan discussed the decline of the sequential story in *Understanding Media*. Many rock songs reflect his discussion by abandoning the uninterrupted narrative. Frequently their lyrics capture snatches of experience, while the music provides a continuity and emotional tenor, creating an audio-visual panorama. Songs center primarily on situations rather than events, and those of the late 1960s, which concentrate on specific moments, do not describe a sequence so much as they relate a feeling toward the whole. They portray and interact with the emotional significance of the event; they sense, experience, and live the scene, rather than observe and record it. Good examples of this genre are Joni Mitchell's "Woodstock," Crosby, Stills, Nash, and Young's "Ohio," and the Jefferson Airplane's "Won't You Try/Saturday Afternoon."

To illustrate the difference between rock songs and mainstream reporting, and their respective audiences, a comparison may be made between Ralph Gleason's account of the Golden Gate Park Be-In of January 14, 1967, for the *San Francisco Chronicle*[3] and the Jefferson Airplane's song, "Won't You Try/ Saturday Afternoon," part of their *After Bathing at Baxter's* album of January 1968, which later celebrated that same event.

Gleason, one of the first journalists to be entranced by the Sixties rock phenomenon, was an articulate and respected commentator on the subject. After serving as a bridge between the *Chronicle* audience and the rock world, he went on to be a founder and editor of *Rolling Stone* magazine. Yet, despite his understanding of the events going on around him, Gleason reported the Be-In as an observer, an outsider looking in. Restricted by his medium, his readership and his role as reporter, Gleason found the gathering of tribes to be a "nonspecific mass meeting" with its participants "interested in the great light show of nature and themselves." He wrote of "designer's dreams," "clean long-haired males," and even included the necessary sexual fantasy in the form of an innocent, nude three-year-old child. The entire coverage consisted of observations and implications rather than actions and sensations.

In the Jefferson Airplane song, on the other hand, the event was "a time for growing and a time for knowing love." Described in terms of "silver sunlight," the Be-In provided a way to "meet someone," "see," and be "set free." Although the lyric was difficult to distinguish, the jubilant music and the phrases heard relayed the message. The song presented the scattered sensations of the day, mentioned LSD as a major catalyst (a subject totally ignored by Gleason), and allowed the listener to experience the emotions of the moment. Furthermore, it urged others to create similar scenes in their own lives—"Won't you tryyyyyyyyyyyy." The song not only recorded an involvement with the world and life, but advocated it, an approach completely anathemic to the typical, passive news report. This is the way in which rock serves as an art of illustration even when it tells no story in a traditional sense.

Arts of conviction and persuasion either set forth the fundamental convictions and realized ideals of a society, or create images to persuade people to form different beliefs. Usually arts of conviction are substantial and assume architectural or sculptural forms, while arts of persuasion are more ephemeral. Rock music in the middle and late 1960s primarily functioned as an art of persuasion. Consciously and unconsciously it propagated an alternate way of viewing our society and induced its audience to consider, if not accept, new values and beliefs about how life should be lived. The songs had a tremendous effect upon their listeners and were one of the greatest forces in the creation of the period's much publicized "generation gap." Rock reflected the growing discontent of certain young people and gave it a voice. It permitted individuals to know they were not alone in viewing the dominant culture as repressive and forced many young people, who might have merely accepted the America culture in terms of their parents, to scrutinize their society more closely.

By becoming the premier art form of the counterculture of the late 1960s, rock reached an apex. At its pinnacle the music was a powerful sound to behold. Boldly proclaiming itself to be the crown of creation, it reflected and reinforced the realities and aspirations of its audience. It was "what was going down." Through its acid infused dimension a glorious tale, suffused with rebellious, triumph-bound visions, came to life.

However, the late 1960s are but one aspect of a larger whole. If any significance is to be attached to the rock experience, the history of its development must be grasped, and this must be done in light of its social context. By considering the continuum of rock, from the great domestic annoyance of the 1950s to the 1970s music to consume by, a clearer conception can be achieved of where we have been and where we are bound.

An Historical Framework

Rock may be traced through four major stages:

1955–1959:	inception
1959–1965:	formulation
1965–1969:	maturity
1969–present:	stylization

The initial period, sparked with intuitive creation, was a time of cultural transition when the old ways were deemed inoperable and a new approach to life tentatively emerged. People began to realize the possibility of ordering the world in terms of their own experiences, and new forms, reflecting the emerging frames of reference, exploded upon the scene. The loudest of these new forms was rock 'n' roll. Embodied in such personalities as Elvis Presley, Bill Haley and the Comets, Chuck Berry, Little Richard, and Jerry Lee Lewis, rock 'n' roll burst upon American life as a totally new, and to many a discomforting, sensation. It was energetic, raucous, and sexual, the antithesis of what passed as life in fifties' America. Like a beacon, it beckoned to those floundering on the stagnant sea of middle class complacency. It was denounced, defended, thwarted, stifled, and eventually sterilized as the 1950s turned into the 1960s and the inception period merged into a time of transition.

In this second era, those who were consciously aware of the new form attempted to explore and express its possibilities in a systematic way. At first, record companies intent on capitalizing on the new fad, undertook such explorations. Their attempts to package rock 'n' roll castrated the genre and decimated its early vitality. Eventually, however, artists with a deeper affection for the music than corporate record producers came to the fore, and from the summer of 1963 onward a more serious, "grassroots" music, reminiscent of the mid-1950s rock 'n' roll, appeared. Such performers as the Beach Boys, Beatles, and Rolling Stones, and later Bob Dylan, the Animals, and the Byrds, introduced new forms and new combinations of old forms, and reinstated the individual as the measure of musical experience. These artists revitalized the earlier rock 'n' roll sound, and in time this forceful music was coupled with more meaningful lyrics to create a new style, commonly referred to as *folk rock*.

Once this new style was formulated, the path was clear for the mature expression of the new orientation. A golden age, presaged by Bob Dylan's *Highway 61 Revisited*, blossomed with the advent of psychedelic rock. Such "great masters" as the Beatles (from *Sergeant Pepper* to the end of their collaboration), the Jefferson Airplane, Jimi Hendrix, Janis Joplin, the Who, the Rolling Stones, the Doors, and the Cream, perfected the rock idiom. Entering through the door opened by Dylan's personal and acerbic lyrics, the musicians became the shamans of the age. Through their amplified artistry the thoughts of a generation spewed forth and a dormant culture came to recognize itself.

This golden age could not be maintained once the desired perfection was found to be unattainable and disillusionment set in. With this rude awakening from the utopian dream, a fourth, and apparently final, protracted period of stylization has followed. The visions and aspirations of the late 1960s have faded with its audience's dwindling confidence in its ability to control the world. Rock continues as a style, deftly nurturing itself, maintained by habit, inertia, or the veneration of long usage. Elaborately self-conscious, it has assumed a multitude of forms, ranging from heavy metal to fusion, 1950s revival to glitter, southern country rock to the California sound, disco to punk and new wave. It has become an accepted part of American civilization, as much in tune with daily life as Barbie dolls, Budweisers, Ban Roll-On, and Big Macs. Assimilated into the ebb and flow of middle-class society, stripped of its antagonist role, rock has evolved into a respectable, albeit superficial, element within the larger matrix that is America. Divested of any deep social meaning, it is now an end in itself, to be played with, refined and eventually polished for the delectation of connoisseurs, whose appearance has marked the final stage of decadence.

This four-phase sequence of development is not unique to rock, and may be observed in much of human creation. Art historians have discussed entire ages, such as classical Greece, renaissance Italy, and colonial America, in terms of similar patterns.[4] By ordering our musical experiences of the past twenty-five years within such a context, we may step back and more objectively view the dramatic changes which have marked rock's brief existence. Such a model facilitates the analysis of the immediate past and present, and makes the entire scenario more comprehensible.

NOTES

[1]For a further explication of art's traditional functions, see Alan Gowans, *The Unchanging Arts* (Philadelphia and New York: J.B. Lippincott Company, 1971).

[2]A further discussion of the drug songs of the mid-1960s appears in Chapter Five.

[3]For Gleason's account, see Ralph J. Gleason, *The Jefferson Airplane and the San Francisco Sound* (New York: Ballantine Books, 1969) pp. 40–43.

[4]See Alan Gowans, *Images of American Living* (Philadelphia and New York: J.B. Lippincott Company, 1964) pp. 120–123.

2

In the Beginning

"If it screams for truth rather than help; if it commits itself with a courage it can't be sure it really has; if it stands up and admits something is wrong but doesn't insist on blood, then it's rock 'n' roll."

Pete Townshend

Combine a traditional European ballad form with an irregular Afro-American rhythm, a vocal and/or instrumental ejaculation to break up or distort the melody, and in 1955 you have a new sound. They called it rock 'n' roll, and it differed remarkably from the popular music presented on *Your Hit Parade* and sung by the likes of Patti Page, Eddie Fisher, and Rosemary Clooney.

The major distinction between rock 'n' roll and Tin Pan Alley lay in its use of musical forms derived from the blues, especially its rhythm. Rather than accent the strong (first and third of four) beats in a song, rock 'n' roll accented the off (second and fourth) beats, and threw teenagers into a mild state of hysteria with its pa-BOOM, pa -BOOM, instead of the more sedate Boom-pa, Boom-pa. The new music also drew heavily upon the blues for its structure embracing the traditional twelve-bar blues phrase structure of $4+4+2+2$, and using the dominant type 7 chord. In comparison, pop composers wrote in a 16- or 32-bar form, usually with all four-bar phrases, and preferred major 7 and 6 chords and minor 7 chords. Furthermore, rock 'n' roll relied on the typical I–IV–V blues chord progression almost exclusively, creating much simpler harmonies and melodies than the pop establishment with its penchant for more sophisticated,

7

variated chord progressions, faster harmonic rhythms, and bridge sections. Sometimes rock 'n' roll also employed bridges, a rarity in blues songs, but limited the frequency of chord changes, following the country and western model of "going to the IV." Pulsating around its beat, rock 'n' roll made sophistication seem irrelevant and Tin Pan Alley seem schmaltzy. It knocked everybody over and made an amazing break with the past.

Rock 'n' roll drew heavily upon the rhythm and blues for its substance. This Black, urban style of music had gained a considerable following during the late 1940s thanks to the full-time programming of it by a number of radio stations, including WDIA in Memphis. The influence of such rhythm and blues performers as Louis Jordan, Muddy Waters, Clyde McPhatter, Joe Turner, Roy Brown, Howlin' Wolf, B.B. King, Little Walter, and many others can easily be detected in the rock 'n' roll music of the 1950s, and such songs as Louis Jordan's "Saturday Night Fish Fry" (1949), Stick McGhee's "Drinkin' Wine Spo-Dee-O-Dee" (1949), Professor Longhair's "Rockin' with Fes" (1951), J.B. Lenoir's "Let's Roll" (1951), and the Dominoes' "The Deacon Moves In" (1952) are for all intents and purposes musically identical in character to what would later be called rock 'n' roll. However, to white audiences rock 'n' roll was new and different, and very quickly established itself as the premier music of the nation. It attained such status not on its musical qualities alone (indeed, some critics questioned if it had any musical merit), but rather through its fulfillment of certain social needs.

As a number of people have noted,[1] from the start rock 'n' roll could be viewed as a teenage cult with its own distinct deities, values, and patterns of behavior. Transcending mere entertainment, it was alive, unrestrained excitement, stimulation, and action. To fully appreciate the significance of the new music, and to understand its place in American society, it should be viewed as a social experience, as an art form produced by social interaction, with its own situationally emergent symbolic meanings.

BACK TO THE BASICS: SEX

From its hazy inception[2] rock 'n' roll has been associated with sex and antisocial behavior. For example, on September 9, 1956, Ed Sullivan's *Toast of the Town* televised a performance of Elvis Presley from the waist up in an attempt to mollify any fears of impropriety. Despite such measures, Jack Gould, the television critic for the *New York Times,* still took offense. In his review of the program's main attraction, Gould recounted Presley's burlesque-like behavior in previous television appearances and declared that the wordless singing and tongue movements, which Elvis engaged in during the Sullivan show, were disgusting and especially distasteful.[3]

As late as 1958 Sigmund Spaeth, the editor of the *Music Journal*, condemned Elvis's "filthy" performances with their "whining, moaning and suggestive lyrics" which "blandly offered a vicarious sexual experience."[4]

Although rock 'n' roll's "leer-ics" in general received inordinate criticism,[5] few nasty lines ever reached the white listening audience's ears due to a lack of airplay. Rare exceptions, such as "Woman Love," Gene Vincent's sensual surprise on the flip side of "Be Bop a Lula" (1956) did happen along, but rock 'n' roll's eroticism emanated primarily from its aura, its beat, and if you were lucky enough to see a concert, its live performance. The pervasive intensity of sound, for so it seemed in the mid-1950s, compelled wanton expressions of freedom, emotional release, and physical movement. These outbursts, coupled with Elvis's notorious gyrating pelvis and the obvious musical associations with rhythm and blues songs, which frequently express more lurid lyrics, spelled only one thing for monitors of morality: S-E-X, the corruptor of youthful innocence, the downfall of civilization.

Such moral indignation and criticism reflected the social context of the time. A society that had objected to the use of the words *seduction* and *virgin* in Otto Preminger's *The Moon is Blue* (1953) certainly would not abide the obvious lasciviousness of rock 'n' roll. A reaction was inevitable; that the reaction was not more vehement—after all, the decade's equivalents of Morton of Merry Mount[6] did not find themselves pilloried—further revealed the complexion of the period.

The time was one of transition, leading to the redirection of accepted social norms and art forms, and the emergence of new ones such as rock 'n' roll.[7] The reknowned scholar, Max Lerner, recognized that at mid-century America was "engaged in a complicated struggle in the building up of definitions as to what is permissible and truly expressive in the area of sexual behavior."[8] Old values and norms, including the small town, genteel sexual codes, that dominated American life for so long, were on the verge of crumbling. Although they received outward support, a number of sexual codes had become empty forms. Subjected to "patterned evasion," the codes perpetuated hypocritical masks of propriety in the face of general acceptance of clandestine violation. Sociologist James Woodward labeled the practice *functional deviousness*.[9] The Everly Brothers depicted this hypocrisy in "Wake Up Little Susie" (1957). The song revels in the plight of a couple who supposedly went to the movies and "fell asleep." Waking at four o'clock in the morning, the boy tries to rouse his date, while fretting over what to tell her mama and pop and all their friends who'll say "ooo-la-la." The parents, representatives of social authority, were the major obstacles with which to contend. The teasing "ooo-la-la" by the peers, while embarrassing, is not harsh or critical, but rather a light-hearted jibe at the couple for being caught. The song's music and delivery supported the classmates' casual attitude, and implied that whatever the couple did it was not that bad. However, the parental sword of Damocles hung over Susie and her boyfriend, and their reputations were badly blemished. Such was life in the 1950s; hollow propriety ruled all.

The increasing covert sexual activity, reported by Alfred C. Kinsey and his associates, began to foster, if not demand, more realistic representations of sex. Rock 'n' roll, like *Playboy* magazine and the French films of Brigitte Bardot, responded to this demand, found a ready audience, and introduced a more open approach to sex in middle-class lives. In presenting this new public eroticism, rock 'n' roll contributed to the social dialogue that redefined permissible sexual behavior, and helped lay the foundations for the sexual revolution of the late 1960s.

So reads one level of reality. However, another parallel, more immediate level also existed within the minds of the young. To rock 'n' roll's audience the music was primarily a way of getting loose. The teenager of the 1950s, restricted by a perceived excess of social control, viewed rock 'n' roll as a means of escape. In many ways the new sound might have functioned as a sex substitute, satisfying adolescent psychological needs similar to those gratified by adults through sex. Like sex, rock 'n' roll provided an emotional release and response to the subliminal rebellion that fermented under the decade's apparent consensus. It was vivacious and offered an individual identity in the world of the organization man. It provided a moment's pleasure, a suspension of regular life, and, in short, made young people feel good.

Many adults understood the music in these terms. *Look* magazine reported, "It is impossible to deny that rock 'n' roll has a sensual sound. But, in the name of fairness, it must be added that the music is vital, exuberant and affirmative."[10] Others were not so openminded. From Asbury Park, New Jersey, to Santa Cruz, California, city fathers banned rock 'n' roll dances and concerts in civic buildings and dance halls, and at swimming pools. A number of high schools forbade the playing of rock 'n' roll at talent shows and completely tabooed its use at dances. In other communities, chaperones, threw "dirty boogieing" teenagers out of high school dances, and unknowingly gave impetus to the consummation of the act being ritually performed on the dance floor.

Adult overreactions to rock 'n' roll's sensuality only bugged teenagers and solidified their conceptions of the restrictive character of adult life. Teenage sex certainly did exist in America in the 1950s, especially in cars parked at the levies, in the parks, on back roads, and, of course, at drive-in movies. However, any objective person could differentiate between the sex act and rock 'n' roll. The dances that the music accompanied harmlessly simulated copulation from a vertical stance, but a giant gap existed between the real act and the music's vibrant promises of a night to remember in the back seat of a convertible. To many minds, the spirit of Elvis's comments rang true, "They all think I'm a sex maniac. They're just frustrated old types, anyway. I'm just natural."[11]

The American teenager did not view rock 'n' roll in terms of sexual revolution, or even a cheap thrill, but rather as a good feeling provided by their own music. While adults perceived the music to be in belligerent confrontation with society, rock 'n' roll was not intent on revolution, nor did it deliberately try to bait community censors. Rather, the music and its performance presented America's youth with a new, expressive, sensual outlet in a repressed world. It offered an alternative to the antiseptic pap which America's sense of propriety had previously demanded. With the rise of rock 'n' roll came the glimmering vision of a world ordered in terms of individual needs. In short, it appeared as a justifiable, natural extension of freedom, and the young could not completely figure out what the big deal was all about. "I never thought my performing style was wicked. *Wicked*? I don't even smoke or drink!"[12] Thank you Elvis.

Martial Music of Delinquency

Closely related to rock 'n' roll's sensuality were its associations with juvenile delinquency, another aspect of teenage behavior about which adults expressed grave concern.

As early as 1956, *Time* magazine reported:

> *In San Antonio, rock 'n' roll was banned from city swimming pool jukeboxes because, said the city council, its primitive beat attracted "undesirable elements" given to practicing their spastic gyrations in abbreviated bathing suits.*[13]

Music Journal claimed:

> *Aside from the illiteracy of this vicious "music," it has proved itself definitely a menace to youthful morals, and an incitement to juvenile delinquency. There is no point in soft-pedaling these facts any longer. The daily papers provide sufficient proof of their existence.*[14]

And the *New York Times* reported Frank Sinatra as saying that primarily cretinous goons wrote and performed rock 'n' roll, and that its lewd, dirty lyrics made it

the music of delinquency.[15] The equation of Elvis with James Dean's role in
Rebel Without a Cause and the movie *Blackboard Jungle*, which featured "Rock
Around the Clock" as its main song, further reinforced the connection between
rock 'n' roll and delinquency.

Rock 'n' roll was not the only popular culture form to be linked with
juvenile delinqueny in the 1950s, as comic books, movies, drive-in restaurants,
and radio and television crime shows were also indicted as suspected corrupters
of youth's morals. However, the new music was the most obvious deviant element
in the home, as middle-class parents had themselves grown up with the other
insidious entertainments. (True, television was a new medium, but many of its
forms in the early years derived from radio.) The fact that the "primitive," "lewd"
and "vicious" rock 'n' roll songs heard in the homes were associated with Blacks
and/or leather-jacketed, greasy-haired, usually swarthy-complexioned hoods had
an unsettling effect upon domestic tranquility. Although social workers reassured
middle-class parents that juvenile deliquency was a product of working class,
urban environments, and poor parental supervision, (implying that such problems
don't occur in the suburbs), the term, nonetheless became a scare word that put
adults on their guard.

Much of what an adolescent did outside the house was unknown, but rock
'n' roll was a known, present within the home itself. Many parents overreacted
to its presence, further reflecting the society's security-through-conformity
attitude. Rock 'n' roll became one of the few agents that polarized parents and
their children. Various defenders of the music attempted to stem and redirect
parental overreaction, including Dinah Shore, who told *Dance* magazine:

> *Frankly, I feel Rock 'n' Roll can be healthy and stimulating. It has certainly
> brought back dancing of an athletic variety. I think that's a lot safer for
> morals than the cheek-to-cheek, almost motionless dance pattern to slower
> tempos. Athletic dancing is good for the body.*
>
> *... I want to make it clear I don't like some songs with double entendre and
> risqué lyrics. Those I abhor.*
>
> *Rock 'n' Roll can't harm youngsters who have acquired a proper foundation
> at home. . . . We should give our children the right background and then
> learn to trust them. In a few years the fuss will die down and a new idol,
> in the tradition of Sinatra–Ray–Presley will be upsetting the parents of a
> new generation.*[16]

Even though Dinah told them rock 'n' roll was just a fad, many parents could
not be molified.

In many respects, rock 'n' roll was equated rightfully with delinquent behavior, a traditional form of teenage deviation, dating back at least to the early nineteenth century.[17] The delinquent stressed prowess and demanded an adventurous lifestyle of thrill seeking. Usually associated with the lower classes of society, the delinquent's rebellion was social in nature, as compared with the political dissent of radicals or the bohemian rejection of cultural norms.

More emotional than cerebral, the deliquent followed the code of the warrior, while maintaining such traditional American values as individualism, success, and material comfort. However, despite the retention of these broad cultural values, much juvenile delinquency was based upon the creation of peer-defined groups that did not identify with adult norms. Sociologists and social commentators suggested that peer status, a quest for a sense of momentary power, and an escape from boredom movitated delinquent actions.[18] These theoreticians viewed delinquency as primarily an individual reaction to a person's inability to achieve socially accepted goals. By establishing an alternate means of defining individual success, delinquent behavior reaffirmed individual worth in the face of failure within mainstream society. As such, delinquency was not so much a symptom of alienation, as a reaction to it. It was a young person's attempt to develop a sense of self in a stifling society.

In part, rock 'n' roll's popularity lay in its connotations of delinquency. The music corresponded with the delinquent style and satisfied similar needs, only in a less extreme, perhaps more middle-class manner. It offered excitement without risk, defiance without disrespect, and allowed listeners the opportunity to associate themselves with an identifiable community of peers with its own forms and values apart from the accepted norms of society. In essence rock 'n' roll provided its predominantly middle-class audience with a vent for its discontent, a form of excitement, and a sense of group identity, while it pursued its socially prescribed goals.

Elvis

The superlative icon of rock 'n' roll delinquency/sexuality was the noncorpulent, noncorporate Elvis Presley. The first white performer to expose a national audience to rock 'n' roll, he embodied the hood image with his duck's-ass hairstyle, sideburns, curled lip, moody eyes and, of course, his pelvis. He was obviously "nasty," yet at the same time he was a God-fearing good ol' boy, just interested in a good life, like the rest of us. As one female fan explained, "He's just like a paperback book, real sexy pictures on the cover. Only when you get inside, it's just a good story."[19] While many parents did not care for the packaging, they were grateful for the "good story" in a time of changing values.

After attaining a regional reputation for performing a "new type of music," Elvis catapulted to national fame when RCA Victor purchased his contract from Sun Records in October 1955. Within his first two years at RCA his records sold twenty-eight million copies, and during that one-hundred-and-four week period his songs topped the charts an incredible fifty-five times. In popular music he reigned supreme as "the King," with a string of hits including "Heartbreak Hotel," "Don't Be Cruel," "Hound Dog," "Jailhouse Rock," "Love Me Tender," "Too Much," "Teddy Bear," and "All Shook Up." Around him swirled hysteria, cries of outrage, and shrieks of adulation. He became one of the ultimate issues of the day. You either defended or rejected Elvis, there appeared to be no neutral ground.

Certain adults quickly condemned Elvis as immoral, a "whirling dervish of sex." However the roots of adult fears lay far deeper than the threat of blatant sexuality alone, as John Sharnick perceptively noted in *House and Garden* magazine:

> *Nobody has suggested banning Miss Monroe from public platforms—not in my vulgar circle anyway—and the parallel between her and young Master Presley isn't purely frivolous. One British observer, trying to analyze the peculiar magnetism of America's pet blonde, commented on "the wonderfully complicated business she makes of breathing." It appears to be Presley's special distinction that he makes such excruciating work of singing, another talent that is usually thought to come fairly naturally. The complexities in both cases are similar—which is to say suggestive. The chief difference seems to be that Miss Monroe addresses herself to the boys, and Mr. Presley, by and large, to the girls. Somehow we accept with amused tolerance the whistles and mutterings of the boys, including a good many boys of rather advanced age. But the squeals of the girls embarrass us, and, in the context of the controversy over Rock 'n' Roll, we are frightened of what we imagine to be the consequences. . . .*
>
> *What is really bothering us adults, I suspect, is not that television has chosen to satisfy this teenage audience but that such a distinctive audience exists at all; that within our society there is a large, well defined group whose standards of taste and conduct we find baffling and even terrifying. These are our children, and we want badly for them to identify themselves with us. But somehow we have failed to inspire in them a respect for our own standards. It is young Presley's air of inarticulate sullenness and suspicion when he talks to the adult M.C. that strikes me as much more ominous than the gymnastics he performs while singing.[20]*

Rhetoric against sexual lasciviousness, upholding moral decency, flowed easily from critical tongues. Sex was a known, an identifiable norm, under challenge. Of all norms, it was one of the most sacrosanct. In comparison, an "air of inarticulate sullenness and suspicion" did not fit into any specific or known form of social or moral deviation. Rather than try to comprehend what was happening, American adults found it much easier to dismiss the whole scene as a teenage aberration; they discounted it and hoped it would go away. Meredith Willson, the composer of *The Music Man*, told *Instrumentalist* magazine that rock 'n' roll "just isn't music. It's utter garbage and it should not be confused in any way with anything related with music or verse."[21] *Look* magazine in an article entitled, "He Can't Be—But He Is," described Elvis as mostly nightmare.[22] The music was "something else"; it was "their music." The polarization became real; the issue of rock 'n' roll coalesced in a growing sense of teenage community. The retreat began; children vacated their seats in front of the television set and moved into a special world of their own—a world that focused on the radio. By consulting the music around which the young gathered, a glimpse of the newly emerging community might be caught.

THE WORLD OF ROCK 'N' ROLL

Perhaps the most powerful and vivid images and descriptions of the new world of rock 'n' roll appeared in the songs of Chuck Berry. One of the earliest rhythm and blues performers to draw an interracial audience, his musical style has been one of the most emulated in the history of rock, with the Rolling Stones, Beatles, Beach Boys, and countless others acknowledging the influence of his guitar playing. The direct lyrics that accompanied Berry's captivating music not only defined the new teenage environment, but clearly depicted rock 'n' roll as part of that world. Such classics as "School Days" (1957), "Maybellene" (1955), "Roll Over Beethoven" (1956), "Rock 'n' Roll Music" (1957), "Johnny B. Goode" (1958), and "Sweet Little Sixteen" (1958) envelop the listener in a world of cars, school, adolescence, and rock 'n' roll.

"School Days," in particular, concisely depicts the routine of school, from getting up in the morning to lunchtime, to three o'clock when the students forget their responsibilities at the local juke joint. Within this haven, the song portrays rock 'n' roll as the prime focus of the teenager's free time. Yet the new music was more than just a leisure time activity; it was an expression of freedom to be: "Feelin' the music from head to toe, round and round you go."[23] The song created a metaphor of freedom from the established order and portrayed teenagers doing what they supposedly wanted to do. The sense of freedom, of total unrestraint and physical expression, lay at the core of rock 'n' roll. This liberating vitality provided the allure of Bill Haley and the Comets, Eddie Cochran, Jerry Lee Lewis, Bo Diddley, and Little Richard.

The most vibrant manifestation of the dynamic rock 'n' roll freedom was Little Richard. The total abandonment of his performances amazed and over-whelmed teenaged audiences. A screaming, shimmering, constantly moving, wildly visual performer, he banged and kicked boogie chords out of his piano to create a new level of excitement. Before retiring to a seminary in 1957, he pounded out hit after hit, starting with "Tutti Frutti" in 1955, and continuing with "Long Tall Sally" (1956), "Slippin' And Slidin'" (1956), "Ready Teddy" (1956), "Rip It Up" (1956), "The Girl Can't Help It" (1957), "Lucille" (1957), "Jenny, Jenny" (1957), "Miss Ann" (1957) and "Good Golly Miss Molly" (1958). One commentator accurately characterized these songs as sounding "roughly the same: tuneless, lyricless, preneanderthal. . . . They were small episodes in one unending scream and only made sense when you put them all together."[24] Little Richard defied the requirements of sophisticated lyrics or melody; the physical reality of his performance was an experience unmediated by complex lyrical thoughts. His songs were not intended to be sung throughout the day. People did not hum "Tutti Frutti"; they reacted to it, and the reaction was release, freedom.

The theme of freedom also served as a major focal point in Chuck Berry's "Sweet Little Sixteen." The girl in the song wore tight dresses, lipstick, and high heel shoes at night against the social dictates that denied adolescents such dress. Her freedom of self-expression, however, was only partial, since in the morning she always changed back into a sweet sixteen for school. While express-ing a certain ironic detachment from the established order, the song was also highly cognizant of the priority of that order. In its lyric, the young girl had to beg permission from her parents to go to the show and dutifully returned to school the following day. Similarly, the students in "School Days" were all conscientious workers and eager to pass. The songs expressed a certain discontent with life, yet accepted the status quo and its values.

Even the most forceful antiauthority songs of the period, "Yakety Yak" (1958) and "Charlie Brown" (1959) by the Coasters, "Get a Job" (1958) by the Silhouettes and "Summertime Blues" (1958) by Eddie Cochran, contained ele-ments sympathetic to the ways of the dominant culture. The singers of "Yakety Yak" knew they would not be allowed to rock 'n' roll unless they first scrubbed the kitchen floor. And everyone knew the answer to why people were picking on Charlie Brown—one did not smoke in the auditorium or call the English teacher "daddy-o," and expect to go unreprimanded. Although the audience might have considered Charlie Brown's behavior "cool," they realized it was not how to play the game. While wishing to do as they pleased, teenagers in the 1950s, by and large, worked toward socially accepted goals. Their songs manifested more grumbling about the traditional mores than outright rejection of them. Although offering a vibrant, visceral, albeit momentary, escape from the world, and defining a teenage sense of identity, rock 'n' roll fit into the mainstream of American values.[25] Many song listeners, aptly labeled "rebels without a cause," dabbled in a new world before they grew up, but had no alternative except to follow the American way of life. Perhaps one of the best indexes of the teenager's relationship to society can be found in the decade's songs about love, the most popular musical subject of the period.

Songs of Love

From 1920 to 1955 the lyrics of popular songs produced for white audiences portrayed love as a miraculous occurrence, solving all problems and lasting forever. Supporting this viewpoint, songs of lost love centered on despondent individuals who wallowed in self-pity, and hoped to regain their one and only. In even more extreme lyrical situations, with all hope extinguished, individuals vowed never to love again, or else treasured a fantasy love, as in "Paper Doll."[26]

Rock 'n' roll more or less continued this lyrical tradition. Frequently assuming the form of sentimental ballads, rock 'n' roll songs depicted love as a monogamous, heaven-sent, dream come true, set in a blissful musical context. Such hits as "Only You" (1955), "The Magic Touch" (1956), "One in a Million" (1957) and "Enchanted (1959), all by the Platters, one of the most successful ballad groups, reflected this style. Other songs of the period, including the Penguins' "Earth Angel" (1955), the Moonglows' "Sincerely" (1955), the Five Satins' "In the Still of the Night" (1956), and the Flamingos' "I Only Have Eyes for You" (1959) presented similar views. These songs and others perpetuated the accepted lyrical imagery of love which S.I. Hayakawa characterized as, "wishful thinking, dreamy and ineffectual nostalgia, unrealistic fantasy, self-pity and sentimental clichés masquerading as emotion."[27]

Certainly the most common type of love song, the ballad, displayed a musical form and content similar to the Tin Pan Alley style of pop. However, in the late 1950s another distinctly rock 'n' roll style of love song tentatively emerged. Embodied in such songs as Lloyd Price's "Personality" (1959), the Big Bopper's "Chantilly Lace" (1958), Buddy Knox's "Party Doll" (1957), the

Regents' "Barbara Ann" (1961), and Dee Clark's "Hey Little Girl" (1958), this new love lyric neither accepted nor rejected the established lyrical views of love. Instead it dodged the issue, ignored the romantic lines of love and involved itself with the infatuation of the moment. By concentrating on the here and now, these songs seemed to imply that something other than eternal love might exist.

In songs of lost love, rock 'n' roll lyrics again continued to present a traditional response. When perfect eternal love faltered and became painfully transient, then a state of depression set it, triggered by a feeling of loss. Such songs as Elvis' "Heartbreak Hotel" (1956), the Fleetwood's "Mr. Blue" (1959) and "Tragedy" (1961), Dion and the Belmonts' "A Teenager in Love" (1959), the Fireflies' "You Were Mine" (1959), the Skyliners' "Since I Don't Have You" (1959) and the Everly Brothers' "Bye, Bye Love" (1957), all reflect the accepted lyrical statement of broken-hearted self-pity. While the lyrics retained the appropriate imagery of devastating trauma, these songs deviated from the lost love syndrome in their musical attitude. Jeremy Larner, writing for *Atlantic* magazine, noted that in "Bye Bye Love":

> . . . though the lyrics portray the familiar broken heart who cannot go on living without his True Love, the bouncing rhythm of the song conveys another emotion altogether; the desire to thump straight on through all heartbreaks and difficulties. This ostensible lament is really steering-wheel-pounding music. The crybaby lyrics are countered by pure psychopathy, nor is there any resolution of these conflicting feelings. The image presented is that of an extremely tender individual ready to strike out or give up if his dreams don't come true. The protest against the clichés of American adulthood is carried by the music rather than the words, so that the teen-ager can pay lip service to the feelings from which the music proclaims his alienation. It is as if his mind did not know what his body was doing. At the same time he expresses his distress with the conventional life and sex attitudes, he prepares to make his peace with them.[28]

To come to grips with this anomaly, Larner postulated that youth "simultaneously accepts and rejects the values of our society without passing through the stages of questioning." In many respects he accurately assessed the situation. The teenager of the 1950s dated and "went steady" at a younger age than any generation in recent history up to that time,[29] and was too aware, experienced, and optimistic to believe in the eternal broken heart. However, the self-pitying, jilted lover imagery retained close links with the concept of idealized love, which the American public still embraced. Rock 'n' roll songs of lost love reconciled the teenage dilemma between ideal love and the reality of breaking up by giving lip service to the accepted image of love lost, while the music presented a new, nonverbalized, perhaps unquestioning, expression of reality.

The converse of "Bye Bye Love"'s lyric-music relationship also occurred in early rock 'n' roll songs. A number of "cutesie" songs, such as the Royal Teens' "Short Shorts" (1958), the Playmates' "What is Love" (1959), and "Little Miss Stuck Up" (1961), and Brian Hyland's "Itsy, Bitsy Teenie Weenie Yellow Polka Dot Bikini" (1960), sounded insipidly innocent from a musical standpoint, but carried rather positive sexual messages in their simple lyrics. These songs emphasized the wearing of abbreviated and tight attire, swaying with a wiggle when one walked, and advocated more sexually open behavior for teenage girls. (Who wore short shorts? They wore short shorts!)

American teenagers were growing up in a rapidly changing society. America's value system, especially its attitudes toward love and sex, was visibly in transition. Old words remained in vogue, although certain people recognized these to be inoperative, and even restrictive, approaches to life. Rock 'n' roll music emerged as one of the first art forms to respond to the dichotomy between daily practice and the values preached by society by interweaving traditional values with new perceptions and feelings. Although rock 'n' roll accepted the dominant cultural values, it was also separating itself from that culture by creating its own forms and heroes. By expressing a world view couched in terms of individual experiences rather than corporate concerns and gray-flannel demands, rock 'n' roll held out the possibility of reassessing and circumventing societal norms. Chuck Berry's concluding paean in "School Days" clearly expressed the prevailing opinion.

> Hail, hail rock 'n' roll,
> Deliver me from the days of old.
> Long live rock 'n' roll
> The beat of the drum is loud and bold,
> Rock, rock, rock 'n' roll,
> The spirit is there body and soul.[30]

NOTES

[1]For example see Max Lerner, *America as a Civilization* (New York: Simon & Schuster, 1957), p. 857; Charlie Gillett, *The Sound of the City* (New York: Dell Publishing Company, 1972), pp. 19–26; and George B. Leonard, "The Great Rock 'n' Roll Controversy," *Look* 20 (26 June 1956), p. 47.

[2]A variety of people have put forth a variety of dates and events to mark the advent of rock 'n' roll. See Arnold Shaw, *The Rock Revolution* (New York: Paperback Library, 1971), pp. 20–23; Carl Belz, *The Story of Rock* (New York: Harper & Row, 1972), p. 16; Jerry Hopkins, *The Rock Story* (New York: New American Library Inc., 1970), p. 17; and Gillett, *The Sound of the City*, p. 9.

[3]Jack Gould, "Elvis Presley, Lack of Responsibility Shown by TV in Exploiting Teen-Agers," *New York Times*, 16 September 1956, Sec. 10, p. 13.

[4]*Music Journal*, 16 (February 1958), p. 3.

[5]For example, see "A Warning to the Music Business," *Variety*, 23 February 1955, p. 2.

[6]See William Bradford, *Of Plymouth Plantation, 1620–1647* (New York: Alfred A. Knopf, 1952) for an account of an early attempt to repress deviant social action in America. Later, Nathaniel Hawthorne immortalized this event in his short story, "The Maypole of Merry Mount."

[7]For further evidence see J.M. Neil, "1955: The Beginning of Our Own Times," *South Atlantic Quarterly*, 73 (Autumn 1974), pp. 428–444.

[8]Max Lerner, *America as a Civilization*, p. 688.

[9]James Woodward, "The Role of Fictions in Cultural Life," *Transactions of the New York Academy of Sciences*, 6 (1944), p. 311.

[10]George B. Leonard, "The Great Rock 'n' Roll Controversy," *Look*, 20 (26 June 1956), p. 47.

[11]Quoted in Jerry Hopkins, *Elvis, A Biography* (New York: Simon & Schuster, 1971), p. 153.

[12]Quoted in W. A. Harbinson, *The Illustrated Elvis* (New York: Grosset & Dunlap, 1976), p. 33.

[13]*Time*, 68 (23 July 1956), p. 34.

[14]*Music Journal*, 16 (February 1958), p. 3.

[15]Gertrude Samuels, "Why They Rock 'n' Roll—And Should They?" *New York Times Magazine* (12 January 1958), p. 19.

[16]Dinah Shore, "The Rock Beat," *Dance Magazine*, 31 (August 1957), p. 58.

[17]For a fuller discussion of teenage deviation see David Matza, "Subterranean Traditions of Youth," *Annals of the American Academy of Political and Social Science*, 338 (November 1961), pp. 102–118.

[18]For example see Martin Gold, "Juvenile Delinquency as a Symptom of Alienation," *Journal of Social Issues*, 25, No. 2 (1969) 121–135; Gordon C. Zahn, "In Our Image," *Commonweal*, 70 (19 June 1959), pp. 302–304; Irving Spergel, "An Exploratory Research in Delinquent Subcultures," *Social Science Review*, 35 (March 1961), pp. 33–47; Joseph Margolis, "Juvenile Delinquents, The Latter-Day Knights," *The American Scholar*, 29 (Spring 1960), pp. 211–218; and Arthur Miller, "The Bored and the Violent," *Harpers*, November 1962, pp. 50–52+.

[19]Quoted in Nik Cohn, *Rock from the Beginning*, (New York: Stein and Day, 1969).

[20]John Sharnick, "The War of the Generations," *House and Garden*, October 1956, pp. 40–41.

[21]Meredith Willson, "Rock 'n' Roll Assaulted," *Instrumentalist*, September 1958, pp. 92–93.

[22]*Look* 7 August 1956.

[23] "School Days," words and music by Chuck Berry, copyright Arc Music, 1957. Used with permission. All rights reserved.

[24]Nik Cohn, *"Rock from the Beginning*, p. 22.

[25]Herbert London discussed rock 'n' roll's conformity to mainstream viewpoints in "The Charles Reich Typology and Early Rock Music," *Popular Music and Society*, 1 (Winter 1972), pp. 65–72.

[26]Samuel I. Hayakawa, "Popular Songs vs. The Facts of Life," *Etc.* 12 (Winter 1955), pp. 83–95.

[27]Hayakawa, p. 84.

[28]Jeremy Larner, "What Do They Get From Rock 'n' Roll?" *Atlantic*, August 1964, p. 46.

[29]For a discussion of adolescent dating patterns see *Youth: Transition to Adulthood, the Report of the Panel on Youth of the President's Science Advisory Committee* (Chicago: University of Chicago Press, 1974), pp. 115–116; and Joseph F. Kett, *Rites of Passage, Adolescence in America, 1790– Present* (New York: Basic Books Inc., 1977), p. 265.

[30] "School Days," words and music by Chuck Berry, copyright Arc Music, 1957. Used with permission, all rights reserved.

3
The Day the Music Died

April is the cruelest month, breeding
Lilacs out of the dead land, mixing
Memory and desire, stirring
Dull roots with spring rain.

                                    T. S. Eliot

In 1959 the music "died." The creative energies unleashed in 1955 issued their last gasps with such songs as Lloyd Price's "Stagger Lee" and Wilbert Harrison's "Kansas City," while Frankie Avalon's "Venus" and "Why," Paul Anka's "Lonely Boy" and "Put Your Head on My Shoulder," the Browns' "The Three Bells," and Bobby Darin's "Mack the Knife" swirled around them. An era of schmaltz and pimple cream ensued, only to be miraculously decimated in 1964 by a new, revitalizing force, the Beatles. So reads the standard, short history of rock 'n' roll for the years from 1959 to 1964; the unabridged version, while more detailed, tells the same tale, but with a twist or two.

PURE PUKE

From the moment of rock 'n' roll's inception, predictions of its demise steadily appeared. Few had any substance; however, by 1957 songs, such as Tab Hunter's "Young Love," Debbie Reynolds' "Tammy," and Pat Boone's "Love Letters in the Sand" and "April Love," all number one hits, were appearing quite regularly on radio play lists. *Cash Box* optimistically announced:

22

The type of rock 'n' roll that originally excited the kids and made it a subject for national and international debate, has quietly receded into the background and has been replaced with a softer version with emphasis on melody and lyric.[1]

At the time, few, if any, listeners could imagine what the softer sound portended. Over the next two years these contrived productions of the record companies encroached more and more into the realm of authentic rock 'n' roll. By 1960, straight, clean, and insipid teen idols like Paul Anka, Fabian, Connie Francis, Frankie Avalon, Brenda Lee, Neil Sedaka, Ricky Nelson, Bobby Rydell, Bobby Vee, and a host of lesser lights dominated the charts. With the support of the record industry, these new stars homogenized, bastardized, and sterilized the original rock 'n' roll sound. They overrode the music of the previous five years and transformed rock 'n' roll into pop music for teenagers.

Almost all the songs by the teen idols rejected rock 'n' roll's blues origins, and reverted back to traditional pop music forms. Tin Pan Alley arrangers took over production and created a more sophisticated and varied musical palette. They added more complex harmonies, counterpoint, and new instruments including horns, strings, flutes, bells, and the like. They completely negated rock 'n' roll's raw, hard, insistent sound and established teenage versions of "How Much is That Doggie in the Window" as the pop standards of the day. The only similarity between this music and rock 'n' roll lay in the fact that both addressed themselves to the adolescent audience. Having lost its vitality, true rock 'n' roll, for all intents and purposes, disappeared from the American scene.

The sound of teenage defiance, absorbed and remodeled by the spirit of American pluralism, became safe teenage entertainment. Young listeners reentered the mainstream of society and consumed a surprisingly large number of records catering to parental approval. Both Percy Faith's "Theme from a Summer Place" (1960) and Lawrence Welk's "Calcutta" (1961) went gold. Other smash hits of the period included Ferrante and Teicher's "Exodus" (1961), Mr. Acker Bilk's "Stranger on the Shore" (1962), Henry Mancini's "Moon River" (1962), David Rose's "The Stripper" (1962), Kyu Sakamoto's "Sukiyaki" (1963), and the Singing Nun's "Dominique" (1963). At the same time, adults began to accept the new teen culture as the twist became the social rage of 1962. The new dance had been popularized by such hits as Chubby Checker's "The Twist" and "Let's Twist Again," the Isley Brothers' "Twist and Shout," Sam Cooke's "Twistin' the Night Away," and Joey Dee and the Starlighters' "Peppermint Twist." Teen culture now became fashionable, and both *American Bandstand* and *Top 40 Radio* assumed a role reminiscent of *Your Hit Parade*, completely "broadcastrating" rock 'n' roll. Combined with the sack dress, madras shirts, white socks, and crew cuts, the music became a very clean, obedient, and innocent experience. Within this era America confidently advanced with vigor (in President Kennedy's words) toward a glorious future, despite the Bay of Pigs, Selma, Alabama, and military advisors in South Vietnam. The death of rock 'n' roll went almost unnoticed, and certainly did not critically affect the lives of its audience. The adults were right, it was just a fad. Many adolescents clung to their musical form, twisting the night away, while another contingent, recognizing the hollow shell that rock 'n' roll had become, moved on, into the expanding realms of commitment, folk music, and social salvation offered by the New Frontier. Still others retreated into themselves, idolized Alfred E. Newman and philosophically pondered, "A nerd, is a nerd, is a nerd." All went with the flow of society.

Uptown Rhythm and Blues

Besides Lawrence Welk, the teen idols, and the twist, another musical form, uptown rhythm and blues, vainly tried to fill the void left by rock 'n' roll. This style continued the 1950s doo-wop tradition of such groups as the Platters, Five Satins, and Drifters,[2] only with more sophisticated harmonies and elaborately orchestrated productions.

This style presented an option to teen schlock, but in many instances was not far removed from it. The genre included such solo artists as Sam Cooke, Jerry Butler, and Jackie Wilson, the songs of such writer/composer teams as Goffin and King, Leiber and Stoller, and Mann and Weil, the productions of Phil Spector, and the early Motown sound of Martha and the Vandellas, Smokey Robinson and the Miracles, the Temptations, the Supremes, and the Four Tops. The style, however, was preeminently the forte of Black female groups such as the Shirelles, Chiffons, Crystals, Ronettes, Marvelletes, and the Supremes. Their hits, including "Will You Love Me Tomorrow" (1960), "Please Mr. Postman" (1961), "Soldier Boy" (1962), "He's a Rebel" (1962), "Da Do Ron Ron" (1963), "He's So Fine" (1963), "Be My Baby" (1963), "Baby Love" (1964) and "Come See About Me" (1964), readily come to mind when early sixties rock 'n' roll is recalled.

Ironically, the most popular group in the field was neither Black nor female. The Four Seasons, featuring the falsetto lead vocals of Frankie Valli, had eleven top ten records between August 1962 and November 1965, with "Sherry" (1962), "Big Girls Don't Cry" (1962), "Walk Like a Man" (1963), and "Rag Doll" (1964) all reaching the number one spot. The group used the production techniques of the uptown rhythm and blues formula in an uninspired, if not awkward manner. Their widespread success reflected the state of the early 1960s market.

While surpassing teen schmaltz, the uptown rhythm and blues sound was still not up to the quality of the original rock 'n' roll. Not as intense as the best of Elvis, Chuck Berry or Little Richard, these songs too frequently became deeply entangled in mawkish harmonic webs of romance and heartache. Rather than presenting an immediate emotional experience, they struck postures and elicited superficial sentiment. With the major exception of the Motown sound, much of this genre could not survive the British invasion of 1964.

However, certain songs rose above the constraints of the uptown formulas. For example, the Righteous Brothers truly affected their audience with two songs produced by Phil Spector, "You've Lost that Lovin' Feelin'" (1964) and "Unchained Melody" (1965), as did the Drifters with the poignant, but restrained, "Up on the Roof" (1962) and "Under the Boardwalk" (1964). The sympathetic handling of "Will You Love Me Tomorrow?" (1960) by the Shirelles made the song one of the earliest and strongest rock songs to acknowledge the existence of exploitive, transient sex relationships, while Betty Everett's "Shoop Shoop Song (It's in His Kiss)" (1964) opened new sexual frontiers by claiming the kiss to be the only true test of love. But these uptown rhythm and blues songs were the exceptions, as were Del Shannon's "Runaway" (1961), Gary and the U.S. Bonds' "New Orleans" (1961), and Roy Orbison's country-influenced "Only the Lonely" (1960) and "Oh, Pretty Woman" (1964). Such songs represented the high points of a four-year period when it didn't pay to turn on the radio.

The music of the early 1960s contributed to the development of rock with the increased use of the electric bass and vocal harmony, the introduction of the twist, Phil Spector's heavily orchestrated "wall of sound" production technique, and the Motown label. However, these were years essentially of formulation, in which people conscious of the rock 'n' roll style began to explore its possibilities and shape them to fit their needs. The record companies cleaned up rock 'n' roll to suit middle-class sensibilities, and placed it back on the shelf where pop music belonged, next to entertainment. Unable or unwilling to grasp the essence hidden within and behind the original rock 'n' roll sound, these producers failed to understand or appreciate that rock 'n' roll transcended its meager associations with stereotypical teenage concerns. Their homogenized music had little relevance to adolescent life other than its status as a recognized focal point in teenage culture, and record consumption declined in 1960. The industry remained in a slump until 1964.

Recrudescence

While the east coast-dominated record industry rode the crest of rock 'n' roll's reputation, other waves were breaking on the west coast. The surf was up and the Beach Boys rode it across the nation. Producing seven smash albums in twenty-two months during 1962–1964, the group personified and popularized the Southern California surf scene. A smooth harmony, inspired by the Four Freshmen, a moving rhythm and beat, derived from the earlier rock 'n' roll of Chuck Berry, Eddie Cochran, and others, and simple, straightforward and realistic lyrics, combined to form a new, carefree, idyllic sound called surf music. Attuned to the time and place of its audience, surf music represented the initial step toward bringing rock 'n' roll back into the domain of teenage expression.

Rising from the surf scene itself, the Beach Boys spoke directly from adolescent experience unlike the contrived teen idols and uptown rhythm and blues performers. Their songs flowed from the life around them, rather than from standard, rote imagery. They presented plausible visions of surfing, cars, dating, the beach, the drive-ins and rock 'n' roll. Their sounds offered a valid alternative from the lackluster uninspiring teen idols. Although not delinquent in character, the new music and its followers stood up to the world and commanded adolescent respect, for as Brian Wilson noted in "I Get Around," the bad guys knew them and left them alone.

Taking an affirmative stance toward life, the songs of the Beach Boys epitomized a new teen subculture of fine times and sunny days. Their harmonic artistry celebrated adolescent summertime freedom in an affluent, consumer society. The group depicted teen existence on a slightly larger-than-life, heroic level, and established a mythic connection with consumerism and its material comforts. Within their vision of carefree bounty lay optimistic joie de vivre which became the foundation for the love generation, as later presented in such songs as "Groovin'," "Good Vibrations," and "California Dreamin'."

The Beach Boys extolled the glories of California living for only a brief period; Beatlemania broke out, eclipsed them, and redirected popular music.

Incredibly impossible adulating inundation summed up the beginning of nineteen-sixty-Beatle-four. During the first three months of that year, the Beatles, stars gone supernovae, single-handedly rescued the record industry from its era of "profitless prosperity"[3] and produced approximately sixty percent of the industry's single sales. Their first American hit, "I Want to Hold Your Hand," moved from number forty-five on January 18, 1964, to number one in a matter of two weeks, and remained at the top of the charts until March 21, only to be replaced by "She Loves You," which was followed by "Can't Buy Me Love." On April 4, 1964, the first of five weeks to herald "Can't Buy Me Love" as America's top tune, the group claimed the initial five spots on the singles charts with "Can't Buy Me Love," "Twist and Shout," "She Loves You," "I Want to Hold Your Hand," and "Please, Please Me," *plus* the top two albums, *The Beatles' Second Album,* which climbed to the number one position just two weeks after its release, and *Meet the Beatles,* the best selling album in music history up to that time. A week later, fourteen Beatle songs appeared in *Billboard*'s "Hot 100." An astounding record, a phenomenal phenomenon, such figures only begin to tell the story of the frenzied fanaticism with which post-Kennedy America greeted the British singing sensations.

To say the least, the Beatles' reception in America was stupendous. Their music, like that of the Beach Boys, derived from the earlier rock 'n' roll of Chuck Berry, Little Richard, and others. However, the two sounds differed dramatically. The Beach Boys drew from both rock 'n' roll and the pop tradition, composing in both twelve- and sixteen-bar forms and employing a relatively wide repertoire of chords, including major sixes and sevens. They developed a more chromatic sound by temporarily breaking the key of the song in a chord, and used minor key changes and fairly rapid harmonic shifts, with as many as three or four bridges in a song. The group introduced elements of madrigal singing, such as parallel counterpoint, and frequently varied their instrumental and vocal leads during a song. They used an assortment of instruments on their records, and did much overdubbing,[4] which created a clean sound with distinctly separated instrumental tracks. The band also featured Brian Wilson's unique bass lines, which they placed up front, making them one of the earliest rock groups to do so.

In comparison, the Beatles presented a more direct, driving sound, which tended to remain within the twelve-bar blues form with its dominant type 7 chord and limited use of bridges. Theirs was a heavier sound than the Beach Boys with the drums and rhythm guitar up front laying down a very straightforward, dominant rhythm, accenting the off (2 and 4) beats. The early Beatles records were not highly produced, and did not use extraneous instrumentation to augment their two guitars, bass, and drums. Also their Gretsch/Rickenbacker guitars and Vox bass created a grittier sound than the twangy Fender equipment of the Beach Boys. Thus the Beatles played a raucous, libido-releasing music which appealed to and reflected the vitality of youth, and reinjected a rock 'n' roll pulse back into teen awareness.

The lyrics accompanying this music adhered to traditional Tin Pan Alley and rock 'n' roll subjects. Listeners were immersed in the innocent, if not innocuous, wonders of eternal love and the bum-out, but bouncy, sorrows of love lost. "I Want to Hold Your Hand," "I Saw Her Standing There," "Things We Said Today," "And I Love Her," "This Boy," "Tell Me Why," "I'll Cry

Instead," "Don't Bother Me," lyrically perpetuated the state of the art. Devoid of lyrical profundity, yet intrinsically linked to the musical currents coursing through adolescent cerebrums, the Beatles' songs offered an escape, a respite of gaiety to a nation encumbered by an increasingly hostile world.

However, the Beatles did more than just revitalize the sound of rock 'n' roll; their public show reinforced a healthy disregard for authority and redefined the idea of teen idol. Like their music, their "im-media" presence was something different. Their long, over-the-ears hairstyles, and "amiable impudence"[5] (consider their press interviews: "What do you think of Beethoven?" "I love him, especially his poems." . . . "What about the movement in Detroit to stamp out the Beatles?" "We're starting a movement to stamp out Detroit." . . . "How do you find America?" "Turn left at Greenland." . . . "What are you going to do in Washington?" "Sleep." . . . "What do you think of criticisms that you are not very good?" "We're not.") confidently espoused a lighthearted, but decisive, disrespect for social conventions. Cognizant of their outrageous success, they claimed they didn't care, and had the pizazz, the charisma, to pull it off. Where Elvis had assumed a sullen, inarticulate posture against mainstream America, and civil rights demonstrators bemoaned the injustices of the system, the Beatles derisively challenged the seriousness with which people sanctimoniously approached life. Remaining behind a curtain of wit, they flippantly questioned the need to conform to the accepted way of doing things. Their audacious disinterest in fulfilling adult expectations embodied the visions, thoughts and non-aspirations latent within youth culture. As such, the Beatles established the viability of rock musicians as social critics.

Crashing through the portals opened by the Beatles, the Rolling Stones further extended and confirmed the reemergence of rock's antagonistic role, with even longer, shaggier hair, a more raunchy, sneering manner, and leering sinister/sexual songs such as Willie Dixon's "I Just Want to Make Love to You," which Muddy Waters earlier popularized, and Slim Harpo's "I'm a King Bee." Self-conscious rebels, they refused to compromise their dark, defiant posture with even a modicum of Beatle charm. *Variety* advised its readers:

> The Rolling Stones is [sic] not a bunch of cleancut youngsters out to make a buck from innocent kids. The group is tapping on the Freudian vein of savagery in their parlay of frantic guitars and drums, wild vocals, bumps, grinds and twitches.[6]

The magazine later classified the Stones as the "rhythm and blues exponents whose wild and crazy appearance has set them up as a symbol of teenage rebellion against conventional parenthood and authority," and warned, "Although they have rejected the family image their success is following much the same path as the Beatles."[7] With the Rolling Stones, the impudence of the Beatles turned, and belligerently confronted social norms. Through their songs and actions, the group reasserted the possibility that rock music might once again serve as a point around which teenage discontent could coalesce. By moving more and more into the netherworld of social criticism, both the Rolling Stones and the Beatles brought rock in closer and closer proximity to the domain of the "folkies," the singing social commentators par excellence of the early 1960s.

FOLK WAYS

As the sound of the New Frontier's social salvation sensibility, the *folk revival* of the early sixties consummated the thirty- to forty-year budding relationship between the pop and folk scenes, despite the latter's protestations to the contrary. The courtship dated back at least to the mid-1920s when folk music filtered into the national consciousness through recordings, radio programs such as the "Grand Ole Opry" (1925) and an increasing number of published song collections, including John and Alan Lomax's *American Ballads and Folk Songs* (1933). During the 1930s this music of the common people, the working class, became frequent fare at union gatherings, Communist party functions, and left-wing political rallies opposing the fascist Spanish Civil War. Through these associations it gained a reputation as an expression of the liberal conscience, which assured it a respectable place among intellectuals and distinguished it from the music of the middle class.

Despite such associations, the marriage between folk and pop seemed imminent in the early 1950s when the Weavers' "Goodnight Irene" (1950) topped the charts and their "On Top of Old Smokey" (1951) broke into the top ten. However, the investigations of the House Un-American Activities Committee on Internal Security, coupled with the distribution of *Red Channels,* a virtual blacklist of singers, writers, actors, and other members of the entertainment industry with alleged Communist affiliations, assured the suppression of folk music in the mass media and marketplace. It was not until a new generation of untainted folk singers appeared, near the end of the decade, that folk once again could court a popular audience.

The Kingston Trio's "Tom Dooley," although rarely recognized as folk music in 1958, presaged the ultimate arrival of the genre. Rising coincidentally with the declining vitality of rock 'n' roll, folk music offered listeners an alternative to the drivel emanating from the radio. But even more importantly, the sound flourished under the liberal Kennedy administration by building on its Depression era reputation for protest. Aligning itself with the civil rights and ban the bomb movements, the music reached its zenith in popularity. Following the success of the Kingston Trio and Peter, Paul, and Mary, folk groups proliferated and new individuals, most notably Joan Baez and Bob Dylan, came to the fore.

Folk music underwent an identity crisis when it began to receive widespread commercial attention and found itself addressing a primarily urban audience. Performers were evaluated in terms of their "sincerity," "commitment," and "integrity." All judgments revolved around the throbbing question of "authenticity." Peter, Paul, and Mary were deemed too commercial, too harmonious, too clean. Among the ranks of the authentic stood Joan Baez and Bob Dylan until he started writing "finger-pointing" and love songs. However, Dylan was so in tune with liberal causes, that he retained his reputation of authenticity, except in the eyes of stuffed-shirt purists. As such, folk transcended the preservation of a specific musical heritage to become a matter of mind, attitude, and lifestyle. It represented, in a rather selfrighteous way, a reaction against contemporary life. Its dissent differed radically from the earlier rock 'n' roll rebelliousness. Where the latter corresponded to a delinquent approach to life, folk advocated political activism tinctured with a touch of bohemian subterraneanism. Folk protest, while rejecting certain bourgeois norms, remained within the social structure, sought but did not offer solutions, and did not attempt to break loose.

Involved in its sense of social mission and the problem of its own definition, folk, while intruding into the realm of popular music, remained a distinct entity, aloof from mainstream pop. Despite this separation, the folk revival came to exert a profound influence upon the course of rock. With the coming of the Beatles, the vital raw power of electronically amplified music and a driving rock 'n' roll sound opened new doors in many minds. Segments of the worlds of folk and rock merged, as a number of Greenwich Village denizens abandoned the coffee house scene and plugged in their guitars. These evacuees included the members of the Mamas and Papas, John Sebastian and Zal Yanovsky of the Lovin' Spoonful, Roger McGuinn and David Crosby of the Byrds, Steve Stills of Buffalo Springfield, and Paul Simon, not to mention Mr. Folk himself, Bob Dylan.

With this infusion, many folk characteristics began to find their way into the rock world. The most apparent, and frequently cited, of these was folk's penchant for meaningful lyrics, but other less obvious factors also prevailed. Folk musicians, following the path blazed by Bob Dylan, already had begun to move from a traditional form that was handed down to them to one characterized by inner direction. The shift into rock freed folkies from the concerns of

authenticity and liberal expectations, thus accelerating their inner-directed incli-
nations. This, in turn, reoriented the rock genre as well. Folk also brought to
rock its messianic "gonna change the world" attitude, a canonized use of drugs,
an abandonment of formal, prescribed attire for performers, and the idea that
lifestyle and music should reflect each other. When coupled with the revitalized,
Beatle-ized rock, a potentially potent art form resulted, which predicated rock's
coming of age.

Folk Rock

Bob Dylan may have best summed up folk rock when he declared folk music
to be a bunch of fat people. The new musical direction of Dylan, the Byrds,
Simon and Garfunkel, the Mamas and the Papas, the Lovin' Spoonful, Donovan,
and a host of others entailed not only a movement toward a more dynamic,
volatile sound, but a shift away from an apparently moribund form which was
no longer appropriate for life in the 1960s. Compared to the Beatles' music,
folk was sterile, otiose, if not obese. It was also pretentious and closely associated
with increasingly unresponsive liberal politics.

Moving away from the old, stodgy prescribed ways of "maturity," to a
new, young adventure ("My Back Pages" to the max), folk rock injected a
joyously alive sound into the flux of popular music and presented the rock world
with the option of greater lyrical pertinence and sophistication. "California
Dreamin'" (1966), "Do You Believe in Magic?" (1965), "Mr. Tambourine Man"
(1965), "Sounds of Silence" (1965), "Go Where You Wanna Go" (1966), "Day
Dream" (1966), "59th Street Bridge Song (Feelin' Groovy)" (1966), "Summer
in the City" (1966), "5-D" (1966), "Eight Miles High" (1966), and "Strange
Young Girls" (1966) presented a new, heroic, inner-directed, magic-mythical
wonder world of drugs, freedom, and exuberance. The Byrds, Lovin' Spoonful,
and Mamas and Papas all stressed harmony, as had the Beatles, while developing
musical styles distinctly different from the Britishers and from each other.
Although judged soft and light-hearted by today's standards, these groups innova-
tively expanded the parameters of the rock sound by creating a very solid and
unique musical intensity for their time.

To appreciate this sound, imagine 1965, when Ralph Gleason described
to his *San Francisco Chronicle* audience the Lovin' Spoonful, "one of the leading
groups of the new, adult rock 'n' roll idiom," at the hungry i,

> *The electric guitars roared, reverberated, and twanged and the drums
> slammed and banged and rocked and rolled and the voices sang out unto
> the wilderness of faces . . .*[8]

Those not familiar with the Spoonful "were frankly dazed" because their music "takes some exposure to before what is going on behind the loudness can seep through to you." Entranced by the Spoonful's music and "casual costumes (Goodwill-surf-and-ski-army-surplus-exotic-vacation style)," Gleason found the music "exciting" and an "expression of freedom" and "a new age."

Similarly Paul Jay Robbins, reporting for the *Los Angeles Free Press,* one of the earliest underground newspapers in America, described the Byrds at Ciros.

> *Their singular method is to unite, in a dynamic and irresistible adventure, the techniques and honesty of folk music, the joy and immediacy of r & r, and the virtuosity of jazz. . . .*
>
> *Their material includes Seeger and Dylan songs, delivered in a way which magnifies the material into a gestalt of meaning . . . the sound is so right you can't deny it. . . . Dancing with the Byrds becomes a mystic loss of ego and tangibility; you become pure energy someplace between sound and motion and the involvement is total.[9]*

In 1965 folk rock was an astonishing new sound. Its development, coupled with the introduction of the strong and distinct music of such British groups as the Animals in "The House of the Rising Sun" (1964), the Kinks in "You Really Got Me" (1964), and the Zombies in "She's Not There" (1964), mark the period of late 1964–1965 as a peak in rock's formulation. More surprises followed.

NOTES

[1]*Cash Box,* March 1957.

[2]The uptown rhythm-and-blues tradition precedes the advent of rock 'n' roll, featuring such groups from the late 1940s, early 1950s as the Ravens, Orioles, Dominoes, Clovers, and Drifters. The style derived from such antecedents as the Ink Spots, Mills Brothers and gospel singing. For more information see Philip Grocia, *They All Sang on the Corner* (Setauket, New York: Edmund Publishing Company, 1974); Bill Millar, *The Drifters* (New York: Macmillan, 1972); Tony Heilbut, *The Gospel Sound* (New York: Simon & Schuster, 1971).

[3]"Disk Biz Flips After '63 Flop," *Variety* 19 February 1964 p. 49.

[4]Overdubbing seems to have been primarily a West Coast phenomena in pre-Beatle rock 'n' roll. Besides the Beach Boys, overdubbing was used by Phil Spector and Eddie Cochran. California also appears to have developed its own "backbeat" as well with two claps on the second beat and one on the fourth. Again, the music of Eddie Cochran, Phil Spector, and the Beach Boys all evidence this sound.

[5]Vance Packard, *Saturday Evening Post,* 21 March 1964, p.36.

[6]*Variety,* 24 June 1964, p. 50.

[7]*Variety*, 26 August 1964, p. 45.

[8]As quoted in Ralph Gleason, *The Jefferson Airplane and the San Francisco Sound* (New York: Ballantine Books, 1969), pp. 31–32.

[9]As quoted in Bud Scoppa, *The Byrds* (California: *Los Angeles Free Press*, July 1965).

4

Enter the Counterculture

"It [Music] is by no means like the other arts, the copy of Ideas, but the copy of the Will itself, whose objectivity the Ideas are. This is why the effect of music is so much more powerful and penetrating than that of the other arts, for they speak only of shadows, but it speaks of the thing itself. . . . I recognize [in the melody] the highest grade of the objectification of Will, the intellectual life and effort of man."

Schopenhauer

By the summer of 1965 a new, more sophisticated, socially aware, electric rock sound had emerged. The Rolling Stones' "Satisfaction" topped the charts for most of July and August and shortly thereafter Barry McGuire's "The Eve of Destruction" attained similar status. In August of that year the Byrds released the album *Mr. Tambourine Man,* which featured several Dylan songs placed to an electric sound, including the title cut, which as a single had reached number one on June 26, 1965. Dylan, himself, also released in August *Highway 61 Revisited* with "Like a Rolling Stone" as its opening number. By September, Simon and Garfunkel's "Sounds of Silence" was being heard on the radio, and their album of the same name appeared in February 1966. Across the Atlantic the Who released "My Generation" near the end of 1965, and the Beatles underwent a metamorphosis as alluded to by *Rubber Soul* (October 1965) and confirmed by *Revolver* some ten months later. The winds of change were gathering force and gusting; captured by the billowing sails of youth, they pushed America ever closer to the psychedelic age. One only had to listen to know the nation was destined for a future quite different from that conceived by Lyndon B. Johnson and the Eighty-ninth Congress. The times were indeed a-changin', but in a totally different direction than anyone could have imagined in early 1964 when Bob Dylan recorded that proclamation. The liberal tradition was dying; the nation's hope for a brilliant future lay splattered on the streets of Dallas. The public, still numbed by the presidential assassination, somnolently watched a televised America drift inextricably, and eventually explosively, into the Vietnamese "police action." They saw L.B.J. of the South sign into law the country's most liberal civil rights act. They viewed the incredible Eighty-ninth Congress as it ground out act after act of major legislation (eighty-nine laws in ten months!) in its attempt to better the human condition. But many Americans remained unconvinced of the significance of it all and unaware of their relationship to it. A common view: "They told me if I voted for Barry Goldwater we'd start bombing North Vietnam. I did, and they were right." They were in a new world and didn't know it. The old political ways were useless and unresponsive, despite the glowing names applied to programs such as "The Great Society," "The War on Poverty," and "Urban Renewal."

The system, the establishment, could not keep pace with the leaps and bounds demanded of it. The time was *NOW!*, but the government preferred to stay on schedule, to play the game according to the rules. As the problem-solving mechanisms of society, the government, and the corporate way of life, broke down and proved themselves to be ineffectual; the social order, its beliefs, values and procedures, came to be viewed as repressive, a problem in itself. Stifled by the game as it was being played, frustrated people took their balls and went home, with intuition as their only guide.

America rests in national stalemate, its goals ambiguous and tradition-bound instead of informed, clear, its democratic system apathetic and manipulated rather than "of, by and for the people."

Not only did tarnish appear on our image of American virtue, not only did disillusion occur when the hypocrisy of American ideals was discovered, but we began to sense that what we had originally seen as the American Golden Age was actually the decline of an era. . . .

Our work is guided by the sense that we may be the last generation in the experiment with living. But we are a minority—the vast majority of our people regard the temporary equilibriums of our society and world as eternally-functional parts. In this is perhaps the outstanding paradox: we ourselves are imbued with urgency, yet the message of our society is that

*there is no viable alternative to the present. Beneath the reassuring tones
of the politicians, beneath the common opinion that America will "muddle
through," beneath the stagnation of those who have closed their minds to
the future, is the pervading feeling that there simply are no alternatives,
that our times have witnessed the exhaustion not only of Utopias, but of any
new departures as well.[1]*

In the midst of this individual reorientation to the government and its social
manifestations, rock music took root, sprouted, and grew. Nourished by a rock
'n' roll heritage of youth-oriented distinctiveness, antisocial associations, and
good times, the rock songs from 1965 onward evolved more and more into a
major art form that expressed the new order of thinking emerging on the streets
of the nation. The new music was the force that united London and San Francisco
to create an electric international youth movement. Its constant broadcast made
the movement of the 1960s more widespread and recognized than any which
came before, and provoked a variety of politically motivated actions, such as
riots and demonstrations, which in turn led to further media publicity for the
discontented young. Such public visibility provided an exaggerated sense of
community and a timely pervasiveness which inspired a sense of ultimate victory:
they had the guns, but we had the numbers, or so Jim Morrison informed us.

Through the songs, the thoughts and values of a generation coming of age
were heard. Denouncing conventionalism, hypocrisy, and empty and unreal
character, the lyrics presented an ideology based on sharing, equality, introspection, individual autonomy and honesty, antimaterialism, spontaneity, originality,
and self-actualization. These lyrics provided their audiences with the words to
fit the feelings and thoughts inside their heads. Or as Tim Findley reminisced:

*We lived at 45 revolutions per minute and moved at a decibel range that
put it all in code. It was the thing which set us apart from the Your Hit
Parade generation that made us feel unique, like charter members in some
secret society. Not all of it made sense, but all of it was meaningful and
later on the music came down from people like Dylan and Baez as legends
being told in our own time and in our own language, until some of the time
you didn't know if you were living out the lyrics or the lyrics were talking
about your life. It all moved faster than we were able to think about it, and
for a while our lifestyles changed almost as fast as the Top 40 charts.[2]*

ELECTRIC SOUNDS
FOR AN ELECTRIFYING AGE

Coupled with the lyrics was a fresh, dynamic, powerful music. At the heart of
this sound lay electricity, which provided an incredible force and volume. The

electric guitar, the origins of which date back to the mid-1930s when such big band guitarists as Leonard Ware, Floyd Smith, and Charlie Christian experimented with the amplification of their instruments; and the electric bass, invented by Leo Fender and introduced by Monk Montgomery of the Lionel Hampton Band in 1953, became new instruments when placed in the hands of acid rock musicians. They fully explored the rainbow of ramifications opened by the union of electricity and music.

Just as drugs altered perceptions and introduced new patterns of thought, so too did electricity modify the reality of sound. Developing literally unbelievable distortions, guitarists unveiled previously inconceivable dimensions of musical experience that interlocked with the ever-expanding planes of consciousness to form the foundations of the counterculture. Wah-wah pedals, fuzz boxes, volume knobs, tremolo bars, and Marshall amplifiers offered infinite potential for weirdness. The performers further accentuated these possibilities by pulling strings, playing behind the bridge, running a pick along the strings, creating feedback, and transmitting guitar sounds through Leslie speakers. Within the studio further effects were achieved by running tapes backwards or at wrong speeds. The period was one of invention, presided over by the wizardry of Jimi Hendrix, Pete Townshend, Jerry Garcia, Roger McGuinn, Jeff Beck, among others.

To add further to the new age's new sound, groups began to introduce exotic instruments, such as the recorder and sitar, and became freer in their composition as well. Jazz-inspired improvisation quickly established itself as a hallmark of such San Francisco bands as the Jefferson Airplane, Grateful Dead, Big Brother and the Holding Company, and Quicksilver Messenger Service. Each player moved in his or her own direction, and frequently, as in the case of the Jefferson Airplane, only a strong bass line held the music together. Bass players such as Jack Casady of the Jefferson Airplane, Chris Hillman of the Byrds, Jack Bruce of Cream, and Phil Lesh of the Grateful Dead greatly expanded on the bass line, playing the instrument more like a guitar than a bass. In so doing, they further demonstrated the heightened sense of individuality blending with the cosmos that pervaded so much of acid rock.

The San Francisco bands also wreaked havoc on popular notions of harmony and melody. They were deliberately outrageous in their melodies, often playing outside the constraints of the key, incorporating more melodic skips than previously deemed appropriate, and featuring chromatic harmonies which broke with musical logic. Rhythmically the majority of their songs retained the twelve-bar blues form, but they introduced odd phrasing, such as $4\ 1/2 + 3\ 1/2 + 2 + 2$, instead of $4 + 4 + 2 + 2$. Songs with sixteen and thirty-two bars also appeared, and occasionally songs such as "White Rabbit" (1967) completely dispensed with the standard formats, just building up to a gradual, Bolero-like climax.

Groups began to move away from 4/4 time, with much of the Beach Boys' *Pet Sounds* (1966) done in 7/8 and the Grateful Dead's "Eleven" (1970) in 11/8. Like the age, the music was a conscious break with the past. People began viewing rock music as "art" and its lyrics as poetry. The form became recognized as a valid intellectual expression rather than just a diversion. As such the period 1965–1970 was indeed the period when rock came of age. It reflected, reinforced, and spread the youth culture. One entity fed off the other. Furthermore, as foreign and domestic crises increased, the nation as a whole began taking cues from the dissonant young, and helped to make their music one of the era's most potent arts of persuasion.

ARTS OF PERSUASION

Usually ephemeral in character, arts of persuasion are vehicles that expose a society to new or different beliefs. By either denouncing the old ways as ridiculous, if not downright destructive, or portraying a better approach to life, usually in utopian terms, arts of persuasion question the fundamental values and hierarchies of a society. Exemplified by such past forms as the etchings of Hogarth and Goya, and the cartoons of Nast and Daumier, arts of persuasion have consciously advocated changing the existing social order and its patterns of life. Rock music did the same thing during the late 1960s.

Rock was admirably suited to fulfill a persuasive function. It already had an antisocietal tradition with an established "us versus them" attitude, a friction capable of producing sparks. Furthermore, its infectious beat and loud, driving sound thumped into the mind, penetrating cranial recesses, setting new brain waves into motion. Readily available on singles and albums, the music could be possessed and controlled by individuals, unlike other mediums of mass communication such as television or motion pictures. Listeners could play and replay *their* music at *their* will in *their* homes. Such a repeatable experience further enhanced the effectiveness of the medium as a communicator of ideals and discontent.[3]

While the turntable allowed rock to be an individual experience, other mediums, most notably radio, but also concerts and movies, helped create a communal sense of identity within the rock scene. Placing the individual action within an audience setting, radio provided a social context for the new music. However, this was not the only role Marconi's invention played in the development of rock, as it also made possible the mass dissemination of the sound.

With the advent of television in the early 1950s, radio lost its broad-based audience support. Forced to rechannel its efforts toward specialized tastes, including those of Blacks and adolescents, stations such as WINS in New York, WHB in Kansas City, WIBG in Philadelphia, KSAN in San Francisco, and WKMH in Detroit opened the public airwaves to the roar of rock 'n' roll. Further enhanced by concerts and movies, the new music made the radio an essential element in the swirl of teenage existence.

Following the payola scandals and the triumph of *American Bandstand* as a major transmitter of clean, popular rock 'n' roll, radio lost much of its effectiveness as an alterate means of communication. With the implementation of Bill Drake's streamlined "Top Forty" style of programming, radio followed the music of the early 1960s and beach blanket movies back into the mainstream of American life. Here AM radio seemed doomed to dwell, as playlists virtually ignored such groups as the Cream, Jimi Hendrix, the Mothers of Invention, and the Grateful Dead, and emphasized the Monkees, Petula Clark, Paul Revere & the Raiders, the Seekers, Herman's Hermits, and Gary Lewis and the Playboys. Fortunately, underground FM radio rose after 1967. A 1965 Federal Communications Commission ruling required stations in cities of more than 100,000 people to avoid duplicating AM-FM programming for more than 50 percent of their daily schedule. This helped produce an alternate radio style that included acid rock in its programming.

Catering to a progressive rock audience, the new underground FM stations expanded the growing sense of an emerging counterculture. Their innovative program formats featured a playlist of noncommercial rock, album cuts (sometimes entire albums) less advertising, and less of a preoccupation with the time, news, and weather. This led AM stations to loosen up their style as well, and reinforced the notion that the world was starting to move in a new direction, changing to accommodate the views of the rock audience.

Concerts added another dimension to the rock community, as did the underground press and a variety of movies. Live performances transubstantiated the spiritual body of the anonymous radio audience into a corporeal entity, a virtual congregation of rock fans, feeding off each other's energy and the power of the music. Here the records and radio came to life. The concert environment, frequently augmented by a light show and elevated by audience and performer drug use, created a transcendent experience that glorified and celebrated the new generation.

Combine FM radio, concerts, movies such as *The Graduate, Easy Rider,* and *Yellow Submarine,* heavy television and press coverage, and the sudden proliferation of underground newspapers, and it is no wonder that Americans began to become aware of a fully developed counterculture in their midst. The mass communications network informed the populace at large that the young were reshaping and redefining their world, and the primary evidence of such a change was the presence of rock music with its socially relevant sounds.

Numerous sociological content analyses of rock lyrics[4] indicate an enormous increase in social/political themes in the music of the late 1960s. During this period lyrical expressions of discontent assumed highly skewed proportions when compared with the earlier moon-June song topics. These lyrics critically examined societal beliefs and values insofar as they affected the quality of life. While many songs questioned the establishment's viability, other songs, although not subjected to sociological study, presented an alternative to American life which was embodied by a misty utopian world of peace, love, and happiness. Such sounds of optimism as "San Francisco," "The Word," and "All You Need is Love," elucidated a positive approach to life, which was to supplant the old ways.

Vitally linked to the core of the emerging "make love, not war" generation, both the sounds of protest and utopian glory provide insights into the perceptions, motivations, and aspirations of the discontented young.

The Voice of Discontent

The discontent of the 1960s adhered to many traditional lines of argument, especially in its denunciation of the oppressiveness of the system and its economic ordering of priorities. Such dissatisfaction with America's civilization can be traced back to the romantic transcendentalist thought of the 1840s and 1850s, and runs through the labor movement from 1876 onward and in the Populist and Progressive movements of the late nineteenth and early twentieth centuries. Yet the disillusionment of the 1960s remains unique because of its pervasiveness and its expression of the adolescent fear of sacrificing freedom, adventure, passion and individuality to the normative dictates of society. Revolted by the definition of conventional adulthood, it rejected the entire status quo. Rather than point to specific problems, the discontented young struck out to discover a new set of social forms which more closely approximated their life ideals. With this departure, the movement struck a new note, a blues note, in the history of protest.

From the 1950s onward, intellectuals labeled the increasingly observable discontent, "alienation," and analyzed its roots in such books as *The Lonely Crowd, Growing Up Absurd, The Sane Society, The Image, The Quest for Community, The Uncommitted, The New Industrial State, The Power Elite, The*

Mechanical Bride, and *The Pursuit of Loneliness*. These books delineated and discussed in detail the various factors which each author felt contributed to the increased feeling of alienation. The decline of "intermediate assocations," such as the church, family, and small community; the decreasing amount of "meaningful work"; the expansion of the military-industrial complex, coupled with the growing autonomy of the executive branch of government; and the populace's increased awareness of living in a world of images created by the mass media and advertising, were viewed as explanations for the growing social unrest.

While intellectuals scrutinized and attempted to decipher the conditions creating a disparity between America's ideals and its actualities, a generation of young people were growing up amidst these alienating circumstances. The lives of these young people constituted a day-to-day reaction to an "unreal" world which was all too "real": "a television commercial was always a television commercial as well as a symbol of alienation."[5] This generation enjoyed the many amusements and comforts of a technological consumer society along with an unprecedented degree of freedom due to their affluence and to the Spockian theories of child rearing adhered to by many of their parents. With no commitments to the system they had the best of both worlds, yet many adolescents realized that their lives and values were irreconcilable with their parents. As adults, society expected these people to reject their benign lives of freedom, to become a part of the corporate masses, and to "pay their dues." Many of them did so. Others refused to alter their self-conceptions or forsake the more or less idealized way of life to which they had grown accustomed.

Rather than compromise their individual integrity for the sake of society, they refused to "sell out," attempted to alter their relationship with the dominant culture, and eventually tried to change the dominant culture itself. Confronted by an "unreal" society, these young hoped to "escape to freedom," to withdraw from the social "games," and create new forms. They searched in a new direction, using personal liberty as the foundation for all individual integrity. Expansion of individual perception was emphasized and criticism of middle-class America centered on its failure to act courageously in the face of injustice. Destructive relationships within the larger community needed to be severed and its coercive pressures avoided.

Between 1965 and 1969 rock helped galvanize young people into their own class. The songs reflected the alienating nature of the American political-economic system, and stressed the power of its dominant institutions to dehumanize through the restrictions they placed upon the emotional side of life. Transcending the questioning lyrics of the folk music tradition, the protest songs of the 1960s assumed a more aggressive stance with a direct and gutsy style.

The songs articulated the alienation of the young, and defined their discontent in terms of daily living rather than liberal ideals. By considering certain selected songs of this period, we can focus on the major themes and examine their means of persuasion.

The Songs

There is only one place to start a discussion of malcontent, rebellion, and defiance of social norms in the 1960s: the Rolling Stones. And there is only one song to start with: "Satisfaction." This song topped the charts in the summer of 1965 and many consider it to be the greatest rock song of all time. A driving, captivating music and highly charged chorus carried its message, while its verses attacked the mass media, advertising, and the sexual mores of the time. Mick Jagger briefly discussed this song in a 1968 interview with *Rolling Stone*.

M.J.: I don't think the lyrics are that important. I remember when I was very young, this is very serious, I read an article by Fats Domino which has really influenced me. He said, "you should never sing the lyrics out very clearly."

R.S.: You can really hear "I got my thrill on Blueberry Hill."

M.J.: Exactly, but that's the only thing you can hear just like you hear "I can't get no satisfaction."[6]

Most of the thoughts expressed by rock come in short phrases or series of phrases reinforced by music to create a font of epigrammatic knowledge as well as instant pop clichés. Listeners plugged into rock songs at will and extracted special words while the music maintained the spirit, the integrity of the piece. Phrases like "Come on baby, light my fire," "I'd love to turn you on," "But first, are you experienced? Have you ever been experienced?" rang in the ears of the young, echoed in their minds, and provided life with new priorities, sanctioned by the music. Fragments like these delivered obvious, direct messages to the brain, but surprisingly, much more subtle lines also came through as intent (stoned) listeners absorbed the sounds coming off the spinning platters. However, in "Satisfaction" the message came booming across, and many fans also picked up on Mick Jagger's discontent over not seducing some girl, and smiled at the television man who told how clean a shirt should be, but who couldn't be a man because he didn't smoke the cigarettes advanced in other, more macho-oriented advertisements. "Satisfaction" not only delivered a cry of rebellion, but offered reasons for that unrest, and did so with a biting wit.

The use of satirical argument was a favorite tool of the rock lyric of the 1960s. It was evident in many of the anti-war and drug songs of the era. Cynical inversion or juxtaposition of dominant cultural values and gleeful exaltation in their glaring inconsistencies, were the most devastating means of argument employed by rock against the status quo.

Another hit of 1965, the Animals' "We Gotta Get Outta This Place," presented a more direct line of argument to reflect the thinking of the malcontented young. Set in the dirty old part of the city where even the sun refused to shine, the song's refrain depicts a boy telling his girlfriend they have to get out of that place to a better life. The image of his daddy laying in bed dying after slaving his life away, prodded the boy to reach his decision. The song contained no musical despair despite its bleak lyrics. Rather, an optimism pervaded which was in accord with the resolution to depart from the old ways.

Although it depicted a lower-class situation, the song appealed to the sensibilities of an American audience which was predominantly not working class. The plight of the boy and girl in the song represented an extreme image of what many middle-class youngsters envisioned their parents' lives to be. Daddy was slaving his life away in the name of the company, the organization. For many fathers, work was their lives, but their work wasn't their own. This realization "freaked out" (in every sense of the word) many of the children, and these young people resolved not to let this be their destiny, for a better life was opening up.

By perceiving the ludicrousness of an American economic system with no social purpose other than its own self-preservation and expansion, the conclusions of American youth paralleled the thinking of such social critics as Henry David Thoreau, Henry Adams, Van Wyke Brooks, Paul Goodman, and John Kenneth Galbraith. The Beatles' in "Can't Buy Me Love" (1964) and "She's Leaving Home" (1967) simplistically portrayed this traditional theme of economic priorities stifling human needs. The latter song told the story of a girl running away from home, ironically, with a man from the motor trade, and juxtaposed the parents' lament that they had given their daughter everything money could buy, with the Beatles' claim that love was the one thing money couldn't buy.

The mass media, and in turn the public, quickly picked up on this rationale as an explanation for the rising generation gap. The press revamped the explanation of juvenile delinquency from the 1950s that blamed the problem on parental neglect. However, in the 1960s, the blame was placed upon affluent parents who were more interested in making money than in their children. Many middle-class parents believed this, and experienced much heartache when their children identified with the growing group of discontented young. "Where did we go wrong?" became the big question for parents; they did not seem to realize they were assigning the guilt to the wrong place. The parent-child relationship had not failed so much as had the child-society relationship.

Cat Stevens reworked the theme of the parent-child conflict in "Father and Son" (1971), and placed it in a more accurate context. As in "She's Leaving Home" this song juxtaposed the words of the parent with those of the child, only now the child spoke for himself. The father, content with his security, placed his material comforts above any ideals or sense of morality. He dismissed his son's outrage as naiveté, suggested marriage as a solution to his anger, and advised his son to think of everything he had, for he would be here in the future, but his dreams might not. The son, however, placed his integrity above the material benefits offered by the system. While the father desired security in an apparently insecure world, the son demanded integrity from a world apparently devoid of morality and justice. He did not begrudge the father his views, but decided he must start out on his own path of fulfillment.

Although the song offered no hint of the boy's solution to his moral anxiety, it delineated the difference in generational attitudes. The Beatles' simple allegorical denunciation at wealth without love was supplanted by a more complex, better construed statement of contrary world views, of compromise and stability versus integrity and social change.

The older generation's possessive clutching at material security might be explained in terms of their past experiences—the Depression, the Second World War, and an orientation toward success. Freed from these chains, a segment of the new generation, while anticipating, if not accepting, prosperity as a right, rejected security, and denounced the environment of insurance policies, terminal employment, and Madison Avenue-created bliss as one step removed from life itself. The modern world did not allow the individual to confront, experience or appreciate the sensations this planet had to offer. The Jefferson Airplane's "Crown of Creation" (1968) decreed that the stability striven for by American society could only be found among the dead. Preferring not to be fossils in their own time, the group moralized, "Life is change, how it differs from the rocks," and moved out, along with the son of "Father and Son," to find new worlds.[7]

The stagnation associated with society's obsession with security became the topic of numerous songs of the period. Couplet after melodic couplet flowed from Simon and Garfunkel records projecting the alienated situation at all levels of society, spelling doom for all, from the wealthy, and reworked, "Richard Cory" (1966) to the anonymous "Most Peculiar Man" (1966). The inescapable maze-like "Patterns" (1966) of corporate America had to be eluded somehow, for predetermined adulthood at best only offered the sophisticated vacuity of "Dangling Conversation" (1966), so whispered "The Sounds of Silence" (1965).

In a more direct manner Ray Stevens in "Mr. Businessman" (1968) and the Byrds in "Why" (1967) also portrayed the repressive tyranny of the older order. The former cynically dissected what passed as life in the corporate world, and the latter, with the help of a driving, demanding music, repeatedly questioned the life-denying attitudes of certain parents. Even the Cream, whose music primarily basked in a heavy, but optimistic, "Sunshine of Your Love" (1967), "Sitting on Top of the World" (1968) enviro-envisionment, advised "We're Going Wrong" (1967) and apprised their audience of the dominant culture's "World of Pain" (1967) and "Blue Condition" (1967) with no relaxation, conversation, or variation.

In a word, America was ridiculously boring, and no one made this clearer to the rock audience than Frank Zappa and the Mothers of Invention. *Freak Out* (1966), *Absolutely Free* (1967) and *We're Only in It for the Money* (1968) blatantly satirized the "drag" of living in a society of "plastic people" with their corny, empty, alcohol blurred, sexually "hung-up" attitudes, all embellished by a material paradise of brown shoes, t.v. dinners by the pool, and hair spray. Such tours de force as "Hungry Freaks, Daddy," "Help I'm a Rock," "Plastic People," "Brown Shoes Don't Make It," and "America Drinks and Goes Home," replete with appropriate sound effects ranging from orgasmic breathing to insane babbling and animal grunts and calls, presented an image of adult life as teenage amusement/derision. Straight teen culture fared no better than its insipid adult model in "You're Probably Wondering Why I'm Here" and a number of cuts on *Freak Out* which parodied love songs of the 1950s and 1960s.

The Mothers also took television newscasts to task in "Trouble Coming Every Day," and questioned, "Who Are the Brain Police?" Obviously opposed only to the content of media communications, the Mothers of Invention epitomized the use of rock music as a means of acquainting young people with a new way of looking at the world. Subtlety was not the group's forte. They denigrated the dominant culture, and implicitly celebrated those hungry freaks, the outcasts of the Great Society. In so doing the Mothers took message songs to their bluntly honest extreme.

Within two years of *Freak Out*, Frank Zappa attacked the mass movement to freakdom, providing the phony hippies and their psychedelic dungeons with treatment equal to that given to the dominant society and teen culture. After *We're Only in It for the Money*, Zappa forsook his role of prophet for the young and went off to explore new expressions of alienation. Rather than follow the master into the wilderness, let us consider the world of the hungry freaks.

POSITIVE PERSUASION:
THE NEW ETHOS

As early as 1960 Yale psychology professor Kenneth Keniston posited that alienation was a way of life with its own coherent and consistent view of the world.[8] From a three year study of over 2,000 Harvard students, he discovered a number of common precepts which the alienated used to define their attitude toward society. Being very much a silent minority, these youths did not recognize their position as part of a larger whole, and rarely could they lucidly articulate their approach to existence. Through lengthy autobiographies, the Thematic Apperception Test, interviews, and a wide variety of psychological experiments, Keniston extracted and compiled a system of values on which the alienated seemed to base their lives. At the center of the system lay the "aesthetic quest," which involved:

> . . . those goals and values whose main temporal focus is in the present, whose primary source is the self, and whose chief aim is the development of sentience, awareness, expression and feeling.[9]

Other values, flowing around and through this aesthetic quest, stressed a high respect for freedom and individual integrity, and a faithfulness to experience, honesty, and pleasure. Through these values the alienated young protected themselves in an inner-directed bastion against an increasingly other-directed society.

This alienated approach to life festered below the perceptual thresholds of American society throughout the years which saw the inception and formulation of rock music. The early music, while giving vent to discontent, contributed little else to ease the alienated individual's situation, and in 1964 Jeremy Larner accurately characterized rock 'n' roll's followers as "sullen rebels on their way to becoming organization men."[10]

From 1965 onward this scene changed radically, thanks to the initial energy burst of the Beatles, Rolling Stones, and Bob Dylan, who made music respectable once again. Numerous songs came forth espousing and reinforcing the values Keniston had identified five to ten years earlier. These songs gave the alienated lifestyle a voice and the discontented young came to realize they were not alone, but part of a growing community with a common, positive value system.

The Songs

With the possible exception of Bob Dylan's "Like a Rolling Stone" (1965), Jimi Hendrix's "If Six Was Nine" (1968) stands as the ultimate declaration/celebration of the autonomous individual, the alienated ideal. Not caring whether the world turned upside down, or mountains fell into the sea, or hippies cut off all their hair, the song's protagonist declared total freedom from established ways and proclaimed:

> *Got my own world to look through,*
> *And I ain't gonna copy you.*

A Hendrix monologue, in the midst of the song, reiterated the chorus' individualist stance, creating a vivid scene:

> *White collared conservative flashing down the street,*
> *pointing their plastic finger at me.*
> *They're hoping soon my kind will drop and die,*
> *but I'm gonna wave my freak flag high, high. . . .*

The music took the listener gloriously higher. The scene vanished and later reappeared with the barbed reply, "Point on Mr. Businessman, you can't dress like me!"[11]

Such an exhilarating taunt revealed not only the youth's sense of moral superiority, but also part of the motivation behind many countercultural forms involving personal appearance and action. Long hair on males, the female avoidance of make-up and shaving of body hair, and extreme manners of dress served as images of separation from the norms of a repressive, business-oriented society. As expressions of independent will, these forms defiantly proclaimed not only a stance against conformity, but also against first impressions and preconceived ideas of normalcy. With the perpetuation of these innovations by the media and advertising, an increased public awareness of the concept of a counterculture arose with its own philosophy of love, peace, happiness, and eternal sunshine.

The concept of "sunshine" existence stressed an appreciation for the moment and all it had to offer. Life, conceived as a grand exploration, centered on perception, the pleasures of the body and mind, and allowed for deep reflection on Truth. Many songs celebrated the joys of "grooving" on the experiential plane, the pleasures of overindulging and totally engaging the senses and brain. Most of these songs stayed on the surface, presenting the beauty of the present. Simon and Garfunkel's 59th Street Bridge *Song* (All is Groovy)" (1966), the Young Rascals "Groovin'" (1967), "Easy Rollin'" (1968) and "Beautiful Morning" (1968), and Joni Mitchell's "Chelsea Morning" (1969) were all glowing paeans to the senses and the present tense. Others, such as the Beatles' "In My Life" (1965), Joni Mitchell's "Both Sides Now" (1969) and the Byrds' "Just a Season" (1970) placed the scene within a slightly more reflective, "philosophical" context.

If all my days was [sic] hills to climb
In circles without reason
If all I was was passing time
My life was just a season.[12]

Still other songs, such as the Beatles' "Mother Nature's Son" (1968) and the Byrds' "Goin' Back" (1968), employed images of childhood as the vision of sunshine existence. Perceived as the period of life least hampered by the restrictions of social norms and hypocrisies, childhood was represented as a time of freedom, when individuals did as they pleased and interacted easily with the world. In actuality childhood was not as pastoral as these depictions, but its use as an ideal state functioned as proof that a sunshine existence was not impossible. In "Goin' Back" the Byrds recalled a time when they were young enough to know the truth, and declared that, with a little courage people could make every day a magic carpet ride.

All the songs of the late 1960s were not so explicit in their depiction of the alienated value system, but more often than not similar stances were implicit in the songs of the period. However, rock did more than articulate the alienated life style identified by Keniston; it built upon it. Where Keniston had found that the alienated youth of the late 1950s/early 1960s held a nonutopian outlook, visions of utopia now emerged in the late 1960s with rock's enunciation of the "new" approach to life. The Christian ethic of "love thy neighbor . . . ", revitalized and garbed in mod clothing, became the cornerstone of the emerging life style. People tried to accept others as equals, with everyone viewed as a brother or sister involved in the experience of living. In 1967 the Beatles claimed that "all you need is love," and the Youngbloods' hauntingly soft, yet psychedelic, "Get Together" (1969) urged everyone to get together, smile on their brother, and love one another.

Such an attitude encouraged a sense of community among the discontented, and a number of rock songs recognized and reinforced the development of a tangible youth community. The songs served as a common denominator, a shared experience upon which a sense of unity could develop, and the publicity given to the lifestyles and attitudes of rock stars further enhanced and justified the rock audience's vision of an emerging subculture. The Haight-Ashbury section of San Francisco became the earliest publicized community, billed as the new hippie heaven, and the equivalent of the beatnik Greenwich Village and North Beach turfs. With its psychedelic bands living in communal situations, this area appeared to some as a starting point for a growing physical community and became a mecca to which a multitude of discontented youth made pilgrimages. By the

48

time Scott McKenzie recorded John Phillips' "San Francisco" (1967) this community had greatly disintegrated, although the media-induced spirit remained until the end of the decade. Phillips' song jubilantly expressed the emerging sense of optimism and hope, and advised those destined for San Francisco to wear flowers in their hair as they would meet kindred spirits there. Presenting major images of love and change for the good, "San Francisco" celebrated the flower children as the new national saviors. Overcoming the inertia of the 1950s and the post-Kennedy 1960s, a whole generation, with a new explanation, was in motion, heading in a new direction to save America from itself. No matter how simplistic and trite these beliefs appear in retrospect, they did permeate the actions of the young for the remainder of the decade, culminating with Joni Mitchell's "Woodstock" (1970), which described the children of god in terms of stardust and gold, seeking a way back to the mythical garden.

The optimistic spirit of rebirth pervaded much of the music, and is most conspicuous in such songs as the Iron Butterfly's "In-a-Gadda-Da-Vida" (1968) and "Iron Butterfly Theme" (1968), It's a Beautiful Day's "White Bird" (1969), and the Moody Blues' *In Search of the Lost Chord* (1968). Lyrical visions of the utopian Eden to which the inspired young aspired also appeared and may be glimpsed in a variety of rock songs of the period.

Through rather vague images of a world based on emotional release and freedom to be, various songs projected a sense of the new utopia. One of the more explicit, the Blues Image's "Ride Captain, Ride" (1969), envisioned seventy-three men sailing out of San Francisco Bay. They invited everyone, "to ride along to the other shore, where we can laugh our lives away and be free once more," but no one heard their call, so the select departed on their way to a world that others earlier had missed.[13] The song coupled an optimistic lyric with dynamic music to create a sense of a quest underway. With a similar spirit, and guided by a new vision, often obtained by the use of drugs, the young also ventured forth, at least in their minds, on a course which would revolutionize the world. Through drugs, these people felt assured of their belief in the perfectability of humanity, despite all the evidence of history. For them LSD was a new force with which history and humanity had to reckon. Through drug-induced visions, the young glimpsed intimations of the new world, and experienced an exhilarating sense of freedom from societal constraints.

Another song to celebrate the new world vision, "Wooden Ships," first recorded by the Jefferson Airplane in 1970, also employed the ship metaphor. Opening in a post-Third World War environment, a reminder of the present system's capabilities, the song immediately invoked a smile as a universal image of friendship and happiness. From this desolate, yet hopeful, beginning the scene shifted to the wooden ships, free from the strife of the land, the emotionless world of the technocratic state. The singers urged the occupants of the ships to foresake the foreign land and return to a place where they could laugh again, where emotional experiences constituted a viable part of life. Going beyond merely describing an alternative world, the song concluded by imploring its audience to go ride the music, implying that the music and the wooden ships were one. The music itself became a conveyance to freedom and the promised land.

EMOTIONAL FREEDOM AND BEYOND

Rock songs not only informed listeners of the destructive nature of society and pointed toward a better existence, but also provided their audience with a temporary means of relief, of freedom *NOW*. Through the music, listeners found a way to escape the world around them and lock into the "away" dimension. Away from all responsibility, worry and doubts; away to sheer ecstasy and the only genuine freedom, sensation.

Numerous musicians recognized their music as a way to "away" and sang about it. Such songs as the Cream's "I'm So Glad," "Dance the Night Away" and "I Feel Free" (all 1967), the Jefferson Airplane's "If You Feel" (1968), Richie Havens' "Freedom" (1969), and Sly and the Family's Stone "I Wanna Take You Higher" (1969) all celebrated the joyously liberating function of rock by laying down a solid, driving sound accompanied by a simple lyric. Steppenwolf's "Magic Carpet Ride" (1968), although primarily a drug song, also alluded to this aspect of the music when it advised:

> *Close your eyes girl, look inside girl,*
> *Let the sound take you away . . .*[14]

With this the music moved inside the brain and took the listener away from the environment. "Spaced out," beyond the ego, the individual and the music became one.

In his article "Rock as Salvation" Amherst professor Benjamin DeMott felt the music possessed a "quasireligious force," and analytically noted:

> *. . . if one phase of the rock experience is confirmation of what man knows,*
> *the other phase equally telling, is escape from the knowledge. . . . the rock*
> *invitation offers the audience a momentary chance to have it both ways: If*
> *I accept the invitation, I can simultaneously be political and beyond politics,*

intellectual and beyond intellectuality, independent and beyond personal independence.

I can be these contrary things because the rock experience at its most intense is an intimation of engulfment and merger, a route to a flowing, ego-transcending oneness. . . . a thunderous, enveloping self-shattering moment wherein the capacity for evaluating an otherness is itself rocked and shaken, and the mob of the senses cries out: "What we feel, we are." [15]

DeMott described the phenomena which the Lovin' Spoonful tentatively had labeled, "the magic that can set you free." In "Do You Believe in Magic" (1965) this group presented one of the earliest lyrical expressions of rock's close relationship with emotional freedom. In acknowledging that there was magic in the music and the music was in them, the group introduced the public to the magician/musician, a shamanistic role that seemed increasingly appropriate as the decade progressed.

While DeMott cautiously considered the rock experience to be "quasi-religious," others were less conservative. The media picked up on the mystical aspects of rock and further heightened the public's awareness of them with such equations as the Cream's selling more record albums in a twenty-four month period than the *Bible* had sold copies in twenty-four years. Jerry Garcia of the Grateful Dead found:

Now all of the sudden it [rock music] is the vehicle for new cultural changes. I don't know why. It could be that music is one of those things left that isn't completely devoid of meaning. Talk—like politics—has been made meaningless by endless repetition of lies. There is no longer any substance in it. You listen to a politician making a speech, and it is like hearing nothing. Whereas, music is unmistakeably music. The thing about music is that nobody listens to it unless it is real. I don't think you can fool anybody for too long in music. . . . Music goes back way before language does. And music is like the key to a whole spiritual existence which this society doesn't even talk about. We know it's there. The Grateful Dead plays at religious services of the new age. Everybody gets high, and that's what it's all about really. Getting high is a lot more real than listening to a politician. You can think that getting high actually did happen—that you danced, and got sweaty, and carried on. It really did happen. I know it when it happens. I know it when it happens every time. [16]

It was not chance when John Lennon compared the popularity of the Beatles to that of Jesus Christ. The music transcended mere entertainment and political ideology, it proposed a new way of life, a new spirit on a supernatural plane, which it at least partially supported by providing an escape from the present and the old ways of doing things. As such, rock music might be viewed as the twentieth-century psychic equivalent of the nineteenth-century American frontier, which Frederick Jackson Turner postulated served as a safety valve for the pressures of civilization.

Rock music appealed to the primordial aspects of man, to the emotional side of a quasirational creature. The German philosopher/sociologist Georg Simmel felt that only on the emotional level might the masses form a common bond. In this age of the mass man in quest of community many people found a release in rock music and a basis for cultural identification. Within the context of emotional release and unity, the music reinforced the role of the emotions in human life. Through rock music humanity's passionate aspects were elevated to a position equal to or above the rational. Janis Joplin said it all when she explained:

> There was a time I wanted to know everything. I read a lot. I guess you'd
> say I was pretty intellectual. It's odd. I can't remember when it changed.
> But you can fill your life up with ideas and still go home lonely. All you
> really have that really matters are feelings. That's what music is to me. . . .
> That's what this music is all about. It's about feeling. It's about wanting.
> It's about needing and cramming yourself full of it.[17]

Rock emotionally expressed in a rational framework the rising generation's thoughts and feelings, making it the ideal clarion for spreading the word to a world which appeared to be devoid of emotional sensation, if not reason as well. Creating an electrical oral tradition, rock became a center of communication for the youth culture. The music emerged as a positive environment in which the rhetoric might circulate. Rock's mass communications network broadcast a lifestyle which obviously differed from the accepted standards of American society. The dissemination and absorption of its subterranean values reinforced behavioral changes, and as these changes became widespread, basic lifestyles were affected. Rock's role as a reflector and reinforcer of these changes becomes readily apparent via an examination of the major lyrical themes of the period.

NOTES

[1]Students for a Democratic Society, "Port Huron Statement" (Unpublished manuscript).

[2]Tim Findley, "Tom Hayden, Ten Years After Port Huron," *Rolling Stone,* 26 October 1972, p. 37.

[3]For a discussion on rock's persuasive characteristics see Irving Rein, *Rudy's Red Wagon* (Glenview, Illinois: Scott, Foresman and Company, 1972), pp. 73–79.

[4]For example, see Irwin Kantor, "This Thing Called Rock: An Interpretation," *Popular Music & Society*, 3, No. 3 (1974), pp. 203–214; James T. Carey "The Ideology of Autonomy in Popular Lyrics: A Content Analysis," *Psychiatry*, 32, No. 2 (May, 1969), pp. 150–164; Richard Cole "Top Songs of the '60's: A Content Analysis of Popular Lyrics," *American Behavioral Scientist*, 14 (January 1971), pp. 389–400; Hugo A. Keesing, "The Pop Message: A Trend Analysis of the Psychological Content of Two Decades of Music," in *Adolescent Behavior & Society*, ed. Rolf E. Muuss (New York: Random House, 1975).

[5]Ellen Willis, "Dylan," in *Beginning to See the Light*, ed. Ellen Willis (New York: Alfred A. Knopf, 1981).

[6]Jonathan Cott and Sue Cox, "An Interview with Mick Jagger," *Rolling Stone*, 12 October 1968.

[7]Jefferson Airplane, "Crown of Creation" from their *Crown of Creation* album © Icebag Corp., 1968, All Rights Reserved. Reprinted by permission of the publisher.

[8]Kenneth Keniston, *The Uncommitted, Alienated Youth in American Society*, (New York: Harcourt Brace, 1965).

[9]Keniston, p. 63.

[10]Jeremy Larner, "What Do They Get from Rock 'n' Roll?" *Atlantic*, August 1964, p. 48.

[11]"If Six Was Nine," by Jimi Hendrix, ©1968 Six Continents Music Publishing, Inc. and Yameta Co. Ltd. Used by permission. All rights reserved.

[12]Byrds "Just a Season"

[13]Blues Image, "Ride Captain Ride," words and music by Frank Konte and Carlos M. Pinera, 1969 ATM Music. Used by permission. All rights reserved.

[14]Steppenwolf, "Magic Carpet Ride"

[15]Benjamin DeMott, "Rock as Salvation," *New York Times Magazine*, 25 August 1968, pp. 40, 44–46.

[16]Fred Stuckey, "Jerry Garcia, 'It's All Music,'" *Guitar Player*, 5. No. 3, pp. 38–39.

[17]Deborah Landau, *Janis Joplin, Her Life and Times* (New York: Paperback Library, 1971), p. 16.

5

Peace, Love,
and
Alternate Realities

"I have lived some thirty years on this planet, and I have yet to hear the first syllable of valuable or even earnest advice from my seniors. They have told me nothing, and probably cannot tell me anything to the purpose. Here is life, an experiment to a great extent untried by me; but it does not avail me that they have tried it. . . . How could youths better learn to live than by at once trying the experiment of living?"

HENRY DAVID THOREAU

The social history of the late 1960s may be characterized by vehement protests against the Vietnam war, a loosening of sexual mores, and extensive drug experimentation. The discontented young were prime agents in these activities, and through their vociferous stances, these movements became national issues. Rock, as a conveyor of the thoughts and values of the generation coming of age, reflected youth's perceptions of the social changes transpiring in their midst, and further served to reinforce the new behavior patterns.

The themes of war protest, drugs, sex, and love suffused the lyrics of the period, and served not only as an index of personal behavior, but also transcended individual lives to become meaningful metaphors to the emerging counterculture. Vietnam represented the Establishment's destructive tendencies, the drugs ingested by the young were the medicine to overcome the old ways, and the "free love" relationship served as an initial glimpse of the world to come. In short, these lyrical themes provided a sense of communal unity, while reflecting and guiding individual reactions to what was "going down." As such, these lyrics provide valuable insights into the history of the period, and an analysis of them may help to systematize and place in perspective the thoughts and actions of the young in the tumultuous closing years of the 1960s.

ANTI-WAR SONGS

Vietnam, more than any other issue of the late 1960s, forced many Americans to consider the possibility that our nation did not always wear the white hat. Middle-class minds could not so easily explain away the war as they had the civil rights movement. Vietnam was not a regional aberration nor the result of ill-formed decisions of the distant past. Rather, it was the product of the present, and something which could be remedied immediately if the President so decreed. As such, the growing discontent with America's direction coalesced around the question of the rationale behind the war. The issue of Vietnam allowed Eugene McCarthy to topple LBJ and led increasing numbers of people to lose faith in the political process.

For males between the ages of eighteen and twenty-six the war transcended political and philosophical rhetoric and represented an imminent threat to their lives. As the justifications for the war became increasingly dubious, many young men questioned whether the risk of their lives was a reasonable price to pay for American citizenship. More men than the government ever reported felt it was not. They evaded the draft and viewed with disdain the society which found the war to be a chore. An examination of the shifting lyrical themes of the anti-war songs of the 1960s reveals evolving attitudes toward war and America, and further attests to the role of rock as an expression and disseminator of the seeds of discontent.

In the early years of the decade, when thoughts of war confined themselves to speculation on the aftermath of a nuclear exchange, anti-war songs came to the public's attention via the popular revival of folk music. Although denigrated by purists, this revival, with its harmonious melodies, fostered an increased interest in folk music and promoted public awareness of liberal protest in general.

Peter, Paul and Mary one of the most popular groups, recorded several anti-war songs, including Pete Seeger's, "Where Have All the Flowers Gone" (1962), and Bob Dylan's "Blowin' in the Wind" (1963). These songs contained the traditional themes of despair over man's inhumanity to man and conveyed an implicit moral indignation toward those who created wars. War was depicted as beyond the control of individual decision, with simplistic remedies reminiscent of those proposed by Woodrow Wilson at the close of World War I. This genre primarily appealed to the listening audience's sentiments, while leaving the depths of emotion undisturbed.

However, from 1964 onward, as the Vietnam conflict escalated, the anti-war songs began to attain a new dimension. Through the publicity given to Peter, Paul, and Mary's rendition of "Blowin' in the Wind," Bob Dylan's name reached the public's attention, and although he did not appeal to the broad audience enjoyed by his popularizers, his influence was to be sweeping. Going beyond the questions raised in "Blowin' in the Wind," Dylan began to attack those "Masters of War" who built the big guns and the death planes while hiding behind desks in offices. He equated these industrialists with Judas and claimed that even Jesus would not forgive their actions. To such moralism Dylan added a new dimension of hatred as the song concluded with the singer wishing for the war mongers' death.

Other Dylan songs, although not so blunt, depended upon cynical invective to convey the singer's attitude. The extremely ironic "With God on Our Side" (1964) enumerated the wars that America had won in the past with the approval of God. The song dripped with cynicism, and among other things reminded the audience that nations ignored the number of dead when God's on their side.

Other singers followed the new paths opened by Dylan's inventive lyrics. Such songs as Phil Ochs' "I Ain't Marching Anymore" (1965), "The War is Over" (1967), and "White Boots Marchin' in a Yellow Land" (1968), Barry McQuire's "The Eve of Destruction" (1965), the Animals' "Sky Pilot" (1968), and Buffy Sainte-Marie's "The Universal Soldier" (1964) all owe a debt to Dylan's style and reflect the increasing resistance forming against Vietnam, despite the number one position on the charts of "The Ballad of the Green Berets" (1966). These songs all differed from the "Where Have All the Flowers Gone" genre by specifically pointing to the idiocies and incongruities of our society, or by placing the responsibility to decide to fight upon the individual. Perhaps the most powerful of these songs, Buffy Sainte-Marie's "The Universal Soldier," blamed the continuation of the war upon those who complied with the dictates of their society and fought, as they were the ones who served as weapons in the war, and without them the killing could cease. By imputing an individual morality which transcended that of society, these songs placed the earlier humanistic themes into a more pertinent, active context.

By the time these later songs appeared, Bob Dylan had vacated the area of folk and protest, realizing a more basic chaos existed in American society, and from 1965 onward, more and more people came to realize that Vietnam and civil rights were not the issues at stake, but rather the entire American system was itself somehow inherently evil. For any viable change to occur, the entire American system of values and priorities had to be altered.

The anti-war songs of the late 1960s reflected this changed outlook. While all previous protest against war either implicitly or explicitly stressed the inhumanity of war in terms of a higher morality, the songs of the middle and late 1960s needed no further justification for opposition to the war than the preservation of an individual's life. Morality resided within the individual's sense of right or wrong, for no higher morality seemed to dictate society's actions. The anti-war songs manifested the counter culture's acceptance of Polonius' advice to his son Laertes, that "above all things, to thine own self be true." In 1967 this boiled down to individuals telling the government, "Make your silly laws, fight your stupid wars, but don't hassle me." By reassuring the individual draft resistor that others backed his stand, the songs provided support for those people involved in making the heaviest decision of their lives.

The Bob Seger System's "2 + 2 = ?" (1968) reflected and augmented the thoughts of many draft age men. Starting in a humble manner, the song portrayed the situation which most potential draftees confronted: They did not want to go to war, but found they must if their society so demanded. The singer, after being labeled a "fool" and an "upstart" for questioning the rules, recounted the death of a friend in "a foreign jungle land" and alluded to the deceased's girlfriend who just cried and did not understand. When told that his friend died for freedom, the singer resolved:

> . . . If he died to save your lives,
> Go ahead and call me yellow . . .¹

as "two plus two" was on his mind. Starting softly, the music became more and more intense as the story unfolded. In the last stanza the music and lyric struck out against those addressed, as the singer declared he wanted a si.nple answer to the question why did he have to die? The song hit at the core of many young men's doubts and made resisting the draft a matter of survival. Similarly, the Vietnam war gave an added significance to the move away from the dominant culture as men of draft age fought for their lives. Vietnam laid the hypocritical ways of the old system a bit barer, and made the need for change seem essential.

Vietnam revealed all too well that the American way no longer was what most Americans thought it was. Rather than providing a "government of the people, by the people, for the people," American political leaders governed the people as an industrial state, for an elite few. The words of Randolph Bourne, written in the midst of World War I, rang terrifyingly true.

> *The kind of war which we are conducting is an enterprise which the American government does not have to carry on with the hearty cooperation of the American people but only with their acquiescence. And that acquiescence*

seems sufficient to float an indefinitely protracted war for vague or even largely uncomprehended and unaccepted purposes. Our resources in men and materials are vast enough to organize the war techniques without enlisting more than a fraction of the people's conscious energy. . . .

. . . Our war is teaching us that patriotism is really a superfluous quality in war. The government of a modern organized plutocracy does not have to ask whether the people want to fight or understand what they are fighting for, but only whether they will tolerate fighting. . . . We are learning that war doesn't need enthusiasm, doesn't need conviction, doesn't need hope to sustain. Once manoeuvred, it takes care of itself, provided only that our industrial rulers see that the end of the war will leave American capital in a strategic position for world-enterprise.[2]

Anti-war protest would not result in the immediate cessation of the war; the war would continue until the President decided otherwise. Such a realization generated a new anti-war lyric, whose strength derived from its black humor. This form of humor, already well established in the literary works of J.P. Donleavy, Terry Southern, and Joseph Heller, differed extensively from Dylan's earlier sardonic jibes. As the reaction of a powerless individual confronted with a totally absurd situation, black humor ridiculed society's insanity, which in turn reassured the listening audience of their own basic mental stability and provided a cathartic release for pent-up emotions. Country Joe and the Fish's "I-Feel-Like-I'm-Fixin'-To-Die Rag" (1967), which reduced "my country right or wrong, my country" to its most absurd level, perhaps best exemplified this critical approach. In the chorus, with its bouncy, gay, carnival-like tune, a jubilant, unquestioning soldier declared:

> *And it's one, two, three, what are we fightin' for?*
> *Don't ask me—I don't give a damn. Next stop is Vietnam;*
> *And it's five, six, seven, open up the pearly gates—*
> *Well, there ain't no time to wonder why,*
> *Whoopee!—We're all gonna die.*

The verses were equally cutting, urging a need for quick action to capitalize on the "war Au-Go-Go" situation. The verses moved from the less than personal images of the military establishment and Wall Street, each with its own motives for encouraging the continuation of the war, to the concluding verse's entry into the family circle, which again advocated immediate action, this time in language reminiscent of television advertising.

> *Come on Mothers throughout the land,*
> *Pack your boys off to Viet Nam.*

> *Come on Fathers, don't hesitate,*
> *Send your sons off before it's too late.*
> *Be the first ones in your block*
> *To have your boy come home in a box.*[3]

This humorous inputation of crass commercial motivations for the war, through the use of popular imagery and advertising sloganese, linked the war in Vietnam to the American industrial state's value system in general, and was very similar in style to certain turn-of-the-century anti-war poems which denounced America's imperialistic actions in the Philippines. Parodying Kipling's "The White Man's Burden," one author wrote:

> *Pile on the brown man's burden*
> *To gratify your greed;*
> *Go, clear away the "niggers"*
> *Who progress would impede . . .*
>
> *. . . With shells and dum-dum bullets,*
> *A hundred times make plain*
> *The brown man's loss must ever*
> *Imply the white man's gain.*

While another chimed:

> *Rob for the sake of justice*
> *Kill for the love of man.*[4]

Such early-twentieth-century depictions of war as an inversion of Christian values closely paralleled such anti-war songs as the Fugs' "Kill for Peace" (1966) and such Jefferson Airplane pronouncements as:

> *War's good business, so give your son,*
> *But I'd rather have my country die for me.*[5]

By the end of 1968, with the election of Richard M. Nixon to the Presidency looming more and more imminent, the production of anti-war songs tapered off. One of the last anti-war songs of the decade, Country Joe and the Fish's "Untitled Protest" (1969) indicted traditional liberal protest methods of sending "cards and letters" and offering "prayers and praises." The song partially reverted to the more traditional theme of man's inhumanity to man, but did so in much more vivid terms that reflected the trends in televised newscasts. The Fish's black humor still showed itself in such visions as:

Superheroes fill the skies, tally sheets in hand,
Yes, in times of war, keeping score, takes a superman.

These were contrasted with dead oxen baking in the mud, while "fat flies eat out their eyes and bathe themselves in blood."[6]

With pronouncements of this sort, musicians abandoned the field as the futility of protest became increasingly apparent. John Lennon's song, "Give Peace a Chance" (1969) and his "Happy Christmas, War Is Over!" campaign (1969) only further demonstrated the impotence of the anti-war movement, since both reflected a spirit of wishful thinking more than anything upon which to base real hopes for change. The ineffectuality of protest led to campus demonstrations that became more militant in mood as the 1960s turned into the 1970s. These actions served as a vent for frustration, a striking out, rather than just a registration of opposition. The optimism of the 1967 march on the Pentagon had long since dissipated, and so did the anti-war song. People came to recognize that Vietnam was not a disease, but merely a symptom of all that ailed American society.[7] Fundamental changes in consciousness would have to be achieved before any major social changes would transpire.

DRUG SONGS

Drugs, more than any other factor, were the new force upon which youthful optimism for positive change levitated. Powerful hallucinogenic chemicals— LSD, mescaline and psilocybin—altered perceptions of reality and stripped away the authority of social forms. Divested of the mystical, religious functions traditionally associated with the use of comparable "allies" in other cultures, these street drugs did not so much reveal a spiritual dimension as they restructured and created new conceptions of the terrestrial plane. In a culture accelerating at a geometric rate from religious associations, the psychedelic experience was not construed so much as a revelatory glimpse into some ethereal plane as declared by Timothy Leary, but rather as an eerie interpretation of society from a transcendent position.

Drugs dominated the age, and were a new force operating in American society. Not since 1910, when the nation banned the importation of opium, had drugs and their use become a major public issue. The enforcement of drug laws provided additional evidence of the repressive nature of the government, and another area of conflict arose between the youth and the authorities.

Drugs, acquired by the Beat culture from jazz and ghetto encounters, had been passed on to the folk music crowd that populated Greenwich Village in the early 1960s. With the folk community's increased involvement in civil rights and the Black subculture, more and more middle-class whites learned about and experimented with drugs. Such early drug songs as Bob Dylan's "Mr. Tambourine Man" (1965) and the Association's "Along Comes Mary" (1966) described the new life experiences discovered by drug users. The portrayal of drug use in a very positive manner through joyous imagery in these songs evidenced a burgeoning subterranean drug culture on the verge of revealing itself to the nation as a whole.

By 1967 this undercurrent of drug use had gathered a sufficiently large constituency to burst upon the American scene in song. Across the nation youths could be found sitting stoned in darkened rooms, the record player (the only thing functioning) sending out a totally new and bizarre electronic music with equally strange lyrics:

> Picture yourself on a boat on a river
> With tangerine trees and marmalade skies
> Someone is calling, you answer quite slowly,
> The girl with Kaleidoscope eyes . . .
>
> Celophane flowers of yellow and green
> Towering over your head
> Look for the girl with the sun in her eyes
> And she's gone . . .[8]

One instantly knew this was *our* music, and now the "our" was not teenagers, but drug users. A new, and potent, ingredient was added to the generation gap as increasingly large numbers of young people "tuned in, turned on, and dropped out" to become members of the new, exclusive subculture. This new society quickly began to develop its own norms, many of which ran contrary to dominant cultural values.

The drugs named the new music "psychedelic." *Sergeant Pepper's Lonely Hearts Club Band* by the Beatles served as a bridge for conventional sensibilities, and within a short period of time the more extreme sounds of the Cream, Jimi Hendrix, and the Jefferson Airplane emanated, along with the pungent odor of marijuana, from anywhere that young people gathered.

Songs such as "White Rabbit," "Purple Haze," "Eight Miles High," and "Tales of Brave Ulysses" served as arts of substitute imagery, inasmuch as they attempted to recreate the sensations of a drug trip. Although nothing could simulate the acid high, these songs operated as reminders and glorifiers of the actual experience. The songs summed up and preserved the psychedelic experience and accomplished the dual purpose of reinforcing the users and encouraging the uninitiated to try. These new sounds not only reflected what transpired on a drug trip, but also set up a positive framework of comprehension and expectation through which individuals would view their past and future drug-induced experiences.

The Jefferson Airplane's version of Grace Slick's "White Rabbit" (1966) quickly became the anthem of the drug culture. Drawing heavily from the imagery of Lewis Carroll's *Through the Looking Glass,* it conveyed the feeling of being beyond the realm of ordinary life. Encounters with hookah-smoking catapillars, pills that made you larger and smaller, and the White Knight talking backwards bedazzled the mind and further encouraged the listener to heed the Dormouse's words, "Feed your head."

While the Jefferson Airplane's song drew its imagery from the western literary tradition, other musician-songwriters moved beyond this tradition to create striking new images which captured the sensations of the drug-infused moment. Dynamically original, Jimi Hendrix transcended traditional imagery in "Purple Haze" and other songs on *Are You Experienced?* (1967). Dwelling on an experiential plane, the songs bombarded the brain with electrical-musical sensations, disjointed thought processes, and strong temporal and emotional shifts, all reminiscent of an actual drug experience. Lyrically they moved at a speed comparable to Bob Dylan's "Subterranean Homesick Blues" and the music was in a class of its own. According to Ellen Sander, Hendrix had, "turned the electric guitar into a uniquely electronic instrument, he pulled sounds from it no musician conceived of and it was all musically intact, all rock 'n' roll."[8] His music completely "incredibilized" listeners, while others doubted that it was music at all. Hendrix's sound embodied the psychedelic experience, and to a person outside that context no gateway opened for comprehension.

In the spring *American Quarterly* of 1971, Lawrence Chenoweth proved this point when he attempted to view the works of Hendrix and the Jefferson Airplane from a strictly psychological perspective. He claimed "Purple Haze" indicated that the singer's:

> . . . *difficulty in understanding and receiving love was so terribly disorientating that colors and emotions blended chaotically in his mind making him unsure if he was happy or miserable.*[9]

By viewing the song completely out of its social context, Chenoweth did not perceive the total resonance of the piece. He recognized the powerful emotional feeling, but erroneously ascribed it to the traditional musical theme of love. The magnificence of the song and its relationship to the psychedelic experience eluded him.

The Cream's *Disraeli Gears* (1967) also conveyed a powerful feeling for the acid experience. Typical of the album "Tales of Brave Ulysses," through a driving sound, sent the listener on a journey from the leaden winter to the violence of the sun, where the sky loves the sea. Vivid colors in constant motion—a girl's brown body dancing through the turquoise, deep blue ripples carved in the mind, tiny purple fishes running through the fingers—flowed together, chilled the skin and incited the mind. Employing the metric pattern of Tennyson's "Lady of Shalotte" and images from Homer's *Odyssey,* the song instilled in the listener a tremendous sense of heroic adventure or quest, the same spirit with which to approach a psychedelic journey.

A trip was an eight-to-ten-hour adventure into the unknown. No one could foretell where the coupling of their mind and acid would take them, nor what would be encountered. R.D. Laing, in *The Politics of Experience,* likened the psychedelic experience to a "trip into inner space." Rather than traveling to the moon, drug users took to traveling inside their own minds. Despite the claims of *Star Trek,* the human mind, and not space, was the last frontier. In a certain sense tripping might be considered the twentieth-century, urban youth's equivalent to nineteenth-century hunting expeditions. Both activities removed individuals from the day-to-day world and allowed them to interact with their environment on a new level. Obviously the two experiences have major differences. For example, the latter emphasized the participant's mastery over the environment, while the former sought to comprehend it, adjust to it and engage it on its own terms. However, this difference is in itself a telling contrast between the psychic landscapes of the two eras, as each activity ostensibly prepared individuals to better handle their daily lives.

The appeal of grand adventure certainly enticed many people to indulge in hallucinogenic chemicals. The drugs were potent antidotes to the sterile world of the man in the gray flannel suit. As Daniel Boorstin noted in *The Image*:

> While an "adventure" was originally "that which happens without design; chance, hap luck," now in common usage it is primarily a contrived experience that somebody is trying to sell us.[10]

Not only had the word "adventure" become devoid of meaning, but so had much of life. Peter Marin, the director of the highly innovative Pacific High School, claimed society deprived its adolescents of any rites of passage into a sacred or mythical world of any sort. He believed:

> . . . it is precisely this world that drugs replace; adolescents provide for themselves what we deny them: a confrontation with some kind of power

*within an unfamiliar landscape involving sensation and risk. It is there, I
suppose, that they hope to find, by some hurried magic, a new way of seeing,
a new relation to things, to discard one identity and assume another. They
mean to find through their adventures the* ground *of reality, the resonance
of life we deny them, as if they might come upon their golden city and return
still inside it: at home.*[11]

Indeed, the hope of gaining insight into the nature of the world and its relationship
to the individual, accompanied the adventure of the drug experience. As a popular
example of the period's graffiti proclaimed, "Time is never wasted when you're
wasted all the time." The chemicals induced phenomenological vision, slowed
down time (or increased perception), and allowed the ego to be transcended in
a manner comparable to that described by Sartre.[12] Reality blurred, was restructured, and a new world emerged. A number of songs, including Bloodrock's
"Gimme Your Head" (1969) and the Moody Blues' "Om" (1968), attempted to
describe this new realm with its sounds of color and light of a sigh. Through
drugs, America's young encountered another dimension, and just as the earlier
explorers searched for new ways to the Orient in hopes of economic gain, so
the twentieth-century adventurers went out in search of new insights into the
ways of human society and the universe.

The Mamas and the Papas' "Strange Young Girls" (1966) celebrated the
young girls of Los Angeles' Sunset Strip who offered themselves on an "altar
of acid." The song endorsed the opinion that LSD was a positive catalyst for
change. Complimented by a soft, tender music, the song lyrically equated peace
and love with tripping. The chemicals freed the individual from socially acceptable, but restrictive, thought patterns. Returning to a more "natural" ordering of
sensations, the drug-affected mind experienced the world for the first time, in
much the same manner as a child's mind was imagined to do. Reviving Locke's
concept of the *tabula rasa,* individuals attempted to wipe their mental slates
temporarily clean to get a better view of themselves and society.

> *Wisdom flows childlike, while softly talking*
> *Colors surround them bejeweling their hair,*
> *Visions astound them, demanding their share* . . .[13]

The Amboy Dukes, featuring lead guitarist Ted Nugent, also portrayed this
utopian vision in *Journey to the Center of the Mind* (1968). The album opened
with the title cut, which urged the listener to transcend the material realm to a
place where fantasy and fact merge. The song established the album's basic
premise by alluding to the joyous benefits that might be derived if everyone

turned on and journeyed to the center of their minds. The cuts which followed explored various aspects of the drug-induced state of mind, with "Why is a Carrot More Orange than an Orange" being the most memorable title. Such a quasiphenomenological question typified the supposedly profound revelations engendered by drug use and its accompanying reflective moments. The stumbling over the contradictory nature of established verities, no matter how minor, reinforced the drug user's doubts about the validity of the dominant culture's ways. These led to further probing of the question, "How else have 'they' entrapped us with their words?"

In the song "Bass Strings" on their album *Electric Music for the Mind and Body* (1967), Country Joe and the Fish also posited the positive possibilities of individual rediscovery through the use of drugs. Reminiscent of nineteenth-century romantic conceptions of nature, the Fish stressed the use of acid as a means of opening the mind and carrying the individual back to a state where the truth, which lives all around, but just beyond human consciousness, can be grasped.

Little in the established press addressed the positive aspects of the young's drug experimentation. An occasional scientific article was biologically informative, but few reports reflected the street experiences of the drug user. Psychologists disclosed set and setting to be significant factors contributing to drug behavior patterns, yet showed little interest in working with the drug outside the laboratory under decontrolled conditions.

Science was interested in testing the drugs, while the young experienced them and, in turn, tested society. The results of the youthful experimentation were not written and read, but rather were relayed verbally to become part of an emerging oral tradition. As a common shared experience, the drug adventure, like rock music, strengthened the bonds of the youthful counterculture, and served as a vehicle for sociability. Country Joe and the Fish referred to this drug-instilled sense of comradeship in "Flying High" (1967), as did the Beatles in "With a Little Help from My Friends" (1967). Vice President Spiro Agnew, in a 1970 Las Vegas campaign speech, pointed to the Beatle song as one of the many used to "brainwash" America's youth into accepting a "drug culture." The Vice President mentioned his shock upon learning the word "friends" represented marijuana, LSD, and other "harmful" drugs. Such a unique interpretation of the word "friends," certainly not credible on the streets, revealed that the people "up there" apparently knew only that pro-drug messages were transmitted by rock music, but had no conception of how the songs accomplished this end. This lack of comprehension stood as an index of the gap existing between the lawmakers and the people governed by the laws.

The laws banning drugs failed to deter people from using them. Instead they merely confirmed the users' impression of the government's repressive and prejudicial character. Steppenwolf's "Don't Step on the Grass" (1968) reflected this reaction to drug regulation. Its chorus presented, in call-and-response fashion, the official allegations of the government and the young's response to such thinking. While a character called "Sam" considered grass evil, wicked, mean, and nasty, and a corrupter of the American way, the young retorted by calling him an ass, full of bull. The song ended with the sounds of a drug arrest, reiterating Sam's choral assertion of power, that all who disagreed with him would pay.

The illegality of drugs further strengthened the young's sense of community. In an era when possession of marijuana might mean a jail term, smoking with someone added a sacred dimension of trust to a relationship. Furthermore, the act of smoking, as an explicit rejection of certain societal norms, placed the users outside the realms of accepted behavior. The hard-line stance taken by the government in regard to drugs, especially marijuana, deepened the generation gap, and created a tangible area of conflict involving perceptions of reality. The only issue comparable to drugs in solidifying the view of America as a repressive society in the eyes of its malcontents was Vietnam.

LOVE SONGS

Like most other societal forms in the period from 1965 to 1969, the idea of love was reevaluated and its imagery reformulated. From late 1965 onward a new type of love lyric emerged which differed significantly from all previous white popular love songs. During this period songs depicted love as a matter of individual choice, existing on a human level, and subject to change. Songs of lost love did not assume their earlier tragic proportions, and the self-pitying cry-in-your-beer sentiment was avoided. Also the "Dream Lover" syndrome disappeared from love lyrics. These shifts in lyrics brought the love song more into line with the reality of young love, and also corresponded to the growing belief in individual integrity, honesty, and freedom.

The Beatles' *Help!,* one of the earliest albums to disclose the new love lyric, appeared in August 1965. Although containing several songs with traditional love lyrics, such as, "The Night Before" and "You've Got to Hide Your Love Away," the album also featured "Ticket to Ride." Superficially, this song portrayed the typical theme of love lost, as the male egocentrically claimed the girl "oughta do right by me," and did not understand her reason for terminating the relationship. However, the inclusion of the woman's uncomprehended explanation provided insight into a new lyrical focal point on male/female relations.

> *She said livin' with me was bringin' her down,*
> *She would never be free when I was around . . .*[14]

With these lines the Beatles expressed a new view of the love relationship that was supported by the song's music. The woman in the song was not so much interested in a heaven-sent love, but rather in someone who respected her aspirations in life. She desired free love, love which allowed her to be free to formulate her own conception of herself, and she desired a partner who would act as a positive force in her life.

From January 1966 onward the Mamas and the Papas fully explored this new concept of love. This group's unique sound centered on the close harmonizing of Cass Elliott, Michelle Phillips, Denny Doherty, and composer/arranger John Phillips. Their style received a tremendous reception, and within a year of the release of *If You Can Believe Your Eyes and Ears* (1966) the Mamas and the Papas had three albums to their credit. Only the Beatles and Elvis Presley surpassed them in album sales, making them America's first "super group."

The Mamas and the Papas' music was not "steering-wheel-pounding music," for no longer was such an extreme musical expression deemed necessary. Their lyrics conveyed the intention to "thump straight on through all heartbreaks and difficulties," and eliminated the need for the music alone to carry the message. Their soft, yet vibrant music lulled unperceptive listeners, including a reviewer for *Newsweek,* into assuming that their songs were merely harmless adolescent reactions to love.[15] The reviewer failed to notice how drastically young love had altered from earlier times. The lyrics of the Mamas and the Papas mark a major transition in the development of the love lyric in American popular music. Their songs depicted an exciting, dynamic, and flexible love. In "Straight Shooter" (1966) the group advised their lovers to bring them up, not down, and described the perfect mate as someone groovy, who really could move them.

Many of their songs stressed the need to avoid the self-pitying attitude of a jilted lover, so common in earlier popular love songs. Although heartbreak, pain, and sorrow afflicted their protagonists, these characters no longer pined away or wallowed in self-pity. In "I Can't Sleep at Night" (1966) the Papas, while unable to sleep, did not weep over their lost love. "Hey Girl" (1966) expanded on this theme by informing a jilted girl that the breakup resulted from her former boyfriend's problems and that nothing was wrong with her. The Mamas further claimed the guy was only trying to "score," and advised the girl not to let the breakup get her down, as there were other boys in town.

The new reaction to lost love followed recognition of people in love relationships as individuals with distinct aspirations and ideas on how life should be lived. It centered on individuals having the freedom to follow their own way of life. Whenever this freedom became cramped, a relationship was likely to dissolve. Perhaps the best lyrical explication of this point of view can be found in "Go Where You Wanna Go" (1965) which declared:

> You gotta go where you wanna go
> Do what you wanna do
> With whoever you want to do it with.[16]

These lines went beyond their context to become a credo of individual freedom for the generation coming of age in the late 1960s. That such a statement of personal freedom was expressed in a love song has profound implications in the understanding of the youth movement of that period. In the past, the male/female relationship had been portrayed as a bastion of order and security; however, in the late 1960s, the young, in their quest for individual integrity and freedom, willingly sacrificed this mirage to attain what they considered to be an honest relationship between self and life. The values expressed in the love lyric of the period were consistent with the general attitudes held by the young, and as such transcended the subject of love itself. "Go Where You Wanna Go" not only expressed the emerging concept of individual freedom, but also rejected the socially accepted reaction of self-pity, as the girl tried "so hard not to be the cryin' kind." Although experiencing heartbreak, she recognized the other partner in the relationship had his own life to live, and she had hers.

Significantly, the female exercised the prerogative to leave as frequently as did the male in the Mamas and the Papas' songs. The group depicted the people in a love relationship as equals, and shunned the traditional double standard, so obviously present in Dion's "The Wanderer" (1961) and "Runaround Sue" (1961). In "Look Through My Window" (1967) the abandoned boy recalled his lover saying there would come a time when one would stay behind and the other would go. They both realized lovers sometimes parted and that few things are as certain as change. He recognized the other person's freedom to move on, and although sadness was not averted, the boy knew he should let go and join the crowds on the street below his window.

In both "Go Where You Wanna Go" and "Look through My Window" the music expressed the sorrow accompanying the breakup. However, the melodies also contained glimmerings of sunshine, for the mourning was only temporary and another love would follow. In "Even If I Could" (1966) the Mamas and the Papas partially revealed this sense of renewal. In this song, a boy who had been dumped by a girl related his present situation to an earlier experience in which he had left a girl. Knowing the reality of heartbreak, he now realized how his earlier love had felt. However, he concluded that both these transient relationships were very good, and he would not trade them away, even if he could. The temporary love experience was not time lost, but rather a lovely way to pass the time. It was unfortunate if it did not last longer, but "life is change, how it differs from the rocks."

Love no longer traveled only the eternity track. Alternate routes existed, and Gale Garnett's "We'll Sing in the Sunshine" (1964), Buffy Sainte-Marie's "Until It's Time for You to Go" (1965), the Stone Poneys' "Different Drum" (1967), and the Jefferson Airplane's "Ice Cream Phoenix" (1968) served as sign posts, making the new pathways a bit more real. With the acceptance of a temporary love, sex became recognized as a legitimate relationship in itself, and consonant with the emerging "aesthetic quest," songs such as Jeff Beck's "Rock My Plimsoul" (1968) and "You Shook Me" (1968) moved toward lyrically portraying sex as an experience rather than a masculine adventure of exploitation. Thus, rock love lyrics began to expand beyond the limits of prescribed ideals and social morality.

Some people, such as the male in Aaron Neville's "Tell It Like It Is" (1966), wished to retain a conventional conception of love, and admonished the newer, freer ways. In that song the protagonist told his girlfriend to find herself a toy if she wanted something to play with, as his time was too expensive and he was not a little boy. Others discarded the "time is money" point of view and embraced the experiential level of life. Rather than *spending* time with each other, they typically found themselves, like the Steve Miller Band, thanking Mary for the day they *shared* together. Time represented an experience, not an investment, and members of the opposite sex came to be recognized as people rather than possessions. Stressing mutual respect and employing a personal love lyric, as pioneered by Bob Dylan, such songs as the Mindbenders' "Groovy Kind of Love" (1966), the Jefferson Airplane's "Today" (1967), and Quicksilver Messenger Service's "Dino's Song" (1967) brought lyrical love relationships into closer accord with countercultural forms.

How much the drug experience contributed to the altered view of sex and love is difficult to assess. That it had some effect cannot be doubted. Increased perception, heightened emotional levels, and transcendence of the ego all reinforced the newly evolving attitudes toward love and the entire man/woman relationship. Through a heightened drug consciousness, an individual life in harmony with the world, based upon relations rather than conquests, appeared feasible.

A number of love songs alluded to acid trips, such as Country Joe and the Fish's "Grace" (1967) which best disclosed the world of shared sensation and perception. Written to Grace Slick of the Jefferson Airplane, its music placed the listener in a hypnotic state of warm tactileness, as the lyric presented an array of soft, multicolored, glimmering images moving "across the tiny door of my eye."[17] Others to employ acid images in their description of a relationship included the Cream in "SWLABR" (1967) and the Rolling Stones in "She's a Rainbow" (1968), which had a typical Stones sexual undercurrent.

In moving toward a more individually oriented love song, the rock audience still retained the emotional aspect of love. Certain of the Mamas and the Papas songs, and those of other groups, including the Jefferson Airplane and the Beatles, depicted love as a heartfelt, romantic event, "a many splendored thing." However, from 1967 onward these songs appeared less frequently, for the young found profound feelings best left lyrically unexpressed. Perhaps this decline in popularity resulted from rock's audience no longer finding a conventional, public love poetry, such an important part of adolescent culture in 1957,[18] to be a useful or desirable social form. The young of the late 1960s rejected the Tin Pan Alley lyrical imagery as pseudo-love. Instead rock lyrics embraced a more human, temporal view of love, which involved a refusal to actually describe the indescribable emotions involved.

With the acceptance of an unidealized temporal love, the problem of choosing a partner to love came to the fore in certain lyrics. In "Did You Ever Have to Make Up Your Mind?" (1966) the Lovin' Spoonful posed this problem within a bouncy, light-hearted musical atmosphere, which prevailed over the rather serious chorus. The Spoonful presented the listener with such situations as meeting a girl you loved from the moment you kissed her, until presented with her older sister. The song made it apparent that the problem of choice was not one to brood over. As such, the song served primarily as an exaltation of the freedom of choice, rather than an examination of the problem of choice. To have the freedom and mobility to be involved in a situation of choosing overwhelmed the difficulties of the choice itself.

Some people attempted to preclude the problem of choice by eliminating the either/or aspect of the situation. Instead of choosing one or the other, they choose one *and* the other. David Crosby's "Triad" (1968) suggested the creation of a threesome, which in time might add others as in the tradition of Robert Heinlein's waterbrothers in *Stranger in a Strange Land*. Many people thought this option to be a logical extension of free love. If a person was capable of loving several people over time, then it was considered possible to love several people at the same time. The mass media quickly picked up on this point and did much to publicize the increasing sexual freedom enjoyed by the young. Through the press's manipulation, free love was redefined. Rather than referring to a relationship based on individual freedom, free love became associated with sexual promiscuity. In this context the word "free" assumed an economic connotation.

A greater openness to the subject of sex typified the late 1960s, and rock music, building on its rock 'n' roll heritage of sexual associations, reflected the changes occurring in society. In August 1965, *Newsweek* pointed to the Rolling Stones' version of "King Bee" as an example of the increasing sexual awareness in rock lyrics. The article admitted such Broadway songs as Cole Porter's "Let's Do It" were suggestive, but argued:

> *The suggestive songs of today's commercial rock 'n' roll groups are something different: they have no wit, for one thing, but more important they are frankly aimed at adolescents rather than sophisticated Broadway audiences.*[19]

The rock audience might have wondered about the level of sophistication of an audience that found suggestive lyrics which noted birds, bees, and even educated fleas do it, and surely they questioned the need for wit to be included in songs dealing with sex. They no longer needed to hide sexual attraction behind a curtain of cuteness. Just as their life and love assumed a certain directness or honesty, so did their approach to sex. Sex was a significant part of any male/female relationship, and such rock lyrics as the Troggs' "Wild Thing" (1966), the Doors' "Light My Fire" (1967), and Jimi Hendrix's "Fire" (1967) and "Foxey Lady" (1967) celebrated it as such.

The sexual frankness of rock ran ahead of the professed values of the dominant culture, which sometimes led to censorship. One of the better publicized instances of such action occurred on January 13, 1967 when the *Ed Sullivan Show* prohibited the Rolling Stones from singing the word *night* during their performance of "Let's Spend the Night Together." Considering what certain young people already viewed American society to be, this only further exemplified the repressiveness and sheer stupidity which surrounded them on a daily basis. For these people, American society, as represented by television, refused to acknowledge what was happening in its midst, and did so in the name of the sacred concept of "upholding the image." Ed Sullivan had to maintain his image, even though it did not relate to the life of much of his audience. In an attempt to hide certain realities, Ed Sullivan unwittingly revealed the "unreality" of his world of image.

While Ed Sullivan and television in general attempted to maintain their naive position, the radio became more liberated. By 1967 the wave lengths openly celebrated sexual themes, and "Light My Fire" remained near the top of the charts throughout the summer. To hear Jim Morrison sing "Come on baby, light my fire" on AM radio indicated to certain people that America was loosening up. The glorification of sex in song, and its acceptance by AM radio served as an indication of America's amenability to change. Another taboo had been removed, another barrier destroyed, and people felt a little freer.

As the decade advanced, rock songs became more and more sexually explicit, and with the release of *Led Zeppelin II* (1969) an ultimate in imagery seemed to have been achieved. Featuring overtly sexual music and lyrics which offered "every inch" of the singer's love and supplicated the listener to squeeze him until the juice ran down his leg, the album received very little AM air play, although it achieved great popularity. Sex-oriented songs such as these, received much more media attention than did those which reflected the changing conception of the love relationship. As a tangible moral issue, the mass media exploited sex's role as a threat to social norms or an index of social change, and as such the new sexual freedom became a national issue. However, the shifting sexual values were only a part of the period's much larger reevaluation of the male/female relationship and the individual/society relationship. As proclamations of free love, the rock songs of the era indicated a reassessment of values was occuring across the nation, and they were consistent with the evolving conceptions of individual freedom and integrity. As such, rock love songs serve to enhance our understanding of life in the late 1960s.

NOTES

[1]Bob Seger, "2 + 2 = ?"

[2]Randolph Bourne, "A War Diary," *Seven Arts*, 2 (September 1917).

[3]Country Joe and the Fish, "I-Feel-Like-I'm-Fixing-To-Die Rag," words and music by Joe McDonald, © 1965 by Joe McDonald/1978 Alkatraz Corner Music. Used by permission. All rights reserved.

[4]These poems are quoted in Leon Wolff, *Little Brown Brother* (London: Longmans, 1961) pp. 197–198, 270–271.

[5]Jefferson Airplane, "Rejoyce" from their *Crown of Creation* album. © Icebag Corp, 1967. All Rights Reserved. Reprinted by permission of the publisher.

[6]Country Joe and the Fish, "Untitled Protest," words and music by Joe McDonald, © 1969 Joyful Wisdom Music, BMI. Used by permission. All rights reserved.

[7]See Chapter Six for a fuller discussion of America's disease.

[8]The Beatles, "Lucy in the Sky with Diamonds," John Lennon and Paul McCartney, © 1967 Northern Songs Ltd. Used by permission.

[9]Lawrence Chenoweth, "The Rhetoric of Hope and Despair: A Study of the Jimi Hendrix Experience and the Jefferson Airplane," *American Quarterly*, Spring 1971, p. 30.

[10]Daniel Boorstin, *The Image* (New York: Harper Colophon Books, 1964), pp. 77–78.

[11]Peter Marin, "The Open Truth: Fiery Vehemence of Youth," in *The Eloquence of Protest*, ed. Harrison E. Salisbury (Boston: Houghton Mifflin, 1972), pp. 185–186.

[12]See Jean-Paul Sartre, *The Transcendance of the Ego* (New York: Noonday Press, 1957).

[13]The Mamas and the Papas, "Strange Young Girls"

[14]The Beatles, "Ticket to Ride"

[15]*Newsweek*, vol. 68, August 8, 1966, p. 78.

[16]The Mamas and the Papas, "Go Where You Wanna Go"

[17]Country Joe and the Fish, "Grace," words and music by Joe McDonald, © 1967 Joyful Wisdom Music, BMI. Used by permission. All rights reserved.

[18]For a discussion of the role of the fifties love song as a conventional, impersonal, public love poetry, see Donald Horton, "The Dialogue of Courtship in Popular Songs," *American Journal of Sociology*, 62 (May 1957).

[19]*Newsweek*, 16 August 1965, p. 76.

6

The World of Image

The rock songs of the late 1960s brought forth alternate values and visions on many levels. The music was in itself a bold statement with all sorts of fantastic phantasms swirling around and through it. Whether denouncing the war, celebrating drugs, or redefining love and sex relationships, the songs declared freedom, sensation, passion, and life. They made the young aware of themselves, reconfirmed their beliefs and acknowledged, within a positive framework, the changes that were taking place. The sound brought together a generation, created a "mystical fusion"[1] and gave the young a shared experience and an articulate, although not necessarily accurate, expression of what is and what will be. Even more important, rock music transcended dreary reality to offer America an optimistic utopian view of the future.

THE BEATLES

*"When people ask to recreate the mood of the sixties,
they will play Beatle music."*

Aaron Copland

74

No one better personified the new age than the Beatles. With songs such as "She Loves You," "Good Day Sunshine," "With a Little Help from My Friends," "Lucy in the Sky with Diamonds," "A Day in the Life," "Strawberry Fields Forever," "All You Need Is Love," "Here Comes the Sun," (the list goes on) they embodied the spirit of the love generation. Buoyant, bouncy, and bright, their optimism pervaded the period, and from February 1, 1964, to July 4, 1970, they dominated *Billboard's* "Hot 100" with a number one single for one out of every six weeks (a total of 59 weeks) and a top album for one out of every three weeks (116 weeks total).[2]

The Beatles maintained such success, in part, by fulfilling certain traditional pop music roles, creating harmonious ideals, visions of romantic love, and sentimental sojourns in songs such as "Yesterday," "And I Love Her," "If I Fell," "Michelle," "Here, There and Everywhere," "Penny Lane," "Julia," "Something," and "The Long and Winding Road." However, as members of the radical mainstream, the group was anything but traditional. They broadened the range of rock, introducing the listening audience to electronically processed music, and non-rock structures and instrumentation, including full orchestral accompaniment. Consigning conventional conceptions of popular music to oblivion, they stood in the forefront of the "rock revolution," expanding the parameters of popular music in limitless directions. And just as they simply and easily transported popular music into new dimensions, so too their audience felt they could move society onto the new plane of their musical ideal.

From "I Want to Hold Your Hand" onward, the Beatles emanated a supercharged, positive energy for good, and through the years they sustained that power. Under their light, but upbeat, mana-ladden songs, anything seemed possible. They created the fluff of which dreams are made.

> *There's nothing you can do that can't be done*
> *Nothing you can sing that can't be sung . . .*
> *It's eeasy; all you need is love . . .*

Without a doubt they were an "up." Joy accompanied their albums, making them special little highs all their own.

The light musical atmosphere, coupled with the group's willingness to change and experiment, helped set the tempo of the era. They offered something different, something beautiful, and an escape from the mundaneness of the period. By following this bright and cheery path the Beatles' audience little by little rejected and discarded the dominant culture. For as Peter Schrag found in his review of *Sergeant Pepper's Lonely Hearts Club Band* (1967), underneath the psychedelic Beatles' "light fun" lay a "somber commentary on the emptiness of most conventional achievements, most ordinary models of success." The songs on *Sergeant Pepper* declared, "that the conventional world of jobs, money and status is blind, brutal and destructive, that it is full of people who 'hide themselves behind a wall of illusion.'"[4]

More than any other artifact of the period, *Sergeant Pepper* reflected and reinforced the desire for change, to explore alternate ways of life. Its extreme popularity signaled that a profound change had transpired within the youth culture. For the cherubic Beatles to voice such discontent, to declare forthrightly "I want to turn you on," and to support their views with such novel music, was as if John Wayne, Superman, or Mickey Mouse had turned beatnik, and their audience had accepted this as a natural development. With this album the counterculture gained momentum and demanded serious attention, for as Peter Schrag noted, the record represented, "a serious search for better, more engaging things, musically and personally."[5]

With "Lucy in the Sky with Diamonds," "A Little Help from My Friends," and "A Day in the Life," the Beatles stepped outside the mainstream and confirmed that rain or shine were states of mind and that Norwegian Wood was indeed good.

> *She told me to sit anywhere*
> *So I looked around and I noticed there wasn't a chair*
>
> *I sat on the rug, biding my time*
> *Drinking her wine . . .*[6]

The time had come to lay aside preconceived conceptions of life and "get it on," or as Paul McCartney prolixly put it:

> *I used to think that anyone doing anything weird was weird. I suddenly*
> *realized that anyone doing anything weird wasn't weird at all and that it*
> *was the people saying they were weird that were weird.*[7]

Within this spirit grew the basic tenets of the counterculture which the past two chapters discussed. Love, peace, and happiness were proclaimed the order of the day, and new social forms and norms flourished. More than just opposition to America's involvement in Vietnam or suppression of drug use or discrimination against Blacks, the late 1960s rock revolution represented a rejection of the fundamental principles of the American industrial state. Viewing the dominant culture as repressive, devoid of meaning, hypocritical, and detached from life, people began to romantically structure their experiences in the light of Hesse's description of Steppenwolf's position in the 1920s.

*Every age, every culture, every custom and tradition has its own character,
its own weakness and its own strength, its beauties and ugliness; accepts
certain sufferings as matters of course, puts up patiently with certain evils.
Human life is reduced to real suffering, to hell, only when two ages, two
cultures and religions overlap. . . . Now there are times when a whole
generation is caught in this way between two ages, two modes of life, with
the consequence that it loses all power to understand itself and has no
standards, no security, no simple acquiescence.*[8]

By the late 1960s an increasing number of young people felt caught in a time
when two ages, two cultures overlapped; they had "no standard, no security, no
simple acquiescence." They began to see through American society, just as such
intellectuals as Daniel Boorstin and Erich Fromm earlier had.[9] For them the
dominant culture had overextended itself and become divorced from life. Social
forms no longer served individual needs. Machines were in the saddle and rode
mankind. Daniel Boorstin called these lifeless forms "pseudo-events," and the
young labeled them "plastic." Deeper thinkers used other words.

FORMS, CONTENTS, AND SYMBOLS

The turn of the century sociologist/philosopher Georg Simmel theorized[10] that
"forms" defined a society. These forms were the social actions employed by
individuals within a society, their customs, their organizational structures, their
procedures of everyday life, which created in Hesse's terms, a society's character.
Behind these forms lay "contents," the motivations for all social interaction.
These contents encompassed instinctive drives, objective interests, common
purposes, religious impulses, psychic states. In short, they were any force which
brought individuals together. These forces were not in their own right social,
but manifested themselves through the forms created around them. These forms
allowed individuals to be one step removed from the "inherent gravity" of life
itself, while still interacting with life.

*Sociability is a symbol of life as life emerges in the flux of facile and happy
play; yet it also is a symbol of life. It does not change the image of life
beyond the point required by its own distance to it.*[11]

However, sometimes these forms "in a peculiar manner" completely divorced
themselves from their contents, from life, becoming entities themselves. Examples included, art for art's sake, science for science's sake, law for law's sake,
and even sociability for sociability's sake. Historically, Simmel pointed to the

ancien régime of France as a society which reached this level. Numerous young people felt American in the 1960s had attained a similar position.

American philosopher Susanne Langer declared the symbol-making process to be a fundamental human characteristic. She felt symbolization was an "act *essential to thought* and prior to it."[12] The mind did not so much transmit sensations from the outside world, but transformed them. For Langer humans were by nature symbol-making creatures; through symbols they ordered their worlds. However, as Simmel noted, these symbols could become worlds unto themselves, completely detached from life's content. When this occurred, humanity discarded the old forms in favor of ones more closely aligned with reality.

The counterculture attempted to create not only new forms but perhaps new contents as well, for "all you need is love." The music of the Beatles, Grateful Dead, Jefferson Airplane, Janis Joplin, Jimi Hendrix, and many, many others reflected and reinforced this counterculture and its new forms. However, the psychedelic scene was not rock's sole response to America's contentless forms.

Two major figures, Bob Dylan and the Rolling Stones, moved to their own drummers. Both were keenly aware of society's vacuity, its moribund images; but rather than follow an image-bound counterculture, they opted for other alternatives. Dylan, the preeminent symbol of the youth movement, quickly recognized the distance between forms and their contents, and strove to move outside America's social games, while at the same time extricating himself from the webs of images which entangled him as a performer. The Stones, on the other hand, remained within society, and waged war on its forms, distorting them, inverting and twisting them, until they splintered and flew apart to reveal the mutilated life behind.

Although removed from the "peace, love, happiness" trip, the postures taken by Dylan and the Rolling Stones were not completely antithetic to those of the counterculture. They all had a common foe: the dominant culture. As such their views flowed together, and intermingled with each other, despite their differences. Individuals freely drew from all three approaches, to create a complex reaction to American society of the late 1960s.

Dylan

"The most important thing that can be said about Bob Dylan, and the key to a good deal of his success, is that like Jay Gatsby, he arose out of some Platonic Conception of himself. He created himself, which is not unusual, but he was more extreme than most of us; he created himself, name and all,

*from scratch, and rejected all the elements in his past except those which
fit in with his carefully constructed mythology.*"

Lawrence Goldman, 1965

From the outset of his public life, Bob Dylan, as Goldman noted, was well aware of society's forms and understood how to manipulate them to his benefit. Consciously or unconsciously, he discerned the essential essence of the folk scene and created an image of himself which closely conformed to the desired ideal. Rather than perpetuate earlier songs, he perceived protest, "the voice of the common people," to lay at the heart of the folk tradition, and thus, in much the same manner as Woody Guthrie had done in the 1930s, Bob Dylan provided this content (protest) and form (folk music) with new words, embued with his own personality and the immediacy of the present. His straightforward manner appealed to folk music's supporters and his wry sense of humor, excellent handling of lyrical imagery, and glaring animosity for contemporary injustices eventually placed him at the forefront of the folk world.

He knew his genre and reflected its visions, expectations, and prejudices in his manners, gestures, and songs. His popularity derived from lyrical stances couched in terms of simplistic, black-and-white, perceptions of good and evil which still characterized so much of American thinking at this point in time. Expounding the liberal good in such songs as "Masters of War" (1963), "Hard Rain's A Gonna Fall" (1963), "Oxford Town" (1963), "With God on Our Side" (1964), "North Country Blues" (1964) and "The Ballad of Hollis Brown" (1964), Bob Dylan became the poet laureate of the New Left, the crown prince of folk music, and the acclaimed leader of the optimistic, "Times They Are A-Changin'" young.

However, in 1964 America's premier folk singer began to extricate himself from the folk world of liberal causes. He abandoned the crusader's position of advocating positive change from within the system, and assumed a rebellious stance outside the jurisdiction of society. He recognized that the forms of folk music and liberal politics no longer related to their avowed goals of protest and change for the good of the common people. In making such a discovery Dylan was not alone. Others, such as Tom Hayden, also saw that the problem with society was society's norms and forms. For these people, the social issues of the day were all part of a larger world, which was devoid of life-sustaining meaning, content. Or as Dylan later claimed, his older songs were about nothing, while his songs of 1964–1965 were about the same nothing placed within the larger context of nowhere.[13] Dylan shifted gears as he came to realize more was wrong with America than just the bomb or civil rights.

I know there's some people terrified of the bomb, but there are other people terrified to be seen carrying a modern screen magazine.[14]

Just as he had seen through the masks of the "Masters of War," he now saw through American society, including the protest movement. In his eyes Americans were not free because a culture of vacuous forms entrapped them and removed them from life itself. People had to unchain themselves from the tyranny of the images which enveloped them. They had to overcome their fears, their "hang-ups," and seek out individualized lives, if they wished to be free.

To explicate the new terror he perceived in our midst, Dylan moved beyond the liberal tradition of causes and romantic musketeers with their clear definitions of good and bad. Commencing with *Another Side of Dylan* (1964), he shed his earlier folk singer image and slipped into a realm of his own creation, just outside the periphery of folk, and at least a dimension removed from pop. Presenting personal glimpses of life beyond images, he began to tell the world what he wished to express, rather than what the performer was programmed to translate into song. Unlike an actor, he knew what he was saying. And he said it well.

Another Side of Dylan stunned the folk world. It had no bomb songs, no civil rights messages, but instead love songs and gibberish about crimson flames and youth. But what love songs! His style now seemed more direct, more personal; and even more staggering, these straight-forward sounds combined to transcend surface meanings, and reached for a cosmic level of understanding. "All I Really Want to Do" implored a woman to believe that all Dylan wanted to do was be friends with her. He had no desire to simplify or classify, categorize or advertise, define or confine her. In short, Dylan did not wish to do to her what the folk world had done to him, encapsulate her in an image on which to lean. Opening with this offer, the album closed with Dylan requesting the same respect in "It Ain't Me Babe." In the intervening numbers the audience heard the chimes of freedom flashing for the searching ones, the lonesome hearted lovers, and others, including every hung-up person in the whole wide universe. Songs such as "I Shall be Free-Number 10" and "Motorpsycho Nightmare" implicitly ad-dresssed the existence of the image world and ridiculed, used, and abused it. "To Ramona" drove home the need for individuals to avoid phony images, explicitly unveiling the destructive aspects of image expectations. "Worthless foam from the mouth," social dictates, and friends "that hype you and type you," twisted Ramona's head and made her feel she must conform to their ways. Dylan grieved for the troubled, disconsolate woman, and advised:

It's all a dream, babe,
A vacuum, a scheme, babe,
That sucks you into feelin' like this.[15]

Although describing the cause of the woman's depression, Dylan prescribed no
cure, for as he told Nat Hentoff:

> *All I can do is show people who ask me questions how I live. All I can do*
> *is be me. I can't tell them how to change things, because there's only one*
> *way to change things, and that's to cut yourself off from all the chains.*

But Dylan realized "that's hard for most people to do," as more often than not
they "have some kind of vested interest in the way things are now."[16] From his
experience with liberal reform, Dylan already recognized the difficulty of change,
of moving beyond the dominant culture; however, his insight was not heeded,
and an image-based counterculture, declining to confront despair, rose and fell.

Following *Another Side of Dylan,* Dylan jumped through hyperspace and
came out with *Bringing It All Back Home* (March, 1965) and *Highway 61
Revisited* (August, 1965), which devastatingly laid bare his vision of the spectator/
image-bound dominant culture. Featuring a solid, electric music and "flashing"
lyrical imagery, these albums moved Dylan far beyond the folk music world,
and presented exciting new possibilities to the rock audience. Incredibly rapid,
shifting lyrics confronted listeners with a helicopter of thought that conveyed
the singer's spirit with a force no train of thought ever could match. Vivid scenes
cascaded one on top of another, creating a veritable waterfall of ideas, all crystal
clear and together in the pool below.

> *Johnny's in the basement*
> *Mixing up the medicine*
> *I'm on the pavement*
> *Thinkin' 'bout the government*
> *The man in the trench coat*
> *Badge out, laid off*
> *Says he's got a bad cough*
> *Wants to get paid off*
> *Look out kid, it's somethin' you did*
> *God knows when*
> *But you're doin' it again*
> *You better duck down the alleyway*
> *Lookin' for a new friend*
> *The man in the coonskin cap by the pig pen*
> *Wants eleven dollar bills*
> *You only got ten*
> *. . .*
> *Ah, get born, keep warm*
> *Short pants, romance, learn to dance*
> *Get dressed, get blessed*

> *Try to be a success*
> *Please her, please him, buy gifts*
> *Don't steal, don't lift*
> *Twenty years of schoolin'*
> *And they put you on the day shift*

From the opening lines the corrupt world of survival in the street entwined with biting, hard-hitting alienated visions of the sham of normal life. They blended, they blurred, and became one; all part of that greater "nowhere." To survive you had better get wise, open your eyes: "Don't follow leaders, watch the parking meters"; "You don't need a weatherman to know which way the wind blows." And if you didn't already realize:

> *The pump don't work*
> *Cause the vandals took the handles.*[17]

Like everything described in "Subterranean Homesick Blues," the vandals were a product of the system. The system's problem was the system. The visions continued to flow down the record, over the ear, and into the mind . . . "Maggie's Farm," "Bob Dylan's 115th Dream," "Mr. Tambourine Man," and the incredible "Gates of Eden."

The album culminated with "It's Alright Ma (I'm Only Bleeding)." This song opened with the Eliotesque "Darkness at the break of noon," and dissected the contentless forms of the Establishment, and pinned on the specimen board, for all to examine, political parties ("social clubs in drag disguise"), "advertising signs that con . . .," people who say "don't hate nothin' at all except hatred," old lady judges "limited in sex" who dare to "push fake morals," and those who "must obey authority that they do not respect in any degree" and "do what they do just to be nothing more than something to invest in." Although presenting no hope of deliverance, the song reminded Dylan, as well as the listener, "it's only people's games that you gotta dodge," and "that it is not he or she or them or it that you belong to."

Dylan, along with Jesse James and Captain Kidd, remained on the outside, apart from society and its facades, trying not to pass judgment, as he claimed:

> *I mean no harm nor put fault*
> *On anyone who lives in a vault*
> *But it's alright Ma, if I can't please him.*[18]

His critique was vehement and placed the alienated point of view into a comprehensible context and gave it a voice. He catalyzed a flux of inarticulate sensations into perceptions, or as Ken Kesey later recalled:

When you heard Dylan in those first songs he was really talking to you in some way that was not customary linear communication. There'd be a phrase that would strike like Rorschach, setting off a personal image that would start a whole crystalization of thinking and leave your head in a place it had never been before. It's as if, inside of us, there's always been the proper solution, and Dylan tossed in the proper crystals. But the crystals weren't connected. One thought running and connecting with the next, and that one connecting with the next to present an inductive argument. This was imagery leading out and connecting lyrically to form brand new thought crystals in people's heads. And that's as subversive an act as you can possibly imagine.[19]

Dylan had leaped into a void, and made it his own. Leaving his public past far behind he refused to conform to his earlier image, and on July 25, 1965, the shining light of folk music had to abdicate his throne at Newport. A profound change had transpired, but the reality of it all eluded most people as the drama of the images consumed their imaginations. Dylan, the image par excellence of folk, no longer was a folksinger. Dylan, the person as image, recognized the limitations, the distance from life that one experiences as a cultural icon. Transferring his knowledge of self to society, he sought but could not find the greater life behind the symbols. So he abandoned folk, liberal commitments, and society, and in farewell at Newport sang the closing song from *Bringing It All Back Home,* "It's All Over Now Baby Blue." As lyrically powerful and portentous as "Times They Are A-Changin'," the song informed the "new" left, the proponents of change, that it was time for them to change too. Life was not as it appeared and truth did not exist outside the gates of Eden. Discontent was swelling; the time had come to "strike another match" and start anew.

With *Highway 61 Revisited* (1965) the match burned brightly. Dylan spoke from a confident, experienced, "Like a Rolling Stone" position, and continued to build on his "It's Alright Ma (I'm Only Bleeding)" perceptions. Totally in command of its material, the album presented a powerful statement of complete freedom beyond the social constraints and petty concerns of the territory outside the gates of Eden. Mainly, the songs heaped invective upon the perceived superficiality and insensitivity of society, climaxing with "Desolation Row":

. . . a descent into a modern Inferno, an eleven-minute freak show that portrays a world of alienation ruled by madmen, a world in which humanity has been estranged from its possibilities, a world in which man's once free mind has been so totally suffocated by the one dimensional society, that it accepts lies as truth and beauty, permits creativity and naturalness and Eros to be perverted by the social "reality."[20]

Pointing out the pointless, sensing the senseless, the album castigated the old forms and elevated individual freedom. Sometimes spouting merciless, livid animosity, the album offered no compassion for those whose lives were directed by the illusions of others, such as Mr. Jones in "The Ballad of the Thin Man," who as the spectator's spectator, ingested experience as received images and called them his own. At other junctures the album was almost sympathetic, offering a hand to the struggling as in "Queen Jane." Above all *Highway 61 Revisited* was a rallying point for those on their own, with no direction home, and its opening number, "Like a Rolling Stone," became an anthem for the 1960s young.

An album of vivid and timeless impressions, *Highway 61 Revisited* represented Dylan at an energy peak. He not only saw through society's forms, but remained removed from them, playing with and controlling them. He did not passively accept forms as given, but actively molded them to suit his needs. D.A. Pennebaker's documentary motion picture of Dylan's 1965 British tour, *Don't Look Back,* captured this aspect of Dylan's persona in several interview scenes. In adroitly controlled conversational "performances," Dylan turned interview after interview on the interviewer. Realizing that questions determined an interview's content, he began asking his own questions, which led to some remarkable answers.

SCIENCE STUDENT: . . . what is your whole attitude to life? I mean, when you meet somebody, what is your attitude towards them?
DYLAN: I don't like them.
SCIENCE STUDENT: I mean, I come in here. What's your attitude towards me?
DYLAN: No, I don't have any attitude towards you at all. Why should I have an attitude towards you? I don't even know you.
SCIENCE STUDENT: No, but I mean it would be an attitude if you wanted to know me or didn't want to know me.
DYLAN: Well why should I want to know you?
SCIENCE STUDENT: I don't know . . . that's what I'm asking.
DYLAN: Well I don't know. Ask me another question. Just give me a reason why I should want to know you.
SCIENCE STUDENT: Um . . . I might be worth knowing.
DYLAN: Why?
SCIENCE STUDENT: Huh?
DYLAN: Why? Tell me why. What good is it going to do me for me to know you? Tell me. Give me, name me one thing I'm going to gain.
SCIENCE STUDENT: Well you might learn something from my attitude to life.
DYLAN: Well, what is your attitude towards life? Huh?
SCIENCE STUDENT: I can't explain that in two minutes.
DYLAN: Well, what are you asking me to explain in two minutes?[21]

Thus Dylan brought the science student's question full circle and turned it back on him. In the remainder of the interview several similar circles completed themselves in a display of shrewd logical manipulation, which confirmed the presence of a new, superior vision, perceiving truths beyond societal perceptions. The naive, inexperienced science student was not the only soul in *Don't Look Back* to fall victim to Dylan's style. A *Time* magazine reporter was told by Dylan that he was no longer a folk singer, but that *Time* probably would refer to him as one anyway, but it didn't matter because *Time* never printed the truth, and besides, his audience did not necessarily read *Time*. Dylan continued:

> *I could tell you I'm not a folk singer and explain to you why, but you wouldn't really understand. All you could do, you could nod your head, you would nod your head . . .*[22]

Then he proceeded to explain, and all the reporter did was nod his head and blindly assert that Dylan did not understand his position with *Time*. *Time* never used the interview, nor did it cover Dylan's British tour. However, as late as 1968 the magazine still referred to Dylan as a "folk singer."

Dylan's "separate reality" as revealed in *Another Side of Dylan, Bringing It All Back Home, Highway 61 Revisited,* and Pennebaker's *Don't Look Back* defined the dominant culture in terms understood by the alienated young. His explications of "nowhere" reshaped reality and led others to think and sing in his terms as in "Eleanor Rigby," "Nowhere Man," and "Season of the Witch." By the end of 1965 he had laid the foundation upon which lyrical arguments of alienation and discontent would rise, and from which a counterculture, based on utopian interpretations of alienated values, emerged. The counterculture strove to create new social forms to replace the old, to supplant old images of life, with more relevant ones. Dylan, however, saw no wisdom in replacing one image world with another, since it would still be at least one step removed from the truth of life. Having already experienced the heights of imagedom, not once, but twice, first as poet of the new left, and then of the alienated young, he opted for other solutions.

The first steps toward a new stance appeared with *Blonde on Blonde* (1966). With this album Dylan finally attained the neutral position he had alluded to on *Bringing it All Back Home.* He no longer faulted those living in vaults, and like the woman in "Love Minus Zero/No Limit" he knew too much to argue or judge. The stylistic change was as distinct as the move from folk songs to *Another Side,* and Ellen Willis found:

> *Dylan was no longer rebel but seismograph, registering his emotions—fascination, confusion, pity, arrogance, exuberance, anguish—with sardonic lucidity.*

To her, the album depicted a love for the surface world and its "fashionable, sybaritic denizens,"[23] an astute approximation of Dylan's position. But, Dylan, although certainly no longer a rebel, was more than a seismograph. While displaying renewed interest in the world, he did not openly accept it or merge with it. Instead, the Dylan of *Blonde on Blonde* sought a middle ground from which an individual might establish an operable relationship with the human world of image/symbol. The album depicted Dylan in a transitional, questioning period, attempting to determine where to draw the line between accepting and rejecting the ways of the image world.

"One of Us Must Know (Sooner or Later)" portrayed Dylan's dilemma and captured a moment when the singer doubted his earlier perceptions, returned to the image world, suspended his judgment, and attempted to ascertain a more pragmatic approach to life. Throughout most of the song he relied upon a woman's image-based vision, even though it ran contrary to his own. He couldn't see how she could know him, but she said she did, and he believed her. He couldn't see where they were going, but she said she knew, and he took her word for it. Unfortunately, the relationship did not work out; Dylan's original views proved to be accurate, much to the detriment of the deluded woman. Thus a major thrust of the song revolved around Dylan's apology for not exercising his judgment. He didn't mean to do her any harm; she just was in the wrong place at the wrong time. The woman's pain resulted from Dylan's not acting on his perceptions, of his accepting the surface world on its terms. For the remainder of the album he counteracted this opening stance and asserted himself and his viewpoints. However, he refrained from criticizing those who did not conform to his visions of life.

Confronted with a situation similar to that of "One of Us Must Know (Sooner or Later)," Dylan took control of the relationship in "Most Likely You Go Your Way (and I'll Go Mine)." He told a woman who claimed she loved him that she could be mistaken, and though she wanted to hold him, she wasn't strong enough. Thus he decided to let her pass and allow time to determine just who fell and who was left behind. Dylan did not go with the flow; instead he spoke his mind and acted on his preceptions. Such was the mood of *Blonde on Blonde*.

Songs such as "Stuck Inside a Mobile with the Memphis Blues Again," "Leopard-Skin Pill-Box Hat," "Fourth Time Around," and "Just Like a Woman" presented the dominant culture in Dylan's terms, but did not rail against life and accepted the world as it was. In these songs Dylan presented a person coming to terms with society, modifying his previous, staunchly egocentric stance to accommodate the presence of a larger world. No longer completely autonomous, he questioned sweet Marie's whereabouts and the hard character of another woman, and asked the sad-eyed Lady of the Lowlands if he should wait or leave his warehouse eyes and Arabian drums at her gate. The world no longer flowed to and through Dylan, nor did he expect it to do so. He began to reconcile himself to life as it was. He reappraised the dominant culture, still found it wanting, but rather than wage war on its symbolization process, he, like Susanne Langer and others, accepted it as a given, a part of the human condition. However, he retained his right to accept or reject social actions, and his choices no longer displayed the black-or-white polarities of earlier times.

Following a near-fatal motorcycle accident and a reclusive recovery, *John Wesley Harding* appeared in 1968. It revealed Dylan's maturing attitude toward the world. He returned to an acoustic sound at the height of acid rock's reign, but nevertheless the album effused strength and understanding. Jon Landau, in his review of it for *Crawdaddy!* noted:

> For an album of this kind to be released amidst Sgt. Pepper, Their Satanic Majesties Request, Strange Days, *and* After Bathing at Baxter's, *somebody must have had a lot of confidence in what he was doing. Hence the first noteworthy fact about this album is its essential lack of insecurity. Dylan seems to feel no need to respond to the predominant trends in pop music at all. And he is the only major pop artist about whom this can be said. The Dylan of* John Wesley Harding *is a truly independent artist who doesn't feel responsible to anyone else, whether they be fans or his contemporaries. It is implicit, in fact, in his rejection of the formal basis of a rock band on this album that Dylan does not accept what is happening in pop music at the moment.*[24]

With the opening number, the title song, Dylan's ideal image of the person outside society came forth, celebrated through an outlaw who had opened numerous doors, and had never harmed an honest man. The remainder of the record's first side can be viewed as an extended, modern-day ballad of Bob Dylan by Bob Dylan. He recounted his previous positions in the public domain, but did so from the vantage point of the present.

"As I Went Out One Morning" recalled Dylan's experience with the political left, their attempt to make him their own, and his "rescue" by Tom Paine. The following cut, "I Dreamed I Saw St. Augustine," chronicled his movement toward independence, reworking the "don't follow leaders . . .," "it is not he or she or them or it that you belong to" theme, and counseled the audience to go their own way, but realize they were not alone. "All Along the Watchtower" powerfully condensed the visions of *Highway 61 Revisited* and went beyond it to note that while some thought that life was a joke, the singer and his audience knew this was not their fate. With "The Ballad of Frankie Lee and Judas Priest" Dylan stressed the need to preserve individual initiative as an alternative to an image world. After recounting in this song the problems of choice confronted on *Blonde on Blonde,* Dylan transcended his earlier dilemma by advising his audience in a moralistic fashion to help people in their trek through life and not seek out instant paradises.

The album's second side revealed Dylan's new "fate" as "Dear Landlord" confidently developed the position tentatively explored in *Blonde on Blonde.* Dylan acknowledged that his expectations of the world outraced reality, admitted that extenuating circumstances may have contributed to the landlord's position, and concluded he would not underestimate the landlord, if in return the landlord would not underestimate him. Dylan no longer passed final judgments on others; and although he pitied the poor immigrant, he declined to "enlighten" such a person. Furthermore, in "I Am the Lonesome Hobo" he advised people to stay free from petty jealousies, to live by no man's code, and hold their judgments for themselves.

Secure in this relationship to society, Dylan struck out on a new tangent in "Down Along the Cove" and "I'll Be Your Baby Tonight." With these simple songs, Bob Dylan, critic of America's image-based society, disappeared, and Bob Dylan, the popular entertainer, emerged. Heeding the message given "The Wicked Messenger," Dylan delivered no bad news, and instead offered his happy songster services to society, if only for a one night stand.

Thus, by the conclusion of *John Wesley Harding* Dylan had divorced himself completely from his former image and attempted to establish a viable alternative, a singer merely singing his song, a craftsman plying his trade. He retreated from life on the political level to the sanctity of his own life. His next albums, *Nashville Skyline* (1969) and *Self-Portrait* (1970) further supported his new image. The former with its strong country-and-western flavor startled many people, who went into total shock when the latter appeared with Dylan singing such songs as "Blue Moon," "Let It Be Me," and "Take a Message to Mary." An uproar ensued which surpassed the one that greeted his earlier shift away from folk. Some claimed he had sold out, others declared him artistically dead, while still others refused to believe a change had happened, that somehow he was "putting us on." Everyone anxiously awaited his return, which never occurred.

To say the least, with his productions of the late 1960s, Dylan succeeded in moving outside the realms of involved song writing. He finally became a person beyond symbolization, and achieved the freedom he had so valiantly sought since 1965. However, in his movement to such a position he opened many doors, which allowed individuals to better perceive society and their relationship to it.

The Rolling Stones

CATHY: Two years ago my girl friend and I were married and living in Ojai. It was okay, but boring, and all we ever thought about was Mick Jagger. We loved him a lot more than our husbands. So one day we decided: we'll split, get divorces, and move down to the Strip. It was great, you know, hanging around the clubs. We got to know a lot of the groups, but we never met Mick. So imagine how we felt in the Whiskey one night when this guy said he was Sam Cutler and asked if we'd like to be with the Stones when they were in LA, and drive them around and stuff.

"It was Sam who picked me up, and I felt loyal to him, but when we were up at Mick's house the first night—well I'm only human. We were all sitting around, and Mick said he was going to bed. I was really disappointed. But he came down again and started pouring perfume on me, and sort of whispered, "Will you come up with me, then?" I almost died, but I managed to say, "Only if my friend Mary can come too." We had been together through two years, and had a pact not to leave the other out. He said okay.

"It was *funny*, man. I could hardly get it on, I was laughing so hard, but know what was funniest? For two years I had been thinking with every guy, "He's great but he's not Mick Jagger." And then with Mick, all I could think was, "He's great, but he's not Mick Jagger."[25]

While Bob Dylan recognized and tried to avoid and move outside the dominant culture's image system, the Rolling Stones recognized and embraced the world of images. Remaining within the bounds of the culture, they assumed a delinquent posture, defying accepted norms. Rather than create new forms and contents as the Beatles attempted to do, or transcend and finally work within social forms as Dylan eventually did, the Stones negated the accepted standards of society and in so doing created their own explosive image domains of dissent.

An indication of the Rolling Stones' success as image creators became evidence when people declared that Mick Jagger should have played the lead in Stanley Kubrick's film adaptation of Anthony Burgess's *A Clockwork Orange*. These people did not realize that the book preceded not only the film but also the Rolling Stones. Indeed the group adapted much of their image from the novel.

The Rolling Stones' translation of Burgess's fiction into flesh and blood must in part be credited to their manager, Andrew Oldham. According to Keith Richard, "He had a genius for getting things through the media,"[26] and seemed to capitalize on every opportunity to promote the Stones' delinquent image, be it on an album's liner notes (for example, those for *The Rolling Stones Now* [1965]) or news articles with such titles as "Why Do Parents Hate Us?" "Would You Let Your Sister Go Out With A Rolling Stone?" and "When Irish Fans are

Punching." Other Oldham communiqués included a billboard in Times Square
to promote the The Rolling Stones' 1965 American tour, which announced:

> *The sound, face, and mind of today is more relative to the hope of tomorrow
> and the reality of destruction than the blind who cannot see their children
> for fear and division. Something that grew and related five reflections of
> today's children . . .*

For ten days the sign puzzled passersby, capturing their attention, piquing their
curiosity. Then a picture of the Rolling Stones appeared above it, and still another
two days elapsed before ". . . THE ROLLING STONES" was added to the end
of the statement to aid those still bewildered. Such gestures as these and such
epigrams as "The Stones are the group parents love to hate," certainly helped
establish the Rolling Stone image.

Oldham traveled within the traditional formats of the mass media, but the
message behind his forms portrayed an image at variance with those normally
delivered. By confronting the media Dylan outmaneuvered it, and made it
communicate his own message. Through his interviews and songs, he disclosed
the image world as a sham. Oldham and the Rolling Stones embraced this sham,
worked within its context, and assailed its values. Dylan rejected American
society's forms, but these forms intrigued the Stones, even though they found
their content lacking. This primary difference between these superstars determined the images which enveloped them: Dylan was the outlaw, the man outside
society fighting a corrupt world, while the Stones were bad guys, sneering at
society from within its very midst. The malcontented young of the late 1960s
accepted both images.

From the start the Rolling Stones, through their manner, their performance,
their choice of material and delivery, conveyed a rough, derisive image. Once
they began to perform their own material their defiant image solidified and grew.
From 1965 onward songs such as "Satisfaction" depicted a distorted vision of
society, laden with discontent and malevolence. The group recognized the image
world which Dylan fought against in *Highway 61 Revisited,* and laughed at it.
They mocked "The Under Assistant Promotion Man" (1965) for thinking just
how sharp he was, and "put down" those headed for their "Nineteenth Nervous
Breakdown" (1966).

At the same time, however, the Rolling Stones recognized their place in
the world of image. They knew the blonde in "Spider and the Fly" dug the way
Mick Jagger held the microphone, and they reveled in this knowledge. Where
Dylan tried to turn away from such an image world, the Stones moved in on it,

grasped it, and from it created an ego-centered, leeringly sexual stance that expressed disrespect for the world as they found it. The plastic sexual imagery of Madison Avenue paled before the threatening throb of the Stones' sound, which probed the dirty thoughts of society.

Through their malignant music the Stones intimidated the girl who had her diamonds, pretty clothes, and chauffer-driven car, and this music reinforced the group's warning that such women had better exercise caution, for when they played with the Stones they were playing with fire. The dark, almost sinister music greatly contributed to the impact of "Play with Fire." It made the Stones "real," not merely another hyped bauble of the image world. They were not safe sex idols in an antiseptic world of make believe. Rather their musical essence merged with the street, where thoughts became tantamount to action. Play with them, but expect to pay the price.

Aftermath (1966) further enhanced this image. Opening with "Paint it Black," the album immediately reestablished the Stones' dissident stance, and songs such as "Goin' Home" and "Under My Thumb" explicitly perpetuated the sexual leer. "Goin' Home" toyed with the audience, posing as a traditional love song at its start, the tale of a touring singer anticipating a reunion with his girl at home. However, as the song progressed it erased this preconception with less ambiguous, more explicit language, music, and moans, and disclosed that the singer's desire centered on the sexual aspects of the relationship rather than any romantic notions of love.

"Under My Thumb" added another dimension to the Stones' sexual image. Laced with Jagger's sexual asides, delivered with just the right inflection, the song centered on an element of power. Jagger now controlled the girl, who once had pushed him around, and he relished the fact and gloried in this sense of power. On another plane the song revealed the Stones in control of their situation, in command of those who deigned to enter their world, and the undercurrent of the song left no doubt in the listener's mind that the control, the power, had no further end than the gratification of the Stones' sexual desires. The Stones were not "youth leaders," but rather bad guys, defying the moral standards of society.

They did not have the "petty" concerns of Bob Dylan, and they gloried in this fact. "High and Dry," which musically mimicked Dylan, found the Stones turned down by a rich woman who feared they were after her money, leading to the moral of the song: next time find a poor girl. "Doncha Bother Me" and "It's Not Easy" further parodied Dylan. The latter sneered at "Like a Rolling Stone," Dylan's depiction of courage in the face of the void beyond society. In the Stones' hands it became a mere whimpering, deserving no sympathy. That's how hard, how bad these "droogs" out of *A Clockwork Orange* were. And

"Doncha Bother Me" continued the assault by playing on Dylan's desire to abandon the role of youth leader. They used the opportunity to mock both Dylan and the follow-the-leader audience.

Social stances and images did not concern the Rolling Stones, although they did heap abuse on that "Stupid Girl" who lived in and accepted the surface world. However, the Stones made their position clear, they were not talking about the stupid girl's clothes or hair style or even her digging for gold, but rather the values motivating these actions, the vanity, the quest for security. Unlike Dylan they did not do battle with the image world itself, but rather its content, its values.

The group's next album of new material, *Between the Buttons* (1967), further proclaimed their position by exaggerating accepted images of women, almost to the breaking point. The album released their raw, unadorned essence to the world in an attempt to reveal the hypocrisy of the dominant culture.

Once again, the opening number, "Let's Spend the Night Together," introduced the group's antisocial, sexual emphasis, which was to be sustained throughout the album. Then came the flow of women. "Yesterday's Papers" and "My Obsession" depicted women as objects, and handled them in a ruthless, impersonal manner. Discarding one as no longer current and pursuing the other as a possession, the Stones' "badness" now came forth in their heartless execution of social values. The women suffered the ultimate fate of denizens of a consumer-oriented society: objectification and planned obsolesence.

The women in "Who's Been Sleeping Here" and "Amanda Jones" appeared to be on the verge of similar objectification, while others seemed to avoid this destiny, as "Cool, Calm, Collected" and "Complicated" demonstrated. These women knew the right games to play, the right words to say, were very educated, and didn't give a damn. Like the Stones, they commanded their image worlds, but despite their strong lyrical presence, the Rolling Stones' music cynically lorded over them. Any of these women could be the next obsession to fall under the Stones' thumbs if their facades could not withstand an assault by the powerful Stones image. Such was the potential outcome when two image worlds clashed.

Such was not the outcome when the Stones assaulted Pepperland, the territory of the Beatles. Splashing into the psychedelic world with *Their Satanic Majesties Request* (1967), they lost their image in a whirl of joyous love. They could not convincingly sustain their sinister disdain in the Beatle-infested strawberry fields. The album was not well received, its dissonant music did not assist its acceptance, and the songs did little to enhance the group's image. They had to fall back and regroup before exploding again on the rock scene one year later.

With *Beggars Banquet* (1968) the Stones attained the pinnacle Dylan reached in 1965. Outside of society, they saw through the mundane doings of the world with cynical glee. While Dylan found this space uncomfortable, and eventually retreated from it to the simple life of *Nashville Skyline*, the Rolling Stones, not ensnared by any moral compunctions, expanded upon their image, making it larger than life.

> *It begins with a crazed wildcat yelp and the primordial rhythms of hand drums on a rampage. It builds maniacally in intensity, and complexity, the vocal brawling, the drums double gunning, the bass pumping, and the piano twisting the melody and rhythms together like so much heavy two-ply twine. The guitar whines, the voices hoot, and the lyrics blast the consciousness with a pageant of chaos . . . it gets you moving, jiving, and throttles you with its raunchy nastiness, the furious ranting that ranges far beyond the lyrics.*[27]

Thus "Sympathy for the Devil" introduced the Stones' new image, Lucifer, a man of wealth and taste, who'd been around a long time and had taken numerous souls. The malcontented delinquents had transformed themselves into the ultimate personification of evil. From being the bad guys within society they merged into a sinister presence above and able to control society. Their image shift corresponded with the times, which conceived of society as evil as any previous Stones' image. All the cops were criminals, all the sinners saints. The name of the game was power, an insight which the Stones had repeatedly revealed in songs like "Under My Thumb," "My Obsession," and "Spider and the Fly." The Stones with their dark image ironically came to represent the essence of American society laid bare. They were the images of an imageless world, Simmel's world without sociability.

In earlier history the Greeks had been content to portray their beliefs and values in statues of their gods. Other eras accepted even lesser images, but the generation coming of age in America in the 1960s, brought up on television and the motion picture, embraced nothing less than a walking, talking, or rather dancing, prancing, leering, sneering idol. In the closing years of the decade the on-stage Mick Jagger became an embodiment of Moloch, but even more than this, he also represented the "Howl." The Rolling Stones not only reflected the perceived evil of American society, but also gave delinquent vent to individual feelings of helplessness and discontent. They delicately balanced these two functions, and masterfully played them against each other. Maintaining this tension, they moved to the forefront of the rock pantheon.

Their super-enhanced image took shape with *Beggar's Banquet* (1968) and *Let It Bleed* (1969), and in concert the word became flesh. Rising above the world and seeing through it, the Stones laughed at the counterculture's "revolution game" in "Street Fighting Man," and in "Factory Girl" and "Salt of the Earth" mocked and uncompassionately empathized with the working class masses and their liberal supporters. Their songs recognized the rising incongruities as the world of image proceeded to become increasingly detached from life. The group noted the voters' choice of crippling diseases in major elections, collected hare-brained children with ear-phoned heads, and knew the family man-gangster packed a luger and could shove in his knife, despite his religious appearance. The Stones sought no answers or quarter from the world, quite satisfied to turn their attention to "Parachute Woman" and "Stray Cat" sex. They invited others to "Live with Me," although they admittedly had nasty habits and sexual cravings. Without a doubt, the Stones preferred "The Midnight Rambler" to the "Street Fighting Man."

Having never fallen into the responsible leader "bag," their lyrics were not culled over for a possible way of life. Rather they were reacted to. The Stones presented no utopian solutions to society's situation, although they acknowledged we all need someone we can lean on, dream on, bleed on, and cream on, and even offered in "Let It Bleed" to allow people to do so on them. Yet it was apparent from the song's music and delivery that the Stones on whom you could rest your weary head were the same ones who had nasty habits. Listeners ventured forth at their own peril.

The Stones embodied power. They controlled and manipulated the world for their own diversion, sometimes providing relief and other times intensifying their sound, driving it to a frenzy. But, like society, they gave no release, reminding people that war, rape, murder are just a shot away. The only advice they had to give taunted their audience: they couldn't always get what they wanted, but if they tried they might get what they needed (as compared to Rosie in her honky-tonk lagoon telling Dylan that his deubante just knew what he needed, but she knew what he wanted). The Stones accepted the world and their discontents as given, and rather than change the social situation, they attempted merely to get by on their terms. They were "something that grew and related, Five reflections of today's children."

NOTES

[1]Kenneth Keniston, *The Uncommitted*, p. 167, discusses the alienated young's desire for an ego-engulfing "mystical fusion" despite their sense of individual isolation.

[2]Figures from Nicholas Schaffner, *The Beatles Forever,* (Cameron House: Harrisburg, Pennsylvania, 1977), p. 214.

[3]John Lennon and Paul McCartney, "All You Need Is Love" (Maclen Music, Inc., c/o ATV Music Corp. © 1967 Northern Songs Limited. Used by permission.

[4]Peter Schrag, "Facing the Music," *Saturday Review,* 19 August 1967, p. 61.

[5]Schrag, "Facing the Music," p. 61.

[6]John Lennon and Paul McCartney, "Norwegian Wood" (Maclen Music, Inc., c/o ATV Music Corp. © 1965 Northern Songs Limited. Used by permission.

[7]Quoted in Joan Peyser, "The Music of Sound or, The Beatles and the Beatless," *Columbia University Forum,* 10 (Fall 1967).

[8]Herman Hesse, *Steppenwolf* (New York: Holt, Rinehart and Winston, 1929), pp. 24–25.

[9]See Daniel Boorstin, *The Image* (New York: Harper-Colophon, 1964), and Erich Fromm, *The Sane Society* (New York: Holt, Rinehart and Winston, 1955).

[10]A discussion of sociability can be found in Georg Simmel, *The Philosophy of Georg Simmel* (New York: The Free Press, 1950), pp. 40–57.

[11]Simmel, p. 55.

[12]Susanne K. Langer, *Philosophy in a New Key* (Cambridge, Massachusetts: Harvard University Press, 1957), p. 39.

[13]Nat Hentoff, "The Playboy Interview: Bob Dylan," *Playboy,* March 1966.

[14]Quoted in Paul Nelson, "Bob Dylan: Another View," *Sing Out! The Folk Song Magazine,* 16, No. 1.

[15]Bob Dylan, "To Ramona"

[16]Nat Hentoff, "The Crackin', Shakin', Breakin' Sounds," *New Yorker Magazine,* 24 October 1964.

[17]Bob Dylan, "Subterranean Homesick Blues"

[18]Bob Dylan, "It's Alright Ma (I'm Only Bleeding)"

[19]Linda Gaboriau, "Ken Kesey Summing Up the 60's Sizing Up the 70's," *Crawdaddy,* December 1975, p. 35.

[20]Anthony Scaduto, *Dylan* (New York: Grosset & Dunlap, 1971), p. 255.

[21]D.A. Pennebaker, *Bob Dylan, Don't Look Back* (New York: Ballantine Books, 1968), pp. 83–84.

[22]D.A. Pennebaker, p. 126.

[23]Ellen Willis, "Dylan" *Beginning to See the Light* ed Ellen Willis (New York: Alfred A. Knopf, 1981).

[24]Jon Landau, "John Wesley Harding," *Crawdaddy,* May 1968.

[25]Michael Lydon, "The Rolling Stones," *Rock Folk,* ed. Michael Lydon (New York: Dial Press, 1971), pp. 177–78.

[26]Robert Greenfield, "Rolling Stone Interview: Keith Richard," *Rolling Stone,* August 19, 1971.

[27]Ellen Sander, "Beggars' Triumph," *Saturday Review*, 25 January 1969, p. 48.

7

The Seventies

"The most revolutionary thing you can do in this
country is change your mind."

Country Joe McDonald, 1971

During the period from 1967 to 1970 a segment of the American population
dreamed, and hoped to break with or change the dominant cultural values and
institutions of our nation. Rock music, a major conveyor of these people's ideas
and beliefs, broadcast a lifestyle based on drugs, free love, defiance of authority,
and an aesthetic quest involving individual freedom and integrity. Viewed as a
potential vehicle for social revolution, rock became a rallying point for the
discontented people of the period, and, in part, a way of life.

However, between 1969 and 1971 many devotees of rock's way of life
came to realize the societal goals they had hoped to attain were not going to
materialize overnight. A series of political events, including the Democratic
Party's failure to nominate Eugene McCarthy for president in 1968, the police
riot in Chicago, the resulting conspiracy trial of the "Chicago Seven," the
continuation of the Vietnam War and the invasion of Cambodia, despite the
mounting number of demonstrations against these actions, proved the United
States, unlike the walls of Jericho, was not about to succumb to the demands
of youth. With this realization, an air of disillusionment, helplessness, and
cynicism, and a general desire to retrench, if not retreat, pervaded the rock
world. The music noticeably changed, and by 1971 most of the major groups
of the late 1960s had either disbanded or undergone considerable changes in

style. Death had claimed Jimi Hendrix, Janis Joplin, Brian Jones, and Jim Morrison. The Animals, Buffalo Springfield, Big Brother and the Holding Company, Cream, Creedance Clearwater Revival, Doors, Fish, Iron Butterfly, Mothers of Invention, Young Rascals, and, of course, the Beatles had either disbanded or lost their exalted positions in the rock pantheon. New individuals and groups had replaced them, such as Crosby, Stills, Nash, and Young; Led Zeppelin; Jethro Tull; New Riders of the Purple Sage; Flying Burrito Brothers; Allman Brothers; Doobie Brothers; James Taylor; Carly Simon; Carole King; Elton John; Cat Stevens; Rod Stewart; Eagles; and others. Many of these newer bands and performers differed from the rock groups of the 1960s in their tendency toward a softer, more country-rock sound. Others maintained a basic rock sound, but began to take it in new directions and broaden its scope. The focus of the rock scene became more diffused, and its audience looked for a new direction.

REVOLUTION DISSOLUTION

By 1970 members of the rock world realized that no major political changes were about to transpire in America. The deeper economic and military currents that guided the nation's course were not about to shift. Any possibilities for change lay in a more distant future, and the best the people could hope for was the maintenance of their own values within their own lives. David Crosby enunciated the prevailing mood in an interview with *Rolling Stone* editor Ben Fong-Torres in 1970, when he spoke of:

> *The problems we're up against, and those include environmental crime, race crime, political, total obnoxious corruption, and international crime, which is war—all of these problems, man, relate to a power structure that is running this country.*
>
> *We got a whole bunch of people who clearly identify that, and say O.K. now we're gonna just shake this power structure by the roots. Right? I laugh at 'em. I laugh at the SDS and I laugh at those fucking parlor-pink revolutionary kids going around saying, "I'm a revolutionary by trade." Bullfucking pukie. They haven't got any idea what it is, man. They should go watch a newsreel of the last three days of Budapest, and think it over. Asshole kids. They don't know what they are up against, man. You can't convince this power structure to change its course. It's inextricably—a curious word— inextricably involved in its course. I'm trying to explain to people that it isn't the President, it isn't Congress, it isn't the governors. It seems like it, but as far as I can tell, it's an interlocking whole socioeconomic system group.*

*. . . I just am really sick of the revolutionary kids, man. I'm really sick of
the talk and I'm really sick of the kids I see at rallies and stuff. Hey, they're
jokes. Fuckin' revolution, man. They forget that they already ate revolution
alive. That's not happening, man.*[1]

John Lennon expressed similar opinions in 1971, when Jann Wenner asked him
in a *Rolling Stone* interview what effect the Beatles had upon the history of
Great Britain. Lennon replied:

*I don't know about the "history;" the people who are in control and in
power, and the class system and the whole bullshit bourgeoisie is exactly
the same, except there is a lot of fag middle class kids with long, long hair
walking around London in trendy clothes, and Kenneth Tynan is making a
fortune out of the word "fuck." Apart from that, nothing happened. We all
dressed up, the same bastards are in control, the same people are running
everything. It is exactly the same.*

*We've grown up a little, all of us, there has been a change and we're all
a bit freer and all that, but it's the same game. Shit, they're doing exactly
the same thing, selling arms in South Africa, killing Blacks on the street,
people are living in fucking poverty with rats crawling over them. It just
makes you puke, and, I woke up to that too.*

*The dream is over. It's just the same, only I'm thirty, and a lot of people
have long hair. That's what it is man, nothing happened except that we
grew up, we did our thing—just like they were telling us—most of the
so-called "now generation" are getting a job. We're a minority, you know,
people like us always were, but maybe we are a slightly larger minority
because of something or other.*[2]

The dream was over. Reality time had arrived, demanding that the generation
coming of age finally mature, or at least recognize the need to establish an
operative individual-society relationship. The older order existed, and showed
no signs of yielding to the new. The road to revolution was a dead end; a new
path had to be discovered, or as Lennon informed Wenner, "It's over, and we
gotta—I have to personally—get down to so-called reality."[3]

With *John Lennon/Plastic Ono Band* (1970), the music world's prime
proponent of peace elucidated upon his trip toward reality. Finding himself in
a situation somewhat comparable to that of Bob Dylan in 1964, John Lennon
in 1970 assumed essentially the same stance. Rejecting messiahs and visions of
instant salvation in such songs as "God" and "I Found Out," he retreated into
the sanctity of Yoko and himself. Disclaiming belief in *I Ching, Bible,* Jesus,

Kennedy, Buddha, mantra, Elvis, Zimmerman (a.k.a. Dylan), or Beatles, he advised his audience to just "carry on," to seek out individually created lives. As for himself, he turned inward in an attempt to appraise his own identity. Such songs as "Mother," "Look at Me," "Love," and "My Mummy's Dead" returned to primal agonies and questions, and partially reflected the depths of his introspection. Furthermore, the album stood as a reiteration of personal integrity, and reinforced individuals confronting a world bound on molding working class heroes. But more than a sound of freedom or a "Hold on John," the album was a declaration of honesty not only to, but with the self.

The time had come to move inward once again, to retreat into the confines of alienation, reexamine the self, and nurture the 1960s hopes and ideals, yet face up to the realities of the seventies. And John Lennon was not the only rock performer to recognize this need. Among others, the Grateful Dead, who dramatically shifted their style from high psychedelia to country rock in 1970, portrayed the loss of unified direction and the need for their audience to establish individually viable approaches to life in such songs as "Uncle John's Band," "New Speedway Blues," "Box of Rain," "Ripple," and "Truckin'" on their *Workingman's Dead* (1970) and *American Beauty* (1970) albums.

> There is a road, no simple highway
> Between the dawn and the dark of night
> And if you go, no one may follow,
> That path is for your steps alone.[4]

Individuals had to work out their own salvations, discover their own ways.

With this realization, the rock world, which had been so united in its assault on the dominant culture's ways, splintered into a multitude of solutions. This pursuit of individual realities contributed to the decimation of the previous decade's sense of community, and certainly figured in the dissolution of many groups. Eric Clapton explained the breakup of Cream in the following terms:

> We were all rebels from different scenes and that was what kind of got it together. We had this basic thing in common, this sort of anarchistic point of view about music and it was only after a while that I started to realize that it was only one kind of thing. It was aggressive and the kind of group we were, we couldn't provide the audience with sweet music or relaxing music or harmonious things. It was always this onslaught of mad sound, and that was because we didn't have the same ideas about music—we just represented this anarchy towards music and we did start something. But we couldn't follow it through because we could only do that one thing.[5]

The breakup of the Beatles further attested to the variety of alternatives open to rock musicians and their audience, as John turned toward politics, George toward religion, Paul toward show business, and Ringo toward a country-based nostalgia. Everyone indeed had their own realities to pursue.

Soft Rock

Getting down to reality was a disillusioning experience for many, and as acid went flaccid, the simple, soft rock sound of the early 1970s aptly reflected the rock audience's mood. The lyrics turned nostalgic and the music became much mellower, moving mostly into sixteen-bar forms with an accent on the strong (1 and 3) beats. The acoustic guitar was revived, and instruments such as the accordian, mandolin, banjo, fiddle, and acoustic piano appeared with regularity. Also most of the songs returned to three-minute lengths, and frequently employed country-folk chord progressions, which unlike the blues, typically featured a I-IV-V verse and chorus progression with bridges moving from the IV to the I, climaxing on the V, and then returning to the verse. The major seven and six chords also abounded. Soft rock accommodated a variety of sounds ranging from the relatively sophisticated chord voicings of David Crosby to the relatively straightforward finger picking of James Taylor, from the Latino rhythms of Stephen Stills to the influence of traditional Greek music on Cat Stevens; but whatever its style, it smoothed listeners out and let them down gently.

Bob Dylan reintroduced the rock world to country and western music with *John Wesley Harding* (1968) and *Nashville Skyline* (1969), and shortly thereafter the huge success of Crosby, Stills, and Nash confirmed the return of the country element to rock. With *The Band* (1969), Crosby, Stills, Nash, and Young's *Déja Vu* (1970), the Grateful Dead's acoustic albums, and James Taylor's *Sweet Baby James* (1970) country rock came of age. A definite market for mellow rock existed, and within a year albums by a host of new stars appeared, with Carole King's *Tapestry* (1971) and *Music* (1971), Carly Simon's *No Secrets* (1972), Cat Stevens' *Tea for the Tillerman* (1971) and *Teaser and the Firecat* (1971), and Elton John's *Elton John* (1970), *Tumbleweed Connection* (1971), and *Madman Across the Water* (1971) all breaking the top ten in album sales.

These albums conveyed the sense of loss, of quiet hurt which followed the deceleration of "Woodstock Nation." Songs of love lost, those tear-jerking staples of country and western music once again emerged, but now they did not so much mourn the dissolution of a love relationship, as they metaphorically lamented the demise of the love generation. This sense of greater loss, implicit in such songs as Neil Young's "The Losing End" (1969), Crosby, Stills, Nash, and Young's "Four and Twenty" (1970), Stephen Stills' "Do for the Others" (1970) and Carole King's "So Far Away" (1971), explicitly appeared in Graham Nash's "Better Days" (1971) and "Wounded Bird" (1971)] The former advised a deserted lover, who had gone out searching for truth, to get home and remember better days, while the latter urged individuals left alone to face the "wounded bird," to stand their ground and maintain their integrity.

Songs such as these not only acknowledged the sad passing of the psychedelic era, but consciously strove in a low-keyed moderate manner to keep alive the spirit and values of the counterculture. The rush of excitement had dissipated, and the time had come to rise from the ruins of shattered hope, and deliberately move ahead. Like the songs of love lost of the 1960s, soft rock songs admitted the pain of sorrow, but declared the need to move on, to "keep on truckin'," to:

> *Carry on, love is coming*
> *Love is coming to us all.*[7]

Offering encouragement and support to the devout, Crosby, Stills, Nash, and Young, in *Déja Vu* (1970), advised listeners to "Teach Your Children" and recounted the time David Crosby almost cut his hair. Carole King in *Tapestry* (1971), the best selling album in rock history up to that time, told her audience, "You've Got a Friend," optimistically pointed to the land "Way Over Yonder," and reminded people to wake up every morning with a smile and share their love for life with everyone.

In a similar vein, Cat Stevens brightened the moment with "Peace Train" (1971) and the early-twentieth-century hymn "Morning Has Broken" (1971). Emitting a spirit of renewal, these songs reaffirmed the optimistic stance of the late 1960s—the energy release had not been in vain; some good had emerged.

> *Yes, we all know it's better, yesterday's passed,*
> *Now let's all start livin' for the one that's gonna last.*[8]

A settled feeling combined with, and augmented, this positive, reassuring mood. Drifting mist-like through the atmosphere of soft rock, this calm sense of stability created an idyllic panorama of contented family life, which presumably was based on the virtues of love, peace, and happiness. Crosby, Stills, Nash, and

Young's "Our House" (1970), Carole King's "Home Again" (1971), Seals and Crofts' "Summer Breeze" (1972) and Loggins and Messina's "Peace of Mind" (1972) presented new utopian visions of pastoral domestic serenity, of life outside the American mainstream, in virtual unawareness of the twentieth century. These songs recognized that any dominant cultural changes would be long in coming, and established a sense of continuity between the late 1960s and the anticipated better days of the future. They offered hope in the face of despair, and confidently advocated the perpetuation of countercultural values.

Gloom

The shoring up of hopeful anticipation for a fine future was not the sole reaction to the apparent dissolution of the rock revolution. Neil Young's "Helpless" (1970) typified another, not so optimistic, view which reigned during the opening years of the new decade. Escaping to a rural retreat in northern Ontario, the song's protagonist despondently discovered that the shadows of "big birds" flying in the skies still intruded upon his sensibilities, and left him feeling helpless. The music accompanying these thoughts heightened a sense of despair over the realization that viable solutions to society's problems were disappearing. The most an individual could do was escape, and even this was difficult in our technologically advanced society with its remote military outposts.

The Beatles' "Let It Be" (1970) became almost an anthem for the age, for it expressed the prevalent sense of declining individual initiative. An air of resignation prevailed throughout the song, and "Mother Mary," serving as supreme comforter, came to the listeners in their time of trouble and advised them to "let it be." The use of the Mother Mary imagery remained ambiguous. Perhaps her presence implied that religion was indeed the opiate of the people, or possibly her appearance ironically coincided with the changing role of marijuana and other drugs in the youth culture.

Instead of being a positive force benefiting the individual, as in the Association's "Along Comes Mary" (1966), drugs made it easier to acquiesce in the 1970s. They provided a means of escape, relaxation, and came to be employed in much the same manner as alcohol in the mainstream culture. LSD, with its ability to bring people up, declined in popularity, while "sopors" (soporifics, the most popular of which carried the Quaadludes brand name), heroin and other downers increased in popularity. Drugs lost their mystical quality, and rather than becoming an adventure they turned into a social behavior. Instead of opening people's minds and eyes, drugs became a fashionable thing to do. Songs specifically concerned with drugs declined, although some alluded to the then current rage, cocaine.

Escape from the dominant culture was not an unfamiliar action for many of the young. Much of the 1950s and 1960s rock centered on escape or momentary release. However, the new decade offered no place to escape to. One could only aimlessly flee. In the 1960s, when the Doors sang "You're Lost Little Girl," that little girl knew she could turn to the music, to social change, and be found, for the music was her friend, until the end. However, with the early 1970s there was nothing left to do but run, only the Doors no longer were running with her. Individuals had to escape on their own and find their own ways.

Most young people retreated into themselves, although some slipped into the rural commune scene, and others cuddled up to the comfort of exotic religions. Norman Greenbaum's "Spirit in the Sky" (1970), Ocean's "Put Your Hand in the Hand" (1970), Edwin Hawkins' "Oh Happy Day" (1969), George Harrison's "My Sweet Lord" (1971), and of course *Godspell* (1972) and *Jesus Christ Superstar* (1971) reflected to a certain extent this religious avenue of interest. "Amazing Grace" (1971), as sung by Judy Collins, indicated the motivation for the new religiosity: she once was lost, but now was found. Through religion some of the young escaped the dominant culture and moved in what they thought to be a purposeful direction, although some critics, such as Norman Spinrad in *The Children of Hamlin,* equated this new spiritualism with heroin addiction, suggesting it to be no more than a crutch for those unable to handle the world.

However, despite such criticism, contemporary Christian rock continued to grow in the 1970s, featuring such stars as Barry McGuire, B.J. Thomas, Phil Keaggy, 2nd Chapter of Acts, Candle, David Meece, Don Francisco, and Amy Grant. By 1980 *Billboard* formally recognized the existence of this new audience and began to chart "inspirational music," and a year earlier the religious impulse had received further rock support with the release of Bob Dylan's *Slow Train Coming,* Robert Fripp's *Exposure,* Arlo Guthrie's *Outlasting the Blues,* and Van Morrison's *Into the Music,* all within a three-month period.

Without a doubt a profound change had occurred within the youth culture of the early 1970s, of which the religious trend was but one indication. The "Times They Are A-Changin'" flame of the 1960s had been extinguished and, although the embers glowed in such revivalist sounds as Graham Nash's "We Can Change the World" (1971), John Lennon's "Give Peace a Chance" (1969), and Stephen Stills' "We Are Not Helpless" (1970), the spark was gone. More than music would be required to rekindle it.

The young retreated from their confrontation with the dominant culture and reassessed the situation. At the same time that the rock audience began to shift its musical tastes under the pressures of political and psychological "realities," other factors came to the fore in the rock world itself to influence performers to alter their images and musical styles.

HELP! I'M AN ARTIST

By late 1968 many musicians were becoming alienated from their audience. They felt restricted by, yet compelled to live up to, the media images which their audiences embraced. These rock stars came to realize as Dylan had as early as 1964 that by formulating images performers could direct their audience for awhile, but their image quickly trapped them and the fulfillment of audience expectations dominated performances. Many musicians spoke out against their image entrapment, including Eric Clapton, whom many considered to be rock's premier guitarist. He found:

> The bigger you are, the more pressure, the more loneliness, the more fear. I feel I'm almost continually on trial. Every time I step on stage now, I know I am expected to give more than I possibly can. The strain is terrifying.

> . . . All we want to do is be left alone and make music. But because we are called "rock stars," a whole different set of expectancies are thrust upon us—that we have instant opinions about almost everything, that we should set an example to all young people of today by making public statements about drugs, that we should dress and behave like the freaks we are supposed to be.[9]

Similarly, in early 1970 Stephen Stills told *Guitar Player* magazine:

> There are a very few bands in this country that are trying to play music, but a lot of them go to the extent of hiding their music behind some kind of little game they play. . . . Jimi Hendrix has let his music get hidden behind his game. A lot of people let that happen and it's a shame because there are a lot of talented musicians that are varying their true talent.

> . . . It isn't so much what the rock musicians are doing, it's what the kids are doing with the pop musicians. The larger-than-life thing. It's like John Lennon is much more important than Vanessa Redgrave; whereas Paul Whiteman was never more important than Gary Cooper. And therefore, the more all the little pieces of BS that go on with the superstar, the less important your music becomes and the less people seem to realize what you are doing musically.[10]

The softer, country-influenced rock, devoid of explicit political associations, allowed musicians to move away from their positions as social leaders, and return to the music itself. They could claim to be playing music merely for its own sake and for the joy (and money and fame) it generated. However, any viable art form, in some way or another, relates to the experiences and aspirations of its audience. The flaccid rock, with its supposedly backwoods "roots," became readily identifiable with the "back to the land" movement, and reinforced a lifestyle image based on the close fellowship of small groups gathering to nurture common values. Furthermore, it proved to be a superb musical vehicle for expressing the despair accompanying the dashed hopes for immediate change. With this multifaceted role, it quietly and smoothly moved the explosion of the 1960s into the withdrawal of the 1970s. As such, the mellow music, although a lot less political in its stance and style than many of the sounds of the late 1960s, was one of the more socially pertinent rock idioms of the early 1970s.

Other rock forms served similar purposes, including a blues-based British rock, which played an instrumental role in deescalating rock's revolution trip, while allowing it to retain its musical vitality.

British Blues

Following the success of the Rolling Stones and Cream, and to a lesser extent the Yardbirds, a number of blues-based British bands came to the attention of the American rock audience in the waning years of the 1960s. Beginning in late 1967 and 1968 such groups as John Mayall's Bluebreakers, Fleetwood Mac, Spooky Tooth, Procol Harum, Savoy Brown, Ten Years After, and Jeff Beck broke into the American charts. However, with the possible exception of Procol Harum's "Whiter Shade of Pale" (1967), Ten Years After's *Ssssh* (1969), and Jeff Beck's *Truth* (1968), none enjoyed widespread popularity. The socially relevant, drug oriented, psychedelic vibrations soared above and overshadowed these more restrained, less driving, blues offerings.

As the revolutionary spirit fizzled, a second wave of blues-oriented British bands hit the shores of America. They offered a rocking alternative to Crosby, Stills, Nash, and Young's "Country-cherubim music, as pretty and ball-less as that sung by the Italian *Castrati*,"[11] and created a focus around which some of the more dynamic aspects of rock would revolve Groups such as Led Zeppelin, Derek and the Dominoes, Jethro Tull, Rod Stewart (and Faces), a reconstituted Traffic, and an equally reconstructed Savoy Brown and Fleetwood Mac presented America with an alive, yet uninvolved rock. Unencumbered by a folk tradition of meaningful lyrics, social conscience and utopian visions, the music of these bands did not so much serve to communicate thoughts and values as it expressed an emotional release, the outpouring of the will itself. Extremely diverse and liberal in their handling of the blues, these groups kept some spunk in rock with their refreshing approaches. Also, by featuring such talented individuals as Jimmy Page, Eric Clapton, Ron Wood, Rod Stewart, Ian Anderson, and Stevie Winwood, these British bands facilitated an audience reorientation toward the musician as artisan rather than shaman. As such their music found a ready audience in America during the 1970s.

STYLIZATION

"Rock functions at its best when it does not seek to over-generalize, preach, or tell people what to do or think. It is at its best when it is used to explore the experience of the musician and the listener, when it seeks to entertain as well as provoke, when it realizes that rock is not primarily poetry or art, but something much more direct and immediate than either. Rock and roll has to be body music, before it can be head music, or it will wind up being neither."

Jon Landau, July 1968

The demise of the rock revolution in one sense freed rock musicians to practice the "do your own thing" methods of the alienated young, and many of them proceeded to explore areas of their own particular musical interest. Solo albums abounded as a result, and the music of the 1970s began to disperse itself in a myriad of directions. However, even though rock withdrew from the vanguard of social change, musicians still had to contend with the previous decade's elevation of rock to meaningful experience. People *knew* rock music was more than just superficial entertainment. Rock of the 1960s, so closely associated with alienation's coming out of the closet, and its accompanying quest for purposeful direction, had proven itself to be a powerful and articulate means of expression and communication. It had affected too many people on too many levels to be lightly dismissed as merely a phase.

Although not demanding sociopolitical commentary from musicians, the earlier folk world's cry for authenticity still rumbled through the corridors of rock, contemptuously shouting down superficiality, commercialism, and contrivances. The rock audience of the early 1970s still expected vitality, relevance, and the maintenance of a close tie between rock and life, between musical forms and their content. As a result, during the opening years of the new decade, a variety of rock styles emerged which self-consciously attempted to come to grips with the meaning and essence of rock. Musicians seemed to step back and ask themselves what was rock's function, what were they trying to do with their music. Their musical responses abounded: rock was good times, escape, self-expression, the voice of alienation, social commentary, art, rebellion, sustenance, dance music, energy release, and the celebration of freedom, love, sex, and youth. Around these answers musical styles developed to meet the casual needs of the rock audience. The scene shattered and differing camps formed. Occasionally camps overlapped, as styles often fulfilled more than one role. However, like the blind men in their encounter with an elephant, the various styles of rock stressed only certain aspects of the creature, and the unity of the 1960s was lost.

The ferment of the late 1960s had welded the various sounds of rock into a united, coherent whole. But that synergy of place, time, and music had dissolved with the changing seasons, and the rock world moved from an era of knowing to a period of searching. Removed from the communal context of optimistic change, rock fragmented and each shard had to stand on its own, leading to an increasingly stylized sound in the 1970s.

Whereas during the 1950s and 1960s people had created new musical forms to satisfy their needs, in the 1970s rock was accepted as a given, an established form. Its heritage defined and categorized its various styles and functions; the music was formalized, if not formulaic. With this institutionalization rock's role within society shifted and its impact decreased. Although its musical vitality remained, for surely the 1970s was not a period of musical stagnation, rock no longer was a way of life, nor even a life style; instead it became merely a part of life.

Sustained Shadows

Soft rock, the dominant sound of the early 1970s, not only reflected the disappointment of the period's crumbling expectations, but also nurtured the hopes and ideals of the fading dream of the 1960s. Thus it retained a strong contact with life and sustained the alienated, utopian visions still sweeping through the minds of the former love generation.

Other styles of rock also pushed people forward and replenished their spirit in the face of the ominous presence of "Nixon Amerika." Blues-based bands such as Savoy Brown, Hot Tuna, Taj Mahal, and Derek and the Dominoes well performed this role. Tight and disciplined, yet capable of opening up to full throttle, Derek and the Dominoes' double album, *Layla* (1970), marked a high point in the genre. Featuring the group's leader, Eric Clapton, and Duane Allman on guitars, Bobby Whitlock on keyboards, Carl Radle on bass, and Jim Gordon on drums, this band presented a solid, hard-hitting, electrically amplified blues emotion, so pure and penetrating it rippled over the skin and into the mind. Even though it featured several encouraging songs such as "Keep on Growing" and "Why Does Love Have to Be So Sad," with their thump-on-through attitudes, the guts of the album lay in such songs as "Any Day," "Bell Bottom Blues," "Layla," and "Thorn Tree in the Garden," which expressed the heavy-hearted soul of Eric Clapton,[12] and in turn captured the mood of the stymied counterculture. Generating an inner strength in the face of pain and despair, the album conveyed a sense of determined survival, if not renewal—a superb blues statement, which no rock blues band has come close to equaling. With this album the musical promise of the 1970s shone brightly, but few followed its lead, preferring instead to explore the highly charged Led Zeppelin sound.

Other less powerful, but potent, forces also kept the specter of the past alive. The raspy-voiced Rod Stewart and the soulful Joe Cocker reworked earlier material, including that of Dylan and the Beatles, and contributed new songs. Both performers drew freely from soul, folk, and rock antecedents, shaping them, combining them into their own statement. Their vocal styles disclosed heavy soul influences; Joe Cocker was influenced by Ray Charles while Rod Stewart drew inspiration from Wilson Pickett. The bands behind them were superb, laying down a strong rock beat [accenting the off (2 and 4) beats] for both rocking and ballad numbers. The transcendent, resplendent air of "Do I Still Figure in Your Life" (1969), "I Shall Be Released" (1969), "Reason to Believe" (1971), and "Angel" (1972) epitomized the spirit of regeneration present in so much of their music.

Despite Cocker and Stewart's heavy reliance on other people's compositions, their songs convincingly conveyed life's day-to-day hopes, pains, and glories. These two singers made the promise and heartache of idealism real. The audience felt it, and through such songs as Rod Stewart's "Maggie May" (1971), "Seems Like a Long Time" (1971), "Mama You've Been on My Mind" (1972), and "You Wear It Well" (1972), and Joe Cocker's "Changes in Louise," "Just Like a Woman," and "Sandpaper Cadillac" (all 1969) listeners were replenished, comforted, and given the confidence to approach the quirks of existence head-on.

Other songs and musicians performed comparable roles. Led Zeppelin's haunting and evocative "Stairway to Heaven" (1971) absorbed the listener with its invitingly soft, surreal visions of an economically prioritized, consumer trip into the mystic. Focusing on a lady who wanted to buy a stairway to heaven, the band created a striking image of modern society and its affluence-inspired delusions. Discounting such visions, the song forged into a guitar-interlude, above and beyond the stairway on the whispering wind, only to conclude with the resigned knowledge that the lady was buying a stairway to heaven. The song spurned the new industrial state's tunnel vision, but at the same time resolutely acknowledged the immutable character of the dominant fiscal approach to existence. As such the song stood as the ultimate statement of the early 1970s. It superbly summed up the situation, and supported a strong individual stance that transcended societal concerns.

Serving similar sustaining purposes, Traffic's *John Barleycorn Must Die* (1970), *The Low Spark of High Heeled Boys* (1971), and *Shoot Out at the Fantasy Factory* (1973) billowed forth and snaked through the mind. Ranging from cryptic commentary on the rock scene of "The Low Spark of High Heeled Boys" to the promising "Freedom Riders" (1970), these albums established a positive position, a breathing space within which hopes might be protected and nourished. Other songs pointed out the endurance of the "Roll Right Stones" (1973) and spoke of nature's "Hidden Treasures" (1971) down by the river. Furthermore they advised those who felt uninspired, tired, or trapped, not to give up—for tomorrow they might be sailing. Often Traffic employed simple, albeit ambiguous, lyrics, but their almost ethereal, jazz-inspired music provided a profoundly substantive depth. Drawing upon the blues tradition for its fortitude, their music retained a solid, earthbound quality while displaying incredible flexibility. Tight and controlled, it gave little rein to flights of fantasy and suited the retrenchment and search for a viable approach to life of the early 1970s.

By 1973 rock's role as a conscious sustainer of the 1960s inner-directed ideals had all but vanished. Most of the soft rockers had shifted their emphases from cultural to personal concerns; Traffic had disbanded, Eric Clapton was moving in his own direction, Joe Cocker disappeared into obscurity, and Rod Stewart vanished into fame. Occasionally a strong song such as Kansas's "Carry On My Wayward Son" (1976) or Aerosmith's "Dream On" (1973) appeared and reinforced personal escapes to freedom and sane living, but these pronouncements became rarer as the decade advanced. Rock began to address itself to other concerns and turned from a bastion of inner-directed strength back to an other-directed media.

Don't Analyze—Energize

Rather than internalizing the despair of the moment and the hopes of tomorrow, a number of musicians in the 1970s exuberantly confronted the world head-on, full steam ahead, in an attempt to overcome or completely ignore the morass of the period. Thumping straight on through at high energy and decibel levels, they emphasized the physical aspects of rock and provided a means to work out frustrations and celebrate the joys of existence. They reestablished rock as body music.

The more rocking proponents of country-rock, such as Poco, strove to attain in their music rock's physical spirit. However, their genre proved too mellow a vehicle for this purpose, and more appropriate styles rose which better achieved the rollicking intensity necessary for letting loose.

One of the earliest of these styles to gain popularity was the decade's revival of 1950s blues-based rock 'n' roll, as exemplified by Leon Russell, Delaney and Bonnie, and the return of Chuck Berry, Do Biddley, Little Richard and others to the concert stage. As in the case of most rebirths, this movement reflected the present more than the past. A listener need only compare Delaney and Bonnie's rendition of "Miss Ann," featuring Little Richard on the piano, with the 1957 original to perceive the more complex, rocking intensity of the 1970s. Tinctured with a blues and gospel influence, this music not only reminded people of its rock 'n' roll's antecedents, but also sustained its audience's flagging spirits, a function well-performed by the preaching piano of Leon Russell. In reaction to the waning sense of optimism, the rock 'n' roll revival sought to institute a new positive direction in which rock might move. Rather than accurately resurrect the earlier rock 'n' roll, the version of the 1970s tried to recapture and build on its predecessor's vitality and spirit. It hoped to reestablish the rousing good-time aspects of rock as embodied by the frenzied high energy release of Little Richard and Jerry Lee Lewis.

The hard-driving southern rock captured in a contemporary manner the energetic, gutsy spirit which the rock 'n' roll revival set out to resurrect. Combining blues, gospel, and country music elements, such groups as the Allman Brothers Band, the Marshall Tucker Band, Lynyrd Skynyrd, ZZ Top, and the Charlie Daniels Band offered their audiences the opportunity to do some all-out, full-tilt boogieing. Strongly influenced by San Francisco's acid rock, these groups stressed a strong, solid sound, and perpetuated the full-blast dynamics of rock through an exhilerating freedom on guitar.

The Allman Brothers introduced the southern rock style in 1969, but did not gain widespread popularity until 1971. They featured a powerful rhythm section headed by Greg Allman's organ and pioneered the very influential "double lead" style with Duane Allman and Richard Betts playing lead guitars in harmony. Following the Allman Brothers acceptance by a widespread audience, record company doors opened for a large number of southern bands, and national recognition followed for this style. It took some adjustment to accommodate the idea of rock being played by these southerners, who frequently performed in country-western attire. Their image embodied the same shit-kicking, red neck culture that blew away Captain America, discriminated against Blacks, and displayed no tolerance for the counterculture to which it stood in violent antithesis. But the music these bands laid down was so solid that it could not be denied; it overcame initial reactions and during the first half of the decade was one of the gutsiest sounds around. Anyone producing music that good couldn't be bad.

These southern bands shared certain common bonds with the new decade's rock audience. The music and musicians were new, and carried no obvious associations with the false hopes of the 1960s. Also, despite their celebration of some less than ideal traits of the southern masculine lifestyle, their country flavor aligned them with the back-to-the-woods urban ideal. In essence an example of the vanquished Confederacy's sustained resistance to the dominant society's authority ("The South will rise again!"), its spirit created another level of affinity between the southern bands and the retrenching rock audience.[13] Thus in the downward spiral of the 1970s, the south, the dissident young, and the music all came together.

While the Allman Brothers were struggling for widespread recognition, the power-packed Led Zeppelin unleashed an incredible musical storm. Working within a traditional twelve-bar-blues form which emphasized a strong rock-oriented bottom (bass and drum) sound, they differed enormously from the southern bands who frequently featured country-western influenced shuffle drumming and an open-ended boogie style based on riffs rather than twelve- or sixteen-bar forms. Expanding upon the heavy sound of the Cream and adding an overwhelming stage show, Led Zeppelin proved to be the most popular and influential high-energy, hard rock band of the 1970s.

They laid down a dynamic, raucous sound, which featured the outstanding guitar work of Jimmy Page and the shrill vocals of Robert Plant. Raw, loud, and intense, *Led Zeppelin* (1969) blew the rock world away, scrambling acoustic nerves in a dazzling manner. Transmitting "Good Times Bad Times" and "Communication Breakdown[s]," it shook people and left them "Dazed and Confused." *Led Zeppelin II* (1969) confirmed everything heard on the first album and brought its sexual undercurrents to the lyrical surface with "Whole Lotta Love" and "The Lemon Song." Released on October 22, 1969, while *Led Zeppelin* sat at number eighteen on the charts, the group's second offering reached the number two position behind *Abbey Road* in a month. Within another thirty-five days it replaced the Beatles' disc as the top selling album in the country. From that point on every Led Zeppelin album of new material would reach number one with the ironic exception of their fourth album (1971), which featured "Stairway to Heaven," but remained number two behind Carole King's *Tapestry*.[14]

Led Zeppelin's music fulfilled its promise; it made you sweat, and it made you groove. It was not a statement, or even a stance; the social context had shifted too far for it to assume such a role. Rather, this music stood by itself, a celebration of driving, sexual rock. In a class all its own, the group inspired a new generation of bands with a similar heavy sound, which was usually labeled *hard rock.*

Such diverse groups as Aerosmith, Alice Cooper, Bachman-Turner Overdrive, Blue Oyster Cult, Ted Nugent, Kansas, Boston, Foreigner, Journey, Toto, Bad Company, REO Speedwagon, Peter Frampton, Thin Lizzie, Heart, and more recently Van Halen, Knack, AC/DC, and Pat Benatar, all reflected the influence of Led Zeppelin. Varying enormously in style from the hard, heavy Aerosmith to the more harmonious middle of the road Foreigner, to the still more civilized Boston, and from the bizarreness of Alice Cooper to the teeny-bop heart-throbbing Peter Frampton, these bands shared a common ground with their emphasis on a straightforward, rocking sound. Dynamic, driving, and usually loud, they frequently employed the traditional rock lineup of two guitars, a bass and drums occasionally augmented by keyboards. Labeled "hard rock" and "power rock" and "power pop" they featured hammering rhythms, prominent lead guitars, and vocals inspired by Robert Plant. Furthermore, these groups followed the Led Zeppelin lead in adhering to a 12-bar-blues form; however, their blues sound was not as solid or convincing as that of the Led Zeppelin, deriving from rock examples of the 1960s rather than from the original blues players.

Another offspring of the Led Zeppelin was *heavy metal* with its hard, driving sound. Such groups as Grand Funk, Blood Rock, Black Sabbath, Uriah Heep, and more recently Judas Priest, Iron Maiden, and the Scorpians, differed from the hard rockers by emphasizing four- and eight-bar phrases rather than blues or pop structures. Musically simplistic, if not intentionally crude, the heavy metal bands formulated very rudimentary harmonies and melodies through the endless repetition of simple chords with extremely short progressions. Rather than "taking you away" most heavy metal plunged listeners to the bottoms of their souls and left them there, or in the words of Lester Bangs, it created a "fast train to nowhere."[15]

The critics regularly ignored and lambasted both the hard rock and heavy metal bands, usually only considering what they did not do rather than their perpetuation of the "rot 'n' roll" tradition. Delightfully degenerate, many of these groups enjoyed huge followings, nurturing anti-authoritarian, escapist aspirations. By-and-large they generated a simple, unsophisticated rock and compensated for any lack of intellectual depth with power and drive.

Closely related to the spirit of hard rock, *glitter rock* appeared on the scene almost contemporaneously with Led Zeppelin and the rock 'n' roll revival. Primarily a British phenomenon, it produced groups and individuals such as

T-Rex, Slade, Sweet, Mud, Queen, Suzie Quatro, Roxy Music, Cockney Rebel, Gary Glitter, Jet, and Be-Bop Delux. These performers had more of a pop sound than Led Zeppelin and the hard rockers, and frequently employed 16-bar pop forms, orchestration, background harmonies, and sometimes acoustic instruments. A number of them, including Suzie Quatro, Mud, and Sweet, relied upon the songwriting talents of Chapman and Chinn for much of their materials.

Because of its more produced sound, many Americans discounted glitter, or *glam* (for glamour) rock as a teeny-bop sound; however, glitter, as its name indicates, was much more than just music, *it was style*. Sequinned costumes, extensive use of glitter and facial makeup created the image around the music. Like hard rock, it was a reaction against the fizzling rock revolution and its accompanying mood of despair. It represented action, life, and glamour, and provided a respite from the mundane realities of everyday existence, an alternate form for youth identification. In contrast to the prevailing restraint of country-rock with its emphasis on the inner person, the simple life, and backwoods attire, glam celebrated the surface of life, the fantastic, the flamboyant. Highly cognizant of personal image, its influence was pervasive in England, and its sartorial impact could be discerned readily in the costumes and make-up of such international stars as Mick Jagger, Elton John, David Bowie, and Rod Stewart.

Like rock 'n' roll in the 1950s, the high energy music of the 1970s provided a means of cutting loose and rocking out, but did so in a predictable, institutional manner. Creating a channel through which frustrations might be physically diverted, the songs assumed a romanticized heroic posture and stressed the themes of love, lust, carrying on, and alienation. As such they reflected the fantasies, pastimes, concerns, and expectations of a people trying to come to terms with the world.

Others, also faced with the dilemma of a viable societal relationship, intellectualized their difficulties, pondering rather than rocking them away.

Intellectual Expression

At the opposite pole from rock as energy lay rock as intellectual expression, an extension of the 1960s "rock as the poetry of alienation" tradition fostered by the likes of Bob Dylan and Leonard Cohen. Although assuming a number of forms, the most pervasive style featured intimate, self-revelatory lyrics accompanied by a mellow, although sometimes anguished, sound. The style was almost the exclusive property of such soft rockers of the early 1970s as Joni Mitchell, Jackson Browne, Neil Young, James Taylor, Carly Simon, the satirical Randy Newman, Paul Simon, and Cat Stevens. However, a few new faces gained acceptance as well, most notably the rocking, but equally alienated Bruce Springsteen, who was burdened with media hype which proclaimed him the new Bob Dylan.

Representing the residue of the social eruption of the late 1960s, these performers shifted the focus of rock from supporting social changes to preserving the pieces of individual identity and spirit. They stretched Bob Dylan's belief that "all I can do is show people how I live" to its logical extreme by presenting introspective, analytical songs which portrayed the private joys and sorrows of their lives and relationships. Moving in successive albums from self-evaluation and presentation of problems to understanding and resolution, these singers literally recorded their personal development in a novelistic, if not autobiographical, fashion. In many ways reminiscent of sophisticated soap opera, but stripped of all prurient thrills and complications, these albums remained viable so long as they sustained the audience's abiding interest in the performer as an individual or struck sympathetic chords in listeners' lives and imaginations. Indeed, in his biography of Bruce Springsteen, Peter Gambaccini contended that the quality, entertainment value, and mood of these songs were secondary concerns when compared to what the singers perspicaciously revealed of themselves.[16] Exempt from traditional popular music criteria these songs became important for the truths they revealed.

Primarily aimed at an older audience, this realm of rock was boring to anyone not involved in the personalities or who found the truths irrelevant to their situations. In turn, those entrenched in these literary rock forms considered the more energy-oriented rock mindless drivel. However, both intellectual and visceral rock forms confronted the same problem of alienation. Both offered a style of coping, a form of relief, but they did so in different manners. Whereas in the 1960s both approaches were appreciated by the same audience, with the fragmented 1970s these stood as distinctly different genres, each with its own following.

During this period, only one major figure, David Bowie, mediated between the hard rock and intellectual rock camps, and in so doing he created his own "camp" camp. David Bowie expressed through rock a totally freak-o scene, which moved the music onto a different plane. While the soft rockers self-consciously examined themselves and presented a "mature" version of youth of the 1960s coping with their psyches in the 1970s, and hard rock fixed on the moment, Bowie turned and faced the strange changes in *Hunky Dory* (1972). With later albums, from *Ziggy Stardust* (1972) through *Diamond Dogs* (1974), he double pumped and moved outside society in the finest alienated tradition, to reveal a glitter-enshrouded phoenix rising from the decimated spirit of the

1960s. Coiled, alert, impersonally cool, detached, yet alluring, he androgynously skittered along the fringes of a jarring tomorrow today, inviting his audience to partake in a "Moonage Daydream."

He deftly created sharp-edged, apocalyptic visions of finely honed, thin tensions that gave alienation a new style. Presenting fragmented experiences, warped fantasies, and filigreed amusements in a spectacular, perverted fashion, Bowie perfected the "rock as theater" idiom earlier explored by Jim Morrison. Ziggy Stardust was the low spark of high heeled boys incarnate, a mocking salutation to society from the dead, those living on the brink of a hope to be shared.

Bowie's music further contributed to his stance. He created amazingly intricate musical textures by drawing on a jumble of styles which he skillfully meshed into an organic whole. Almost exclusively working within a 16-bar pop format, he retained a strong rock 'n' roll rhythm which accented the off (2 and 4) beats. Comparatively complex, chromatic chord progressions featured fairly rapid harmonic rhythms that really progressed. Like the songs on the Beatles' *Abbey Road* and *Let It Be,* Bowie's songs included composed guitar leads and complex arrangements, relative to rock standards. Much studio production went into his albums, such as overdubs, the continual movement forward of different instruments, and the variation of the percussion instruments. Yet despite its sophistication, the music came off as credible rock, and was by far the most exciting sound happening in the rock world of the early 1970s.

This solid rock sound, coupled with stunning postures, Bowie's highly theatrical singing style, which hinted at a pre-World War II German cabaret spirit, and his lyrical collages opened new avenues for rock, down which punk and new wave performers soon ventured. Bowie himself opted for another route, moving into the more rarified domain of "art rock," starting with *Station to Station* (1976) and culminating with his collaborative efforts with Brian Eno, *Low* (1977), *Heroes* (1977) and *Lodger* (1979). These later albums featured a doubling of synthesizer and guitar to create pastoral, Sibelius-like melodies which were juxtaposed with a hard, driving rock back beat and dramatic vocals. These, and the more recent *Scary Monsters* (1980), created a distinct and desperate rock sound, but became almost too eloquent in presenting their stance, and tended to lose their edge of vitality, a potential hazard in any art-rock synthesis. However, these works nevertheless blazed a new trail for rock as intellectual expression, and further advanced the self-conscious character of rock in the 1970s.

Bowie was not the only star to migrate into the realm of art rock. The metamorphosis of Jethro Tull further demonstrates the gravitation of certain musicians into this area. Although their music always tended toward a light, cerebral sound, accentuated by the wispy flute of band leader Ian Anderson, their earlier albums featured a strong insistent rhythm section, and delicately balanced rock and British folk traditions, while hinting at classical musical structures. Undergoing several changes in personnel, the band moved from its initial blues stance on *This Was* (1968) to a successively heavier rocking sound, interspersed with soft ballads in *Stand Up* (1969), *Benefit* (1970), and *Aqualung* (1971). With the last of these, Ian Anderson came to view the album as a thematic whole, and began to expand his already classically influenced musical style, while retaining a powerful rock content. *Thick as a Brick* (1972), which featured only one cut per side, *Passion Play* (1973), and subsequent albums broke completely with rock frameworks and entered the area of art rock.

As rock in the 1970s lost momentum and direction, a number of people began to probe, usually with their favorite toy, the synthesizer, the borders between rock and classical music, attempting to elevate rock to an abstract, complex musical experience. Rock no longer was a form communicating common ideas in a common musical code. Instead of molding their thoughts to fit the demands of rock forms, some composers now began to manipulate the form to more suitably express their conceptualizations. Earlier, Frank Zappa and Captain Beefheart had advocated such an evolution, and inflicted Zappa's *Lumpy Gravy* (1968) and *Weasels Ripped My Flesh* (1970), and Beefheart's *Safe as Milk* (1968), *Trout Mask Replica* (1969), and *Lick My Decals Off Baby* (1970) upon rock audiences in the name of broadening their horizons. However, at best they enjoyed only a cult following, until the 1970s when Zappa gained in popularity with such albums as *Fillmore East-June 1971* (1971) and *Apostrophe (')* (1974). These later efforts were seriously composed and intricately arranged, but presented a more conventional rock music.

Similarly, England produced a number of high brow rock bands during this period. Such obscure groups as Henry Cow, Can, Magma, Egg, the Third Ear Band, and Hawkwind recorded improvisational, free-form compositions, while others such as the Moody Blues, King Crimson, Emerson, Lake and Palmer, and Yes delved into more popular ethereal excesses. However, by far the most popular art rock band of the seventies was Pink Floyd, with *The Wall* (1979), *Wish You Were Here* (1975) and *The Dark Side of the Moon* (1973) all topping the album charts. The latter, with its literate exposition on alienation, enjoyed the greatest longevity on *Billboard*'s charts of any rock album to date.

Pink Floyd's music differed from that of other artful rockers like David Bowie, Roxy Music, and Brian Eno by employing a more direct and unobtuse lyric and a less jarring sound. They also deviated from the high brow rock bands by injecting into their elaborate sound of synthesizer, cathedral singing, colorful chord progessions, composed guitar parts, a more hard rock sound with heavy drums, and hard-edged vocals. These differences have allowed them to enjoy a larger following than any of the other art rockers. Their music retained a close connection with their audience and avoided moving too deeply into the realms of intellectual expression. Their directness hit home, and as such indicated the balance which should be maintained if rock is to continue to be a popular vehicle for intellectual as well as emotional expression.

The Elder Gods

With the fragmentation of rock into a multitude of styles, a peculiar phenomenon transpired in rock. The major figures of the rock scene of the 1960s did not fade into the past as their predecessors had done. Instead they moved ahead and continued to develop within a rock context. This carryover was unprecedented in rock's history. Prior to the 1970s two alternatives were open to aging rock musicians. Most vanished into obscurity. Some graduated from rock into a more respectable medium or style, such as Elvis's sojourn into motion pictures and Las Vegas, and Jerry Lee Lewis's move into the country-western realm. Others became nostalgia pieces who repeated previous hits such as Chuck Berry, Bill Haley and the Comets, or Little Richard. To continue to produce new rock material was next to unthinkable; the changes were too drastic and images too firmly entrenched.

However, the stylization of rock and the removal of set image roles enabled performers to shift their styles more easily, and to claim to be musicians plying their maturing trade. Groups such as the Rolling Stones, the Who, the Grateful Dead, and Jefferson Starship, as well as such individuals as Bob Dylan, John Lennon, Paul McCartney, George Harrison, Ringo Starr, Eric Clapton, Stevie Winwood, and Paul Simon became the elder statesmen of rock. Pursuing their own courses, these figures were outside the mainstream of rock in the 1970s, while still very much a part of the overall music scene.

In many respects their appeal paralleled that of the introspective, personal singers using rock to express themselves. People were attracted to their personas; listeners tuned in to hear what the stars had to say, to get inside their current "bags." Few had any new profundities or revelations to contribute. With the possible exception of Bob Dylan's *Slow Train Coming* (1979), featuring such cuts as "Gotta Serve Somebody," "Gonna Change My Way of Thinking," "When You Gonna Wake Up," and "Slow Train," no rocker from the 1960s made any enduring statement for the 1970s, and it might be argued that Dylan's album caused less stir than the news of his conversion to Christianity. In the main, the major artists of the 1960s suited the temperament of the rock world in the 1970s, producing little to last beyond the moment.

Easy Listening

Somewhere between the self-expressive, intellectual, art rock style and the high-energy heavy rock style stood Elton John, Steely Dan, 10 cc, Fleetwood Mac, and others who primarily emphasized a soft sound with a beat. As the successors to the middle ground between rock and pop, which had sat vacant since the demise of the Beatles, they kept things light while laying down a lively sound.

Elton John, in collaboration with Bernie Taupin, restored the pop-rock bridge which the Beatles had built, and was one of the few people to successfully cross it. Slipping into the American rock scene in 1970, amidst the soft rock explosion, he quickly established his own niche. His music differed from that of the other soft rockers, as he brought the drums up front and employed rapid harmonic rhythms, which accented the beat, to give his music more bounce. His catchy, and slightly romantic tunes stuck in the mind and tugged at the heart. When compared to his more serious, and even sullen, contemporaries, Elton John emitted a ray of joy. Listeners embraced his amiable music when it sidled up to them, making him unbelievably popular.

Seven out of eight Elton John albums from *Honky Chateau* (1972) to *Rock of the Westies* (1975) reached number one, and during the period from July 15, 1972 (when *Honky Chateau* first reached number one) to November 29, 1975 (the last week *Rock of the Westies* was number one), his albums topped the charts one out of every three weeks, for a total of thirty-nine weeks. His albums had enormous staying power on the charts, with *Madman Across the Water* remaining on the charts for fifty-six weeks, and *Don't Shoot Me, I'm Only the Piano Player* lasting eighty-nine weeks. This meant that Elton John frequently had two to four albums on the charts at any one time. At no time between June 1972 and the end of 1975 was there no Elton John album listed on the charts.

To a world without Beatles, Elton John was the next best alternative. His songs brightened the moment, and allowed listeners to have their sentiments stroked and their sensibilities unprovoked. With his collection of outrageous glasses, platform shoes, and glitter galore, Elton John played out his rock 'n' roll fantasy as rock's answer to Liberace. He injected some light-hearted glamour into the music, and like "Mr. Kite" he guaranteed a splendid time would be had by all.

However, by 1976 Elton John's shooting star burned out. His music seemed to lose its spark, the dynamite John-Taupin team split apart, and the source of innocent pubescent sexual fantasy revealed he was bisexual. Behind all these turn lay the hero's tragic flaw; he lacked the Beatles' magic. Despite his enormous popularity, a distance existed between his material and the concerns of his audience. His position in rock might be compared with that of Peter, Paul, and Mary in the folk scene of the early 1960s. Both emitted the proper signals but communicated little of substance, as their medium was indeed their message. Elton John offered vitality in the form of pretty songs with a beat; he touched people, but couldn't move them. As a performer he went no deeper than the larger-than-life, nude, cardboard cutout used to promote his 1972 tour. He functioned as a surface embellishment of rock, a major prop of the seventies, incapable of profoundly influencing or affecting his audience. He offered a respite from life, but rock had been so much more.

Fleetwood Mac, who quickly filled the gap left by Elton John, provided a bit more. They had a fuller, more balanced sound, with a harder edge. Unlike Elton John they used no orchestration, the electric guitar replaced the piano, and they presented a more dominant rock bass to create a stronger rhythmic thrust. They generated a genuine and powerful energy, and their haunting songs evoked the romance, passion, mystery, and tension of life and love.

Starting as a British blues band in 1967, the group underwent a number of permutations in personnel and style, through which only the rhythm section of Mick Fleetwood and John McVie remained constant. Moving from the blues into a softer, smoother sound, the group's penchant for rock ballads became evident with *Future Games* (1971), which saw Danny Kirwan mature as a songwriter, and introduced the talents of Christine McVie and Bob Welch. Later albums, such as *Bare Trees* (1972) and *Penguin* (1973) continued this direction, but the band did not attain extensive popularity until the release of *Fleetwood Mac* (1975), which included the newly recruited Stevie Nicks and Lindsey Buckingham. *Rumours* (1977) followed and remained at the top of *Billboard*'s "Hot 100" for twenty-nine weeks, selling over eight million copies and placing the band at the pop-rock pinnacle of success.

The group's repertoire predominantly centered around songs depicting love as an individual experience, with a variety of moods, twists, and changes. In their songs love was more than just warm gush, and although they explored the romantic, all-consuming qualities of the emotion, such songs as "Sentimental Lady" (1972), "Rhiannon" (1975), "Crystal" (1975), "Warm Ways" (1975) and "You Make Loving Fun" (1977) did not pander to clichés. Furthermore their tactile, sensual music and occasional bedside lyrical setting never allowed the listener to lose sight of the sexual aspects of a relationship, keeping everything very down to earth.

Besides portraying the beauty and comfort of love, Fleetwood Mac also acknowledged its difficulties and elusiveness. "Did You Ever Love Me" (1973), "Monday Morning" (1975), "Over My Head" (1975), "Say You Love Me" (1975) and "Landslide" (1975) all displayed love in a less than ideal state. They expressed the doubts and uncertainties of love, its shifting moods and its potential to subjugate individual development. Through such questioning songs as these, the group presented the AM radio audience with different facets of the love relationship than simple perfection or grievous loss. They elucidated the concerns and experiences of their listeners and set them in a positive framework, making the imperfect less than catastrophic, a situation open to individual reconciliation.

The group also placed the loss of love within an individual frame of reference, as *Rumours* (1977) revealed. Recorded during the dissolution of the love relationships of all five group members, the album captured the multiplicity of reactions to love lost coursing through their minds. The songs expressed the confusion and pain of parting, with its accompanying venom, as well as the anticipation of a better tomorrow. However, underneath the totality of responses lay the ethos from the 1960s of free love, which "Go Your Own Way" and "Dreams" explicitly stated:

> Well, here you go again,
> You say you want your freedom
> Well who am I to keep you down . . .[17]

Herein lay the essence of Fleetwood Mac; they celebrated a sense of love taken from the 1960s within the more stable context of the 1970s. With the passage of time, they were able to express the age of acid's inexpressable feelings toward love, and they did so in a penetrating, convincing manner. Avoiding standard rhetoric and sentiments, they seemed real, because they presented direct images taken from the heart and imagination, the realms of love. Thus the group transcended the more banal approaches which very easily turned pop rock into pap rock. Fleetwood Mac maintained a valid connection with life by synthesizing soft and hard rock to create a reflective, celebratory vehicle capable of supporting individual beliefs in addition to offering enjoyment and a charge of energy.

Groups such as the Eagles, Doobie Brothers and America worked in a genre close to that of Fleetwood Mac, by playing soft rock with a dominant rhythm section and featuring vocal harmonies in parallel counterpoint reminiscent of the Beach Boys. Expressing the vigor of youth and the joys of freedom, the early albums by these groups perpetuated the idea that life should be approached as experience.

Dealing with "Life in the Fast Lane" (1976), the Eagles lampooned the "Earlybird" (1972), and extolled the life of the outlaw on the road in such songs as "Takin' It Easy" (1972) and "Twenty-One" (1973). The Doobie Brothers presented similar themes of free and easy living in "Travelin' Man" (1971) and "Growin' a Little Each Day" (1971), as did America in "Ventura Highway" (1972). The most popular of these groups, the Eagles were among the first soft rockers to inject some excitement into their music, which they accomplished by employing various bluegrass-inspired "G runs," having the bass accent the strong (1 and 3) beats while the drums accented the off (2 and 4) beats, and highlighting major chord changes with a shot of acoustic guitar. Rather than bemoan the dissipation of the counterculture, they picked up the spirit of the 1960s with little or no thought,and continued on with an innocent, bouncy, romantic world view. As such the aura of the late 1960s pervaded their music in a manner similar to Fleetwood Mac's. Indeed, much of the music of the 1970s either reflected the sense of rock revolution from the 1960s or reacted to its demise. It was not until the mid-1970s that distinct creations of a new time began to emerge in a consistent manner.

Disco

Just as the twist was the first readily identifiable new dance, and initial rage of the 1960s, so too *disco* was the first publicly recognized dance and sound of the 1970s. Rising out of an urban context, primarily within the gay, Latino, and Black communities, the music began to attract a widespread audience in the mid-1970s, with such songs as George McCrae's "Rock Me Baby" (1974), KC & the Sunshine Band's "That's the Way (I Like It)" (1975), "Get Down Tonight" (1975), and "(Shake, Shake, Shake) Shake Your Booty" (1976), Wild Cherry's "Play That Funky Music" (1976), and Donna Summer's "Love to Love You Baby" (1975) all breaking into the top 10 on both the pop and rhythm and blues charts. However, it was not until after December 1977 when the movie *Saturday Night Fever* was released that the music made its big splash. Following the lead of John Travolta and the pied piper sounds of the Bee Gees, people literally lined up to wait their turn to make the scene and dance, dance, dance.

During 1978 and 1979 disco reigned supreme and was heard incessantly on the streets, in the boutiques, and at the gatherings of the chic. A *Los Angeles Times* article on February 21, 1979 estimated that the disco industry was worth over eight billion dollars. The music dominated *Billboard*'s single and album charts during 1978 and 1979, with close to forty percent of the positions on each chart. The Bee Gee's *Saturday Night Fever* (1977) sold over fifteen million copies in America and thirty million worldwide, making it the biggest selling movie soundtrack in history. WKTU-FM New York, after going over to an exclusively disco format in July 1978, had by December 1978 an unbelievable 11.3 percent of the city's listening audience, as compared to a previous .9 percent, which precipitated the reprograming of numerous stations. Also the high sales volume of such singles as the Village People's "Y.M.C.A." (1978) (twelve million copies), the Bee Gee's "Stayin' Alive" (1977) (six million copies), and Chic's "Le Freak" (1979) (four million copies) led such stars as Rod Stewart, the Rolling Stones, the Beach Boys, Paul McCartney, and Dolly Parton to record disco songs. The music was definitely "in" to the joy of many and the disgust of others, whose "disco sucks" attitude reflected the deep polarization within the musical world of the 1970s.

Disco music and its social scene were superficial and mindless energy releases, filled with sexual overtones, glamour, a strong consumer ethos and an ego-oriented sense of communal ritual. The music itself was characterized by metronomic trap drumming with the bass drum and high hat closed on the strong (1 and 3) beats and open high hat playing on the off (2 and 4) beats. The songs universally employed the same tempo, between 125 and 134 beats per minute, and used very simple chords or riffs. Sometimes songs utilized only one chord, or emphasized the I chord with a brief IV progression. This was pure and simple dance music, centering on the beat with all other aspects of a song serving as embellishment. Even the performer was relegated a secondary role. Producers such as Giorgio Moroder, Cerrone, Jacques Morali, Tom Moulton, Freddie Perren, and Bernard Edwards & Nile Rodgers, emerged as the star creators of the sound.

A few performers did transcend the faceless standardization of disco, including Donna Summer with her distinctive voice and highly hyped "Hot Stuff "/"Bad Girls" (both 1979) image, causing her hair style to replace that of Farrah Fawcett's on the streets of America. Also the Village People's frank sexuality and tongue-in-cheek "Macho Man" (1978), "Y.M.C.A." (1978), and "In the Navy" (1979) gave them a recognized, although not emulated, image. However, aside from these two "larger than life sex totems,"[18] other performers such as Sylvester, the Brothers Johnson, Sister Sledge, Gloria Gaynor, Chic, Kool and the Gang, Shalamar, were essentially faces in the crowd, receiving no more or less attention than their devotees gyrating on the dance floor.

Indeed, the music may well have been secondary to the action on the boards. For at the heart of disco lay the scene, the performance, for which everyone dressed up and played their part. It was a statusphere with starring roles for all, the apotheosis of self-centeredness. As such disco provided entertainment for the moment, and then, like all diversions and most bad dreams, it disappeared. Disco became the distant past overnight, swept under by the deluge of rock's New Wave, which offered new costumes, new roles, and a harder sound.

Punk and New Wave

Punk, another distinct movement of the 1970s, gained widespread attention in 1977 and 1978, just as disco was beginning to climb to the top of the music world. Primarily an English movement, it had little immediate impact beyond that island, although its repercussions were felt in America and elsewhere. Within the extremely diversified, but increasingly normal, controlled excitement of the rock world, punk infused an imaginative, radical element, something totally different for the time. It reminded people that rock could still serve as a focal point for an otherwise vague social situation. It generated rabid enthusiasm, rather than mass appreciation, at a time when most rock was not especially exciting. However, it was a bit extreme, with its publicized safety pin jewelry, excessive and distorted application of facial cosmetics and hair dyes, exploitation of Nazi imagery, and display of kinky sex paraphernalia and wardrobes. Also the audience's habit of "gobbing" (spitting) rather than applauding to show appreciation, and shunning heterosexual activities on the dance floor, where pogoing (jumping up and down) was a favorite dance style, rasped against the social grain. As such it never made it big. Most people did not readily identify with the scene, having not reached such an advanced stage of disgust, revulsion, or boredom. Even in England a large concert crowd numbered only about two thousand.

Punk emerged as a reaction to the high rate of unemployment among Britain's youth and the ho-hum character of rock at the time. Anti-adult, anti-upper class, and anti-rock establishment, it abhorred the status quo even more vehemently than the previous counterculture, which punk rejected with the rest of the past. Unlike that old counterculture, however, punk found no viable new direction in which to move. It only offered its negation of social norms as a vehicle for expressing outrage and a relief from "Babylon."

Musically and culturally punk drew from a range of diverse elements, most of which dwelt close to the borders of accepted reality. From the glitter rock of David Bowie came a sense of nihilism, gender confusion, role playing, obsessive individualism, and fragmented self, as well as a feeling for impending apocalypse with triumphant, super-alienated "peoploids." Iggy Pop, a haunting American specter, contributed stiff, jerky movements, an aura of violence, and a penchant for self-laceration. The New York underground rock scene, so deeply steeped in the vanguard art of Andy Warhol via the Velvet Underground and Lou Reed, inspired a raw, minimalist, primitive rock, a sense of the avant-garde opposition to the artistic establishment, and a feel for the street, as initially (1972–1973) conveyed by the glittery New York Dolls, and later (1975–1977) by Patti Smith, the Ramones, Television, Blondie, and the Talking Heads. Other influences included the rockabilly rhythms and simple beat of fifties rock 'n' roll, and Jamaican reggae with its cultish separateness and lyrical emphasis on a utopian delivery from alienation and Babylon. Punk amalgamated these various responses to alienation, mixing them with responses to the British social scene, and became the avant-garde style of the rock world

Prior to the 1970s the idea of a rock avant-garde was inconceivable. First, no one took the music that seriously. Second, rock was always viewed in terms of a united rather than a fragmented youth culture. Finally, the music was not self-consciously viewed as an established tradition. The closest the late 1960s came to an avant-garde was in Frank Zappa and Captain Beefheart's ridiculing the tastes of the rock audience and society in general. However, with punk the entire rock establishment was indicted as lethargic, decadent, complacent, and unresponsive to the times and the audience's needs. The punks advocated a return to basics, and created an extremely simple, underproduced sound, which often seemed painfully amateurish if not totally incompetent. The bands strove to destroy the distance between the performers and audience, to obliterate the concept of star and the audience's expectations of quality, and in return provided release, an opportunity to frenzy out and associate with total social anarchy. Johnny Rotten, the lead singer for the Sex Pistols, claimed the group was into chaos not music, and that they wanted to be amateurs, which some critics felt made a virtue out of necessity.[19] To further advance the punk message, *Sniffin Glue*, the first and most popular punk "fanzine," in a bit of self-parody, featured a drawing of three finger positions on the neck of a guitar, and advised, "Here's one chord, here's two more, now form your own band." A spirit of total autonomy and vitality pervaded the early period of punk as bands made and distributed their own records and fans published their own typewritten fanzines. The punks in essence developed their own salon, and with it their own subculture.

The subculture might best be described as a late 1950s "blood joke" set to music—and made a way of life.* It reeked of total disrespect for all social authority and sensibility. Bands with such names as the Sex Pistols (with Johnny Rotten and Sid Vicious), the Clash, the Damned (with drummer Rat Scabbies), the Sniveling Shits, X-Ray Spex (with lead singer Poly Styrene), the Vibrators,

---

*Remember those rib-tickling stomach-retchers?

the Radiators from Space, Stiff Little Fingers, the Buzzcocks, the Adverts, the Castrators, and the Slits created such musical moments as "Anarchy in the U.K." (1976), "God Save the Queen" (1977), "Belsen Was a Gas" (1977, Sex Pistols), "London's Burning" (1977), "Career Opportunities" (1977), "White Riot" (1977, the Clash), "Terminal Stupid" (1977), "I Can't Come" (1977, the Sniveling Shits), "Oh Bondage Up Yours" (1977, X-Ray Spex), "Gary Gilmore's Eyes" (1977, the Adverts), and "Orgasm Addict" (1977, Buzzcocks).

The most reknowned group, the Sex Pistols, managed to be banned from BBC radio, barred from public performance, attacked by the police, denounced in Parliament, and beaten and razored in the London streets, all of which their lead singer, Johnny Rotten, claimed not to understand, as all the band tried to do was destroy everything.[20]

As a subterranean tradition punk, as its name indicates, most closely aligned itself with a delinquent posture, but internalized the sense of violence. Rather than strike out against the social vacuity and authority by breaking the law, punks taunted and provoked the accepted order through a deliberate "if you don't like it, I do" attitude. Their use of Nazi and other perverse imagery did not stem so much from any ideological affinity as from a desire to shock. When asked why she wore a swastika one punk replied, "Punks just like to be hated."[21]

The movement heroically destroyed idealism and idealistically denounced heroism. It saw no hope for the future,but still worked for a better tomorrow. It rejected the rock establishment, but willingly accepted its contracts, when offered. Such contrary behavior patterns understandably arose, for although punk infuriated public standards, it provided little more than a limited joy of communal subversion, which could not accommodate the positive energy bristling underneath the movement's surface. Stymied by its contradictions and its own constraints, including an inability to expand beyond the borders of the United Kingdom, punk faltered, and following the 1978 breakup of the Sex Pistols, collapsed.[22] A more stylish New Wave sound eclipsed punk, presenting a hard-edged, alienated resignation with which a much larger audience could comfortably identify.

New Wave, the music industry's respectable promo name for punk, quickly asserted itself as a movement in its own right. As a more musically sophisticated outgrowth of punk, it absorbed the surviving punk talents (the Clash, and John [a.k.a. Rotten] Lydon's Public Image Ltd.), the vestiges of the New York underground (the Talking Heads, Ramones, and Blondie), several detached elements from the British rock scene (Elvis Costello, Dave Edmunds, and Nick Lowe), and an effusion of new groups who responded in a middle-class way to the punk scene (the Cars, the Police, Devo, the Pretenders, B-52, and Cheap

Trick). More of a posture than a stance, this music perpetuated the alienated atmosphere of punk without its gleeful perversion, horror, defiance, or terror. It retreated from warped chaos to create, more often than not, detached, impersonal, if not cynical scenarios of life and love, although a number of performers tempered their alienation with a surprisingly positive outlook, as might be heard in Dave Edmunds' "Sweet Lisa" (1978), the Ramones' "Baby I Love You" (1980), Pearl Harbor's "You Got It" (1979), Elvis Costello's "What's So Funny About Peace, Love and Understanding" (1978), and the Talking Heads' "The Good Thing" (1978).

Stylistically, New Wave music was much more diverse than punk, and the name became a catch-all title liberally bestowed upon almost any progressive group in the early 1980s. The bands ranged from the highly produced, commercially-oriented Cars, Blondie, and the Ramones, to the more stark, artful Talking Heads and Public Image Ltd., with groups such as Devo somewhere in the middle. Lyrical statements ranged from the heavily political stances of the Clash to the romantic, good fun of "We Got the Beat" (1982) by the Go-Go's. The sound varied from the B-52's early 1960s pop/rock music to the heavier, Kink-like sound of the Pretenders, to the Captain Beefheart-influenced Magazine, Pere Ubu, and Siouxsie and the Banshees, to the jazz-inspired Lounge Lizards, Defunkt, and James "Blood" Ulmer, to the blues-based Fabulous Thunderbirds, Rock Pile and Mink Deville, to the more country-western, rockabilly orientations of Elvis Costello, Rachel Sweet, and Robert Gordon. Their musicianship improved slightly over punk's proud amateurism, so, for example, a New Wave chord progression might move from C to F#, instead of C to G. However, some groups, such as the Plasmatics and the Bow Wows Wows, were more stimulating visually than acoustically.

As opposed to the rock 'n' roll and rock music of previous decades, New Wave derived primarily from a highly stylized white rock music tradition. Generally sparse and uncomplicated, New Wave music drew from a number of antecedents, however, Lou Reed must be viewed as a seminal figure, with his style and spirit running through much of the sound. He invited his listeners to "Walk on the Wild Side" (1972) and accept the bizarre as the norm on such albums as *Loaded* (Velvet Underground, 1970), *Lou Reed* (1972), *Transformer* (1972), and *Rock 'n' Roll Animal* (1974). With his child's-eye approach, practiced nonchalance, and frequent juxtaposition of terror and naiveté, Lou Reed's shadow looms large behind the New Wave show. Other profound influences include Jonathan Richman and the Modern Lovers with their straightforward music and frequently positive viewpoint; Captain Beefheart (often by way of Frank Zappa) with his engaging poetic imagery and discordant, jagged musical textures which included poly- and a-rhythms; Roxy Music with their mechanical vocals; and Brian Eno with his technologically advanced studio techniques.

The style was a deliberate statement on the nether regions of alienation from which it supposedly grew; however, occasionally it became a bit too transparent or self-conscious to be believable. Rather than dwell on the ideals of alienation, as the counterculture had, New Wave performers portrayed alienation at a self-centered extreme. Songs such as Blondie's "Heart of Glass" (1978), Joy Division's "Love Will Tear Us Apart" (1980), and many of the Tubes' satirical compositions, such as "White Punks on Dope" (1981), as well as Devo's messages on the "devolution" of humanity, emphasized the more detached, callous aspects of alienation. Frequently featuring passionless, unemotional vocals, which the producers often reinforced through a high mix and various filters and processes, these songs crystalized no stunning revelations, but instead served more as a backhanded commentary on modern society, a slightly more extreme declaration of the already known. They presented few alternatives to the present, apparently content to offer relief via a snide aloofness from sociability.

Like so much music in the 1970s, New Wave attempted to address and lessen the problems existing between the individual and an alienating society. Rather than seek any solutions to problems, it strove to alleviate the discomfort through its "howl." Like an aspirin, it knocked out the pain of the moment, but did not address itself to the cause of the headache. It represented one more standardized musical posture which a listener could choose to adopt in an attempt to cope with the mainstream. By providing a new role to act out, New Wave fittingly concluded the first decade of rock's stylization.

So It Went

During the course of the 1970s, rock developed into an accepted and established respite from society, presenting a variety of musical releases. With an audience which spans several generations in age, the rock world of the 1970s saw a diversity of albums, Carole King's *Tapestry*, Pink Floyd's *Dark Side of the Moon*, Peter Frampton's *Peter Frampton Comes Alive*, the Bee Gee's *Saturday Night Fever*, and Fleetwood Mac's *Rumours*, attain eight-digit sales figures. Furthermore, on the air waves *My Life in the Bush of Ghosts* intertwines with the specter of the Doors as eclecticism becomes the order of the 1980s. And this eclecticism not only characterizes the rock audience, but its performers as well, as Blondie's *Autoamerica* and Debbie Harry's *Koo Koo* demonstrate. Amorphous and highly stylized, rock music has returned to the mainstream of American life.

Having established itself as more than a fad, rock has become a normal part of growing up in America, attaining an institutional status comparable to Big Macs and Coca-Cola. As a recognized pattern within the fabric of society, the sound has continued to broadcast a message of dissatisfaction and has retained its energy and anti-social appearance. However, it has lost its antagonist role. It no longer demands action, only reaction. Like a political cartoon, rock has become a formalized vehicle for social commentary, a self-conscious, established expression of discontent. Given a social sanction, it lost its power to topple Tammany Hall. Presenting a momentary diversion rather than a proclamation for change, rock in the 1970s and early 1980s has come to operate primarily as a pacifier, a social tranquilizer or escape hatch.

POSTSCRIPT: REGGAE

With rock established as a dominant cultural form, a music of the majority, certain new styles of music appeared which catered to specialized audiences. These subcultural sounds, of which *reggae* has been the most dynamic and popular, have rumbled beneath the surface of the 1970s and 1980s. Deviating from prescribed tastes and values, music such as reggae has disclosed a continuing disenchantment with the dominant culture and a search for alternatives.

Rising out of the Jamaican rock steady style (a style which derived from ska and was influenced by American Soul music,[23] reggae appeared on the American scene by way of Great Britain in the early 1970s. Strongly tinctured with a Rastafarian outlook which stressed the deliverance of the Black race from "Babylon" and its "bald heads," the music had an unmistakable Third World African flavor accented by its dominant percussion and bass lines. In favoring this sound, the American listening audience separated itself from the dominant culture, and in many ways resembled the adolescent rhythm-and-blues audience described by David Reisman in 1950.[24] Like the specialty audience of that period, the devotees of the Jamaican sound spurned, for the most part, the offerings of commercial radio, and displayed a stronger sympathy for the Black point of view, and that of the Third World in general, than did the social mainstream. The listeners viewed themselves as part of a distinct subculture and frequently employed their own private language, which primarily derived from the Rastafarian movement.

Reggae embodied a powerful revolutionary political statement that was supported by its lyrics, although the thick Jamaican patois made the vocals incomprehensible to the majority of the American audience. However, the mere presence of the music, with its heavy back-to-Africa associations, embued them with a strong sense of "otherness," which further was augmented by the limited accessibility to the music.

Like the race music of the 1950s, reggae was not readily available through normal distribution channels. Less than twenty-five radio stations across the nation programmed the music in any regular manner prior to the late 1970s, and even today it is rare to hear reggae music on any of the major commercial radio stations, or even the so-called progressive FM rock stations. Furthermore, reggae records received limited distribution in America, with Chris Blackwell's Island Records the only major reggae label readily available. It featured such performers as Bob Marley, Jimmy Cliff, Toots Hibbert and the Maytals, Peter Tosh, Burning Spear, the Heptones, and producer-performer Lee Perry.

Occasionally various major record companies have signed a reggae musician in the hope that the music might become the next big sound. Thus Columbia recorded Johnny Nash's "Hold Me Tight" and "Stir It Up"/"I Can See Clearly Now" (both written by Bob Marley, 1972); Capitol released a number of records by Inner Circle during the mid-1970s; and A & M presently features Dennis Brown's music. However, as long as the music appeals only to a subculture, the major record companies will not pursue its production in any sustained fashion. Thus such major figures as Big Youth, Ras Michael and the Sons of Negus, Sugar Minott, Black Uhuru, Augustus Pablo, and Gregory Isaacs will continue to be available only in specialty shops.

As a specialty sound within the pluralistic American society, reggae survives, and like the rhythm-and-blues music of the late 1940s and early 1950s which eventually merged with white pop and country-and-western to produce rock 'n' roll, it holds the possibility of blending into the American mainstream and moving popular music into a new direction. During the 1970s such songs as Eric Clapton's version of Bob Marley's "I Shot the Sheriff" (1974), Paul Simon's "Me and Julio Down By the School Yard" (1972), and the Rolling Stones' 1976 version of Eric Donaldson's "Cherry Oh Baby," along with a number of recent selections by the Clash and the Police, and Blondies' resurrection of the Paragon's rock steady hit of the early 1970s, "Tide is High" (1981), all reflected the influence of reggae. To date such an amalgam has been easily assimilated into the stylishness of rock, and more than likely any future interaction will continue along this vein. However, as a dissident force reggae offers the possibility of infusing new vitality into rock and as such should not be ignored.

NOTES

[1] Ben Fong-Torres, "Rolling Stone Interview: David Crosby," *Rolling Stone Magazine,* 23 July 1970, pp. 20–27.

[2]Jann Wenner, "Rolling Stone Interview: John Lennon," *Rolling Stone Magazine*, 21 January 1971, p. 41.

[3]Wenner, "Rolling Stone Interview," p. 33.

[4]Grateful Dead, "Ripple," Copyright 1970, Ice Nine Publishing Co., Inc. Used by permission.

[5]Quoted in Richie Yorke, *The Led Zeppelin Biography* (Toronto: Methuen, 1976), pp. 166–167.

[6]Along with the performers mentioned within the text a number of lesser figures also began moving towards a country-rock sound from late 1968 onward. These include Gram Parsons' International Submarine Band, Dillard and Clark's Expedition, the Flying Burrito Brothers, Jimmy Buffet, Jerry Jeff Walker, and John Prine and Steve Goodman.

[7]Crosby, Stills, Nash and Young, "Carry On"

[8]Cat Stevens, "Changes IV" Copyright 1971 Freshwater Music Ltd. Administered worldwide by Island Music Ltd. All rights reserved. Reprinted by permission.

[9]As quoted in Deborah Landau, *Janis Joplin* (New York: Paperback Library, 1971), pp. 124–125.

[10]Michael Brooks, "Stills Moving," *Guitar Player*, 4, No. 3, p. 48.

[11]Ed Leimbacher, "Super Group," *Ramparts*, February 1970, p. 56.

[12]The album's mood stemmed from Eric Clapton's pain after Patti Harrison left him to return to her husband, George. However, this mood corresponded with that of the disillusioned and hurt counterculture audience. Patti eventually divorced George and married Eric.

[13]This affinity between the decimated counterculture and the Confederacy had established itself prior to the southern bands gaining national followings, as indicated by such a song as "The Night They Drove Old Dixie Down," which both the Band and Joan Baez recorded.

[14]Although never reaching number one, the album remained on the charts for one hundred fifty-eight weeks. Carole King's *Tapestry* was the best-selling album in rock history up to that time.

[15]Lester Bangs, "Heavy Metal," in *The Rolling Stone Illustrated History of Rock 'n' Roll*, ed. Jim Miller (New York: Random House, 1980) p. 332.

[16]Peter Gambaccini, *Bruce Springsteen*, (New York: Quick Fox, 1979), pp. 156–165.

[17]Fleetwood Mac, "Dreams," Copyright 1977, 1978 Fleetwood Mac Music & Welsh Witch Music. Used by permission.

[18]Stephen Holden, "Space Age Pop," *High Fidelity*, July 1979, p. 79.

[19]See Dick Hebdige, *Subculture: The Meaning of Style*, (London: Metheun, 1979), p. 109.

[20]John Rockwell, "The Sex Pistols—A Fired-Up Rock Band," *New York Times*, 7 August 1977, Sec. 2, p. 16+.

[21]As described in Hebdige, pp. 116–117.

[22]A punk scene struggled to surface in America as witnessed by such groups as the Dead Kennedys, the Blackouts, the Contortions, X, DNA, the Appliances, the The, the Plasmatics, the Germs, the Adolescents, T.S.O.L., Fear, the Circle Jerks, and Black Flag. However, outside of Los Angeles, American punk did not generate any sizeable audience.

[23]Rather than imitate American Soul, as so many people around the world did, rock steady

musicians and producers adapted certain Soul characteristics while retaining ska's distinctive beat and percussion. A comparative listening to ska and rock steady readily reveals the influence of such Atlantic Soul artists as Solomon Burke, Otis Redding, Joe Tex, Ray Charles, Wilson Pickett and Percy Sledge on rock steady's lyrical attitudes, vocal styles and more pop oriented arrangements. Both Solomon Burke and Percy Sledge still have albums on Jamaican record store charts. This Soul infusion continued with reggae, with Curtis Mayfield and James Brown both exerting an influence on the writing style of Bob Marley. In much reggae of the mid-1970s the echo of the psychedelic Temptations, who were produced by Motown's Norman Whitfield, can be heard.

[24]David Riesman, "Listening to Popular Music," *American Quarterly*, 2 (Winter 1950), pp. 359–371.

8

The Rock Revolution: Ruminations and Reflections

"Well, everything is going to pieces on the one hand, and everything is coming together on the other hand. I think the revolution is over, and what's left is a mop up action. It's a matter of the news getting out to everybody else. I think that the important changes have already happened, changes in consciousness. It's mostly a matter of everything else catching up to that. Everything is traditionally slow—much faster than it has been on earth, but still far, far too slow."

Jerry Garcia

Over the past three decades rock has undergone a number of transformations. It has moved from an abscessed adolescent obsession streaked with rebelliousness, through a consciousness raising stage that articulated alienated utopian ideals, to reach the present day's multiplicity of styles that self-consciously perpetuate the rock tradition. By continuing to perform previous functions, the stylized rock retains a vital position within society, addressing not only adolescent, but adult concerns. It carries a zip, a zing, but little zeal. The earlier sense of collective joy and freedom, of shared common experience, has all but disappeared from the rock scene. A glossy shadow of its former self, rock moves on down the line, a background sound in a world that keeps turning around us, a declaration of alienation and/or joy that goes no further than the periphery of its own musical dimension.

However, rock's impact runs deeper than today's music. The music of the late 1960s made an indelible mark on society, and its imprint still remains. To perceive the extent of rock's cultural influence, forms other than today's music need to be examined. However, prior to undertaking such an investigation we need to move back to the period from 1969 to 1971 and reconsider the dissolution of the rock revolution. Such a step will further illuminate the rock stance of the 1960s against the dominant culture, and provide a better position from which to evaluate the effect of that music.

SNAP, FIZZLE, AND POOF

The rock forms and energy supporting the counterculture gradually faded during the opening years of the 1970s. Their disappearance was a profound and noticeable change, and people were quick to comment upon it. In an attempt to explain the evaporation of the rock revolution three major arguments came to the fore:

1. Rock had become too pretentious and had lost sight of its original purpose.
2. Rock, as a commercial product, could not sustain any viable attack upon the economically oriented dominant culture.
3. The audience did not follow the precepts elucidated in the songs.

None of these viewpoints perceived what was happening, and instead reflected the immediate reaction to the moment rather than any accurate appraisal of the situation.

The first argument myopically viewed rock as primarily a musical form rather than a social phenomena. Arnold Shaw, the author of *The Rock Revolution* in a *High Fidelity* article from April 1969,[1] accurately descerned the rock audience's retreat "into the woods and hills of mountain music," and their acceptance of soul and vintage rhythm-and-blues. He ascribed this shift in taste to a rejection of rock's increasing artiness, which led to a loss of "the raw vitality, eroticism and simplicity of its birth phase." Shaw viewed rock essentially as part of a popular music tradition rather than an integral part of a social movement. Instead of considering the change in musical preferences in terms of the social scene, he claimed that popular listeners could tolerate only a minimal range of deviation and artistic license. However, such an explanation confuses symptoms with causes. The rejection of artiness accompanied the change in taste, but did not cause it. During the height of the counterculture's energy burst, the music's artiness and increased complexity were lauded as positive values, and such well-received albums as the Beatles' *Sergeant Pepper,* the Jefferson Airplane's *Surrealistic Pillow,* and Jimi Hendrix's *Are You Experienced?* deviated from previous popular music in a much more dramatic manner than any of the more pretentious rock material of 1969 and 1970. Also, such aspiring "artists" as Frank Zappa, Pink Floyd, and the Jefferson Starship continued to have large followings in the 1970s, as did many new stars such as David Bowie, Roxy Music, and numerous art rock and New Wave bands, indicating that at least a portion of the rock audience continued to support the pretentiousness posited by Shaw as a motivation for the movement towards the more mellow country-rock sound. As such, an increased artiness may not be viewed plausibly as the trigger for the 1969 turn to different musical forms. As already noted, deeper cultural factors were at work.

Rock as a Commercial Product

Another more popular explanation for the demise of the rock revolution, focused on the music's economic context, its status as a commercial product. In a June 1969 *Ramparts* article, "Rock for Sale," Michael Lydon summarized this position.[2] He recognized rock's "undeniably liberating effect," but also realized rock was "a product created, distributed, and controlled for the profit of American (and international) business." Such a relationship ultimately doomed rock "to a bitter impotence" as the music remained subservient to those whom it attacked, turning a profit for corporate America.

Without a doubt rock is a commercial product, a popular art form with a wide appeal, thanks to mass distribution and advertising. Furthermore, rock has been largely responsible for the enormous growth of the music industry over the past quarter-century. Since 1955 record sales have increased phenomenally, moving from a total of $277 million to over one-half billion dollars by 1959. By 1968 sales had advanced to over one billion dollars, and ten years later that figure had tripled. By 1972 the sale of records and tapes brought in more money than did movies, professional sports, and the theater *combined*. Rock concerts grossed close to five times as much money as Broadway plays. By this time at least fifty music superstars were earning between two and six million dollars a year, which represented a salary range three to seven times higher than America's highest paid corporate "capitalist pig." Rock does make money, and makes it in large quantities.[3] The expansion of the music industry has been stupendous, and as the age bracket of rock's audience continues to broaden, the industry appears to have growth potential, as long as the economy remains sound.

As big business the music industry has developed along lines similar to those of other corporate establishments. During the 1950s the major companies, RCA, Columbia, Decca, Capitol, MGM, Mercury, and later ABC-Paramount, controlled less of the rock 'n' roll market than the independent companies, which included, Atlantic, Dot, Chess, Specialty, Sun, Herald-Ember, Cadence, Liberty, and Imperial. Most of these companies, both the majors and independents, were fairly new to the field, with only RCA, Columbia, and Decca operating prior to World War II. The majors primarily differed from the independents in their capital investment. They not only produced records, but owned manufacturing plants and directly controlled distribution outlets. RCA and Columbia, the two dominant companies in the industry, held their positions mainly due to their affiliations with their parent communications organizations: the Radio Corporation of America and the Columbia Broadcasting System.

The majors approached the peculiar, new rock 'n' roll fad with caution, signing only a moderate number of performers: Elvis (RCA), Bill Haley and Buddy Holly (Decca), Gene Vincent (Capitol), Conway Twitty (MGM), and the Big Bopper (Mercury). In comparison, many of the independents already operated within the rhythm-and-blues market, and thus easily flowed into the new rock 'n' roll scene. From 1955 to 1959 they produced over one hundred top ten hits as compared to forty-six by the major companies.[4] Even through the early 1960s the independents dominated the charts with Roulette, Cameo, Parkway, and Chancellor boasting such stars as Bobby Rydell, Fabian, Frankie Avalon, Jimmy Rodgers, and Chubby Checker.

However, the reign of the independents was short-lived. Commencing with the purchase of Dot by ABC-Paramount for two million dollars in 1957, the independents slowly but surely sold out to major companies, with Warner Brothers-Reprise's purchase of Atlantic in 1967, Electra in 1970, and Asylum in 1973 among the more significant later deals. By the late 1960s the majors were in fairly tight command of the music scene. Capitol featured the Beatles; RCA, the Jefferson Airplane; Decca, the Who; ABC, Steppenwolf; MGM, the Animals; Warner Brothers, the Grateful Dead, Jimi Hendrix, Jethro Tull, Joni Mitchell, James Taylor, Led Zeppelin, and Crosby, Stills, Nash and Young; and Columbia, Bob Dylan, Simon and Garfunkel, the Byrds, Janis Joplin, and Santana. A majority of the independents operated under the majors and relied upon them for distribution, although a few companies such as Motown and A & M remained completely autonomous.

The 1970s brought further consolidation of the industry as the smaller majors had to merge in order to attain a more financially efficient scale. MCA, which resulted from the combination of Decca, Kapp, and Uni records in the late 1960s, added ABC to its organization in the late 1970s, and in the early years of that decade Mercury, MGM, and Polydor records were united under Polygram. This corporation has since added Casablanca, Capricorn, and RSO to its ranks. Thus, as the 1980s began, the "Big Six," (Warner Communications,

Columbia Broadcasting System, Polygram, RCA, Capitol-EMI, and MCA) held a firm position in the music industry, with 1977 figures indicating that Warner controlled twenty-three percent of all record and tape sales, Columbia nineteen percent, and Polygram fourteen percent.

The immediate association with outrageous wealth and an increasingly consolidated corporate system surely has affected rock, but in all likelihood did not contribute to the declining spirit of revolution. By 1968 annual record sales already had surpassed a billion dollars, making the sense of wealth, of churning capitalism, very much a part of rock's revolutionary stream. This presence, however, neither stemmed the flow nor contaminated the water. Indeed, it might have contributed to the stream's floodlike appearance. The record companies filled a demand, and although much of the rock of the late 1960s explicitly stood as the antithesis of the corporate way of life, these companies exerted little or no censorship over rock material. When they did intervene, their concerns usually revolved around the use of obscenity, as in the clash between RCA and the Jefferson Airplane, which the band eventually won.

Thus the revolutionary content of the music was not diluted by the music industry. Indeed, the existence of the record companies as figures of authority, as representatives of the corporate world, heightened the rebellious tension in the songs in certain instances. For example, the Jefferson Airplane's fight to use explicit language became one in a series of metaphors which enhanced the spirit of change, the feeling of us versus them, and the role of musicians as exemplars of the new ways. Their victory transcended their individual battle, representing a step forward for the counterculture itself. As such "Eskimo Blue Day" (1969) and "Volunteers" (1969) carried a triumphant message which outstripped their lyrical and musical contents.

Further evidence of the minimal impact of any corporate influence on the rock revolution may be obtained by a comparison of *Abbey Road* (1969) and *The Beatles* (1968), which the Beatles produced under their own Apple label, with their earlier Capitol works, *Sgt. Pepper* and *Magical Mystery Tour*. Certainly the freedom of their own label did not precipitate a more radical dialogue in their music. The same can be said for albums produced by other musicians who operated their own independent labels such as the Beach Boys, Frank Zappa, the Rolling Stones, the Jefferson Starship, and the Grateful Dead.

Thus the highly commercial character of the music industry did not directly mitigate any of rock's revolutionary fervor. Nor did it do so in an indirect, coopting manner as Steve Chapple and Reebee Garofalo postulated in *Rock 'n' Roll Is Here to Pay*. These investigators of rock's commercial core more or less revamped the theories of the German philosopher Theodor W. Adorno and applied them to rock. Adorno premised all his perceptions of music upon the fact that with the advent of improved mechanical reproduction and more sophisticated means of distribution, a "commodity fetishism" had increased in all areas of modern music, both classical and popular. Music, once freed of its more traditional context of ritual and use, had come to function primarily as a commodity with a value of exchange. Adorno found popular music, including jazz, to be corruptions of earlier forms, a standardized product with a "pseudo-individual" veneer, the sole end of which was its consumption by the masses. This music produced a "commodity listening" which ideally dispensed, as far as possible, with the need for any attentive efforts on the part of the audience; it was "easy listening" music. As a commodity in a capitalist system, popular music implicitly reflected and legitimized the establishment, replicating working conditions within the context of a leisure time. To Adorno, the product orientation of the music destroyed any revolutionary potential which it formerly might have harbored.[5]

Many of Adorno's observations apply to mainstream popular music, and indeed they are quite applicable to much of the rock scene of the 1970s. However, Adorno so intently examined the commercial form of music that he overlooked the range of audience reactions to it, and thus, for example, failed to differentiate between the extremely diverse reactions aroused by jazz in comparison to easy listening music. Similarly, the proponents of "rock as a commercial product which coopted the revolution" failed to adequately acknowledge the tremendous impact rock had on the late 1960s. Rock was the voice of the counterculture; without it no sense of revolution would have existed. Furthermore, people did not passively listen to this music; they "dug on it" and embraced its reality. Espousing alienated values, rock did more than provide merely an illusion of freedom, it conveyed an alternative vision to the prescribed ways of life. By articulately reflecting and reinforcing the social flux of the period, this music transcended its role as a commodity; it was a human force pushing for a better tomorrow.

A Matter of Definition

Rather than attributing to rock's commerciality the cessation of the movement to change the world in a radical way, Jonathan Eisen in *Altamont: Death of Innocence in Woodstock Nation* (1970) laid the responsibility for the belated revolution upon the rock audience. He recognized that the music had created an atmosphere for positive change, but felt the listeners had not followed through.

Instead of transmuting "repressive conditions" and establishing alternate institutions, Eisen felt the hip community, including himself, had basked in a media-created world of delusion, "preferring to live within the comfortable confines of the illusion that turning on is the equivalent of making revolution."[6]

Eisen, Chapple and Garofalo, Lydon, and other activists shared a common misconception insofar as they defined revolution in terms of Che Guevera, or at least an immediate institutional response to the rock world. They laid upon rock their expectations, and these exceeded the actual realms of the music. Although goals such as the termination of the Vietnam conflict were entwined in the fabric of the rock world in the 1960s, the social ferment of the era had a broader scope than political problems. The counterculture was not so interested in changing the social structure as rearranging the American way of life. The essence of rock in that decade was its deprecation of the dominating society's alienating character and its articulation of a set of values which grew in response to that character. It presented the problem and offered a solution, a way of coping. It brought alienated ways of life and thought into the cultural mainstream and placed them in a plausible environment around which grew a "statusphere."[7]

In *The Pumphouse Gang* Tom Wolfe observed people during their leisure time "splitting" from prescribed definitions of social achievement. To nurture self-esteem they established their own "leagues," miniature worlds with their own concepts of accomplishment. These worlds he labeled "statuspheres." Examples included the microcosms created by surfers, hot rodders, motorcyclists, and art patrons. The rock-counterculture statusphere, which Wolfe did not directly address, differed from the others in that it developed standards that were not only apart from but opposed to those of mainstream society. It rejected the norms and values of the dominant culture, and around this rejection grew the idea of revolution.

While the idea of revolution triggered different visions in different minds, the reality of the rock revolution varied tremendously from most traditional expectations. Not only was it nonviolent, but by-and-large it was unassertive. The rock revolution was an alienated movement, not one committed to "the cause." Bob Dylan had warned individuals off that trip as early as 1964, and the Beatles had reminded people that nothing was real, and there was "nothing to get hung about." Causes, however, did exist—freedom to be, do, and feel, openness of spirit and mind, and non-acquiescence to consummate consumerism, plasticity, and repressive authority—but these were individual battles which drew support from and advanced the collective "flower-power" scene. The revolutionaries primarily aspired to "live my life the way I want to," and pledged their allegiance no further. Secure in their stance, they conceived themselves to be examples of how to live, despite the contrary opinions of others.

> *And it really doesn't matter if I'm wrong*
> *I'm right*
> *Where I belong, I'm right*
> *Where I belong.*[8]

Rather than a frontal assault on the establishment, the counterculture proposed an alteration of attitudes, or consciousness, in the hopes that the dominant culture would acquiesce, change itself, and follow a new path.

This movement was at best amorphous, visible only through media reports, the appearances of its more conspicuous proponents, and the sound of rock music. It confronted the dominant culture through the sheer vitality of its existence; its threat lay in its mere presence, rather than in any overt, concerted actions. Demonstrations did happen, the most memorable being the 1967 march on the Pentagon, the 1968 Democratic Convention in Chicago, the Weatherman's attempt to Bring the War Home in 1969, and the confrontations at Berkeley, Kent and Jackson States, and Columbia. But, like the SDS, the National Mobilization to End the War in Vietnam, and the rhetoric of Abbie Hoffman and Jerry Rubin, these old forms in hip clothing vainly attempted to harness, if not exploit, the new countercultural energy. They drew on the exuberant air of positive change for their drive, but never attained overwhelming support. The demonstration against the Democratic Convention in Chicago drew five to fifteen thousand people; the march on the Pentagon thirty-five to one hundred thousand.

In comparison, major groups, such as the Doors, rarely played auditoriums with capacities under ten thousand and frequently performed before audiences of fifty thousand or more; the Golden Gate Park "Gathering of the Tribes" attracted twenty thousand persons, and over three hundred thousand turned out for both Woodstock and Altamont. The politically oriented movements made good theater, which further emphasized and justified the sense of alienated outrage, but clearly they did not represent the thrust of the rock revolution. Indeed, at best they were peripheral factions. The soul of the rock revolution lay in its articulation of the youth culture's alienated ideals and ways, which placed it at center stage, the only action in an otherwise predictable play. Rock was what was happening and young people flocked to be a part of it.

Youth Culture and Alienation

In *The Uncommitted*, Kenneth Keniston discussed the manner in which the youth cultures of the 1950s and early 1960s mediated the strain of adjusting to adult life.[9] He found modern society accepted the existence of youth cultures which systematically disengaged teenagers from the demands of conventional adulthood. These cultures were considered to be a part of normal life, and although definitely non-adult in orientation, they were rarely anti-adult in attitude (delinquent and bohemian stances being the exceptions). Their members assumed they would enter the adult realm, but they had few high expectations concerning their future and disclosed little hope for personal fulfillment. Thus the youth culture served as a breathing space in which individuals reconciled childhood viewpoints with adult demands and developed a sense of identity and inner unity. As a socially supported period exempt from adult standards, it let young people remain outside society without taking an open stance against it. A separate youth culture allowed the young as a group to be "institutionally alienated" from society without assuming personally alienated positions. In essence, the rock of the 1970s has served a similar purpose for a wider audience and age group.

Rock, in the late 1960s, however, signaled the appearance of a dramatically different youth culture. The scenario shifted from the innocuous non-adult world of *Beach Blanket Bingo* and Beatlemania to the anti-adult sphere of *Sergeant Pepper* and Haight/Ashbury. It wasn't cigarettes which "Charlie Brown" now smoked in the auditorium, and instead of asking "Will you still love me tomorrow?" females inquired "Why can't we be three?" Youthful disregard for social norms turned from an attempt to appropriate adult privileges such as sex, smoking, and drinking (vertical deviance) to the creation of new activities and values in opposition to traditional standards (lateral deviance.)[10] A recognized phase of life, intended to mitigate the crush of society's demands on the individual, transmogrified itself and labeled society's expectations and, more significantly, its rewards, "plastic." Rejecting adult values, the youth culture reversed its prescribed role as an institutionalized outlet for alienation, and instead advocated personal alienation as an open way of life. As a result a generation came of age which reconciled the tensions between social forms and individual needs by renouncing the former. They left society behind and went their own way.

The lateral deviance of the youth culture of the 1960s differentiated it from the youthful rebellions of the past. Such deviance, by challenging the status quo of the dominant culture, also distinguished the rock world from innumerable other statuspheres. Featuring alienated values and their non-cause orientation, this deviance was truly revolutionary, in both its form and content, and shook American society.

Various disillusioned critics, including Eisen and Lydon, questioned the depth of the quake. Vietnam continued until even Richard Nixon got bored by it. Marijuana and other drugs remain illegal, love is still a four-letter word, and rock just keeps on rolling along. Certainly the ideals of the coming Age of

Aquarius have not evidenced themselves on a cultural level. However, the attainment of ideals is not the proper measure of revolutions. Political equality did not result from either the French or American revolutions, nor did economic equality spring from the Russian revolution. What did issue from these movements was an overthrow of authority. A similar accomplishment resulted from the rock revolution, only on a more subtle, and perhaps less pervasive, level.

As a vehicle for cultural revolution, rock struck at the patterns of social character which directed individual lives and enforced conformity. It reestablished a viable sense of inner-direction and individual autonomy. Alienated by an other-directed corporate society with its consumption ethos supported by mass marketing and advertising, rock sought to reinstate the individual as the center from and for which decisions were made. "It is not he or she or them or it that you belong to;" "It's my life and I'll do what I want;" "*I* can't get no satisfaction;" "Dig, I got my own world to look through, and I ain't gonna copy you." Such pronouncements placed a high priority on individual integrity and self-respect. The concern over being labeled "Cathy's Clown" or of having friends go "ooo-la-la" disappeared, as the songs of the 1960s defiantly stressed a strong sense of inner-direction and autonomy. By advocating the restoration of a world where individuals were the supposed masters of their destinies, a world where people already inculcated with social values let their consciences be their guide, rock appeared to be not so much the vanguard of a new age, but the last stand of an earlier inner-directed way of life. And in part it was.

However, the social values advanced by rock music clearly placed it in the forefront of the cultural revolution. Articulating the inner-directed, alienated viewpoints enumerated in Keniston's *The Uncommitted,* the music proposed the creation of a new foundation upon which to ground social authority. Encouraged by the music, members of the youth culture cast themselves afloat as the centers of their own universes and relied upon an abiding faith in the integrity of the "aesthetic quest" for their direction. By reflecting and reinforcing the values inherent in this quest—its emphasis on self, freedom, the present, and the development of sentence, awareness, expression and feeling—rock made its mark upon the world.

To assess the impact of rock, we should consider the orientation of the youth culture from which it emerged. Rock served as a vehicle for an essentially passive revolution. It offered an alternative to mainstream society by presenting life-enhancing ways with inner-directed, alienated values. Like the "battles" of youth culture in the 1960s, rock's influence centered on individual actions and orientations, and although the young had hoped for the dominant culture's acceptance of their visions, when "love, peace and happiness" were not embraced the members of the youth culture simply moved on. Some moved into deeper alienation, others into greater commitment, and still others into their own expressions of fulfillment. Although the government showed minimal interest in accepting the ideals of the love generation, the people who lived with the music continued to carry its hopes and ideals into the 1970s.[11]

The rock revolution, however, not only affected its audience; society itself lurched in the youth culture's wake. The young fermented a turmoil not easily quelled, and in recuperating from the upheaval of the late 1960s society accommodated a variety of countercultural forms.

REFLECTIONS OF ROCK

Just as rock was an index of the youth culture in the 1960s, reflecting and reinforcing its beliefs and attitudes, so too other forms appeared in the 1970s which equally reflected the absorption of the movement by the dominant culture. While the music, the vanguard of social change, bemoaned the termination of the revolution, other forms, often modified to the point of perversion, arose which proclaimed the social acceptance of certain aspects of the counterculture.

Madison Avenue almost immediately picked up on the images and rhetoric of the rock revolutionaries. In a manner reminiscent of the young political activists, advertising agencies appropriated the forms of the counterculture in the hopes of gaining support for their own ends. Schlitz beer advocated an aesthetic quest enhanced by alcohol, informed its audience that things only come around once in this world, so they must be grasped with gusto and made the most of. Similarly Seven-Up defiantly moved itself outside the cultural mainstream, bucked conventional values (in soda flavor) and joyously proclaimed itself the "Un-Cola," replete with an abundance of Peter Max-inspired rainbows, fireworks, and stars. Along with such inducements to consume came other peculiar phenomena, including a flood of gurus, EST, encounter sessions, and scientology, all of which attempted to retool individuals for their new inner-direction, and teach them how to do their own thing, to be free, honest, open, and understanding of themselves and others.

Politically, a new assertiveness for individual needs over corporate dictates characterized the early 1970s, and the movements for ecology, women's rights, and consumer protection all partially derived their impetus from the surge of energy provided by the 1960s. On the commercial front, head shops, natural foods, hand-crafted merchandise, water beds and exotic clothing sprang up to meet the more trendy consumer demands incited by the recent revolution. Also a more liberated attitude toward sex and nudity became apparent as society first moved from topless to bottomless dancers and centerfolds, and then quickly adopted a "let's all join in" attitude of streakers, swingers, and socialities on display. And of course, everyone everywhere was enjoined to "have a nice day."

The forms of the counterculture, adapted to the sensibilities of the silent majority, emerged in the mainstream of the 1970s as strange, distorted apparitions, easily recognized as part of everyday life. A peculiar fit, the incorporation of the rock revolution into the dominant culture nevertheless had begun. The excesses of young people in the 1960s, once removed from the glow of the blacklight, became normal and tolerated, although not always totally acceptable. Thus an extremely broad surface permissiveness with little imagination or flair came to pervade the 1970s.

Society recuperated from the upheaval and repaired itself as best it could. This return to "normalcy" entailed two concurrent actions, the assimilation of countercultural forms and styles into the commercial sphere both as products and sales aids (i.e. advertising, shops' interior and sign designs, and the like), and the redefinition of deviant behavior.[12] The former essentially accommodated newly created demands, a simple process under the capitalist system once the market was recognized. The latter, largely media induced, defused the explosiveness of deviant actions through tolerant amusement or by labeling such behavior harmless, trivial, or a part of the mainstream. As the general public became more familiar with sensational conduct, a referential context for such actions was established allowing for easy recognition and labeling as well as new perspectives which rendered such behavior less exotic and more mundane. Thus the public came to accept marijuana "experimentation," if not use, as normal behavior among the young. Furthermore, the insights gained from drug use became trivialized as the visions of the naive and inexperienced. Likewise, many people eventually viewed cohabitation as harmless, and obscenity and nudity lost some of their power to offend.[13]

The absorption of countercultural styles into the dominant culture allowed the social system to continue intact and in control. The recuperation process essentially was a cosmetic one. Although exhibiting a countercultural air, almost all of society's accommodations were superficial manifestations of change; they involved adjustments in outward behavior, but did not evidence any redirection of cultural attitudes. Whims of the moment, perhaps as ephemeral as rock music itself, these new forms and values cannot be viewed as persuasive indexes of any deposed authority. At best they merely indicated an acknowledgement by American society that something profound had happened in its midst in the late 1960s.

To uncover evidence of more lasting social changes which resulted from the cultural explosion of the period, we must move beyond forms and seek out actions or artifacts whose contents reflect the autonomous, inner-directed attitudes of the alienated counterculture, and whose very existence challenge the Establishment, as rock had in the 1960s.

Rock as Architecture

Architecture, the most substantial art form within a society, usually acts as an art of conviction, giving tangible form to a society's beliefs and aspirations. The White House, the Capitol building, and numerous other clasically-inspired buildings throughout the land bespeak the founding fathers' belief that they had reestablished the political ideals of ancient Greece and Rome, the cradles of democracy. Likewise, the austere, functional boxes and impersonal highrises of modern architecture aptly reflect the corporate ideology of recent American society.[14]

With the 1970s a reaction against modern architecture evidenced itself in several areas, including the post-modern movement, the increased attention given to peculiar and fantastic architecture, and an interest in renovating nineteenth- and early twentieth-century houses. These alternatives to architecture's established corporate image may be viewed as an index to a fundamental shift in American thought and taste. They embody strong statements on non-conformity, and through them we may glimpse the perpetuation of the spirit of the rock revolution. This is especially true of the new found enchantment with Queen Anne style homes.

The Queen Anne residence, the stereotypical old house which was broken into apartments and rented to people like Mork and Mindy and Mary Richards of *The Mary Tyler Moore Show*, became during the 1970s, not only a fashionable, but an enviable abode. The style, which previously had been dismissed as garish, "decadent," grotesque, and unworthy of serious contemplation,[15] suddenly returned to favor. Individuals started restoring these magnificent "mansions" to their former grandeur, and even devoted books to them (with San Francisco receiving a disproportionate share of the attention).[16] Opposing all standards of modern architectural taste, the Queen Anne's return to popularity signaled an unmistakable movement away from established architectural norms.

But what does this have to do with rock music? If we consider the fundamental characteristics of the Queen Anne residence and the acid rock song, an amazing number of parallels quickly appear. Both the Queen Anne style and acid rock broke with the classical tradition and used its elements in dynamic and exciting ways. Whereas rock in the 1960s transcended the restraints of the three-minute pop song and exhibited a highly improvisational format with deliberately outrageous melodies and chromatic harmonies which defied musical logic, so too the Queen Anne style decimated the classical, box-like house by employing an asymmetrical composition with irregular floorplan. Turrets extended up towards the sky, and bay windows, balconies, and applied ornamentation disrupted the straight line of the facade. Exuberant, flamboyant, and heavily embellished, the Queen Anne residence sought "to capture the eye and captivate the mind."[17] Each detail demanded its full share of attention, yet was completely integrated into the whole. Likewise, the tendency in rock of the late 1960s for a variety of players to develop their own leads simultaneously resulted in a similar multilayered yet cohesive effect. Both forms spoke strongly of the integrity of the individual and allowed the imagination to soar.

That the Queen Anne style enjoyed a revived popularity almost immediately on the heels of the blossoming of rock was no mere coincidence. The product of the late nineteenth century, the high point of American laissez-faire capitalism, with its strong emphasis on the individual and inner-direction, Queen Anne-style residences embody in architectural form the ideals and values espoused by the rock songs of the 1960s. Symbolically, they stand as exuberant celebrations of an alienated freedom to be, and are the antithesis of modern design and society. Thus a strong link exists between this style and rock of the period. The outlook which created and thrived on rock music could not ignore the allure of the Queen Anne house with its parallel visual signals. Bolstered by their new sense of independence from authority, people moved beyond merely changing their diets or hairstyles and undertook the expense of rehabilitating these structures, and created substantial statements in opposition to prescribed ways and standards of taste. Registering a rejection to other-directed authority, they restored remnants of the past to declare tangibly the continued well-being of the countercultural spirit. The presence of these houses radiates a bright hope that the ideals of the 1960s have taken root.

EPILOGUE

The revived interest in the Queen Anne style of architecture is a substantial, albeit oblique, expression of the continued existence of the values extolled by the rock music of the 1960s. Other evidence, more germane to the topic of this book, also abounds.

Within the recent past three major events have revealed the hold which the musical spirit of the 1960s still exerts on contemporary American society.

The lingering longing to reaffirm the faith of the young burgeoned forth with the funeral obsequies following the assassination of John Lennon, the Central Park reunion concert of Simon and Garfunkel, and the Rolling Stones' 1981 American tour. All three events represented a coming together of masses of people to publically express, if not reaffirm, their sense of identification with the values of the 1960s, to feel once again that common hope and to remind themselves that the spirit still abides within them. Embraced not only by the aging members of the psychedelic youth culture, but surprisingly, also by many still in their youth, these events were not acts of nostalgia, but rather displayed a veneration for a shared sensibility.

The first, and by far the heaviest, of these events started on Monday night, December 8, 1980, with the shocking murder of John Lennon. His death shattered any dream of a Beatle reunion, and represented the loss of a major icon within the reposing counterculture.

Countless people—over 100,000 in New York's Central Park, another 30,000 in Liverpool, several thousand in Boston, Chicago, Melbourne and other urban areas around the globe, and still smaller groups in numerous towns and hamlets—fittingly observed a silent vigil in his memory at 2 P.M. Eastern Standard Time, December 14, 1980. For months afterward, Beatles songs somberly issued forth from the radio, a consistent, haunting eulogy for the man and the era. John Lennon was truly everywhere, and his spirit became again deeply imbued within the American psyche.

The death of the man did not signal the death of the era. If anything, Lennon's assassination fixed within the minds of people the tremendous impact the 1960s and its music had made on them and the world. In part, this consciousness led half a million people to gather in Central Park nine months later to listen to the reunited Simon and Garfunkel. Stirred by a rekindled memory, one of the largest crowds in the history of American music,[18] almost doubling Woodstock's attendance, assembled on September 19, 1981 to hear once again the sounds of silence, and reexperience the sensation of unity, of coming together and enjoying the pleasure of the shared moment. The autumn nip in the air could not refute that the summer of love was still alive.

Equally telling was the Rolling Stones' 1981 American tour, which opened to a crowd of ninety thousand at Philadelphia's John F. Kennedy Stadium six days after the Simon and Garfunkel performance. Building on the energy generated in Central Park, Stones fever inundated city after city, laying them to waste. "The World's Greatest Rock 'n' Roll Band" played to packed house after packed house during the three-month tour, with ticket demands far outstripping seating capacities. Every Stones' tour is something special, as a sense of transcendent autonomy, tinged with malevolence, pervades the concert atmosphere. The energy, drive, and aura of the band surpass audience expectations, and through the live performance the Stones' mythic image, so finely honed in the 1960s and maintained in the 1970s, is renewed, perpetuated. The audience, having partaken of a transdimensional ritual, return to their lives replenished. Yes, a Stones tour has always been an incredible, memorable event. However, the 1981 American tour, viewed by over two million paying people, assumed an even greater air.

Constant speculation over this being the aging band's last tour helped generate numbers of fans. People reached out to garner a final memory for the future, grasping at the Stones as a major presence, a vestige of an era about to pass. The turnout was tremendous. In Seattle, the Kingdome was filled to capacity twice, a crowd equal in size to nearly a quarter of the city's population; the two San Francisco shows drew the largest paid crowds in Bay Area rock history; and in New York four million ticket requests were received by mail in a fifty-six hour period for the five metropolitan area shows, which would accommodate approximately one hundred thousand. Couple such numbers with the enormous stage set in Philadelphia, the giant video screen in Syracuse, the cherry picker in Los Angeles, tremendous amounts of money (with ticket sales alone grossing over thirty-four million dollars), the incessant programming of Stones' hits on the radio, and the extensive national media coverage, and the tour took on epic proportions, presenting a stunning statement on the group, their time, and their music.

All three events, the Lennon funeral, the Simon and Garfunkel concert, and the Rolling Stones tour, derive their significance from the overwhelming response they elicited. But more than just numbers, these events also had a spirit. They were not belated acknowledgements of the past, as was the rock 'n' roll revival of the early 1970s, nor were they comebacks of the order of Neil Sedaka or Frankie Valli. Rather than exercises in nostalgia or resurrection, they were large-scale demonstrations that the good vibrations had not as yet disappeared, that the invisible atmosphere which surrounded the late 1960s sensibility was still capable of generating high energy. These three highly charged moments were but events in a continuing tale, fragments to once again show us that "The Time Has Come Today." Without a doubt, the time will come again, and again.

NOTES

[1]Arnold Shaw, "Rocks in Their Heads," *High Fidelity,* April 1969, pp. 48–51.

[2]Michael Lydon, "Rock for Sale" *Tamparts*, June 1969, pp. 19–24.

[3]These figures appear in "The Rockers Are Rolling in It," *Forbes*, 15 April 1973, pp. 28–30 + ; "The Gorillas are Coming," *Forbes*, 10 July 1978, pp. 41–46; and Steve Chapple and Reebee Garofalo, *Rock 'n' Roll is Here to Pay*, (Chicago: Nelson-Hall Inc., 1977), p. 14.

[4]Charlie Gillett, *The Sound of the City* (New York: Dell, 1972), p. 76.

[5]See Theodor W. Adorno, "On Popular Music," *Studies in Philosophy and Science*, vol. 9, No. 1 (1941); Theodor W. Adorno, "A Social Critique of Radio Music," *Kenyon Review*, 7, No. 2 (Spring 1945); and Gillian Rose, *The Melancholy Science, An Introduction to the Thought of Theodor W. Adorno* (New York: Columbia University Press, 1978).

[6]Jonathan Eisen, *Altamont: Death of Innocence in Woodstock Nation* (New York: Avon, 1970), p. 16.

[7]For a discussion of the concept of statusphere see Tom Wolfe, *The Pumphouse Gang* (New York; Bantam Books, 1968), pp. 3–10.

[8]John Lennon and Paul McCartney, "Fixin' A Hole" (Maclen Music, Inc., c/o ATV Music Corp. © 1967 Northern Songs Limited. Used by permission.

[9]For a discussion of youth culture, see Kenneth Keniston, *The Uncommitted* (New York: Harcourt Brace and Co., 1965), pp. 341–351; and *Youth: Transition to Adulthood, the Report of the Panel on Youth of the President's Science Advisory Committee* (Chicago: University of Chicago Press, 1974), pp. 112–125.

[10]A discussion of vertical and lateral deviance within the counterculture appears in John Robert Howard, "The Flowering of the Hippie Movement," *The Annals of the American Academy of Political and Social Science*, 382 (March 1969).

[11]For a discussion of the retention of values of the 1960s in the 1970s see, Rex Weiner and Deanne Stillman, *Woodstock Census* (New York: Viking Press, 1979).

[12]An analysis of a similar recuperation process involving the defusing of the punk subculture is discussed in Dick Hebdige, *Subculture: The Meaning of Style* (London: Metheun, 1979), pp. 92–99.

[13]This loss of shockability has led deviants to become more extreme in their actions in the hopes of offending the keepers of propriety. An excellent case in point would be the punks.

[14]See Alan Gowans, *Images of American Living* (Philadelphia and New York: J.B. Lippincott, 1964), for a discussion of architecture as a reflection of social beliefs.

[15]Proponents of the modern style of architecture have always been quick to belittle the Queen Anne and other "derivative" styles. Siegfried Gideon went so far as to declare that no credible architecture emerged from the late nineteenth century, the high point of the Queen Anne revival.

[16]For example see Judith Lynch Waldhorn and Carol Olwell, *A Gift to the Street* (San Francisco: Antelope Island Press, 1976); Thomas Aidala and Curt Bruce, *The Great Houses of San Francisco* (New York: Alfred A. Knopf, 1974); Elizabeth Pomada and Michael Larsen, *Painted Ladies, San Francisco's Resplendent Victorians* (New York: E.P. Dutton, 1978); and Judith Lynch Waldhorn and Sally B. Woodbridge, *Victoria's Legacy: Tours of San Francisco Bay Area Architecture*, (San Francisco: 101 Productions, 1978).

[17]Aidala and Bruce, *The Great Houses of San Francisco*, p. 29.

[18]The only crowd to surpass the Simon and Garfunkel audience converged on Watkins Glen in 1973 to participate in the Grateful Dead and Allman Brothers Band's Summer Jam.

Further Reading

The following list contains the major works that have appeared on the subject of rock music and the social scene in which it emerged. We found them to be invaluable sources of information and recommend them to any reader who wishes to gain a fuller sense of the rock world. A number of titles (designated by OOP) are out of print. We included these publications because they flesh out the music and its times further and contribute to our understanding of rock's history. Many of these books still can be found in libraries and used book stores.

ROCK IN GENERAL

BELZ, CARL. *The Story of Rock*. New York: Oxford University Press, 1969.
   Attempts an analysis of rock from the standpoint of folk art. A primary difficulty with this examination is its consideration of rock in terms of folk rather than popular art.
COHN, NIK. *Rock from the Beginning*. New York: Stein and Day, 1969. (OOP)
   An impressive assessment from a British point of view.
FIRTH, SIMON. *Sound Effects: Youth, Leisure and the Politics of Rock 'n' Roll*. New York: Pantheon, 1982.
   A well-trained academician strives to address the masses in a simplistic, yet ponderous, manner. Less concerned with the music than with rock as an example of the pop process.
GILLETT, CHARLIE. *The Sound of the City*. New York: Outerbridge and Dienstfrey, 1970. (OOP)

A highly respected history which is very strong on the pre-Beatles era. The author displays a strong interest in the role of the record companies and the influence of rhythm-and-blues on the music.

HOPKINS, JERRY. *The Rock Story*. New York: Signet Books, 1970. (OOP)
Places a strong emphasis on rock of the 1960s, although it does cover the earlier rock 'n' roll in a better than adequate manner.

MILLER, JIM. *The Rolling Stone Illustrated History of Rock 'n' Roll*. New York: Random House, 1980.
The most recent comprehensive overview of the subject, with articles written by major critics in the field. This is the only general history to venture beyond 1970 in its treatment of rock.

SHAW, ARNOLD. *The Rock Revolution*. London: Crowell-Collier, 1969.
Covers pretty much the same territory as Jerry Hopkins' *The Rock Story*.

THE FIFTIES

MILLER, DOUGLAS, and NOWAK, MARION. *The Fifties*. New York: Doubleday, 1975.
This is a most important book covering the socio-cultural history of the period. Includes a very good chapter on rock 'n' roll.

Several books have been published which address themselves solely to the history of rock 'n' roll; these include:

BUSNAR, GENE. *It's Rock 'n' Roll*. New York: Wandered, 1979.
Examines rock 'n' roll according to its various styles and forms.

SHAW, ARNOLD. *The Rockin' Fifties*. New York: Hawthorne, 1974.
Covers much of the pre-rock music of the decade.

GURALNICK, PETER. *Feel Like Going Home*. New York: Outerbridge and Dienstfrey, 1971.

GURALNICK, PETER. *Lost Highway*. Boston: Godine, 1979.
Both books are first-hand accounts written in a highly readable fashion.

GREENFIELD, JEFF. *No Peace, No Place*. New York: Doubleday, 1973. (OOP)
Has an excellent chapter on the meaning of rock 'n' roll to an adolescent of the 1950s.

A number of biographies also provide further insights into the period:

GOLDROSEN, JOHN. *Buddy Holly: His Life and Music*. Bowling Green: Popular Press, 1975.
The definitive work on this rock 'n' roll idol of the 1950s.

LAING, DILYS. *Buddy Holly*. New York: MacMillan, 1972.
Another view of this short-lived star.

DEWITT, H. *Chuck Berry: Rock 'n' Roll Music*. Fremont, California: Horizon Books, 1981.
An examination of Chuck Berry's career.

CAIN. ROBERT. *Whole Lotta Shakin' Goin' On: Jerry Lee Lewis*. New York: Dial, 1981.
A good overview of this rocker's career, including his later country and western years.

HOPKINS, JERRY. *Elvis*. New York: Simon and Schuster, 1971. (OOP)
The best of a large number of books written about Elvis. It provides excellent insights into the relationship between Elvis and the cultural scene of the 1950s. This book and Jerry Hopkins' *Elvis, the Final Years* (also out of print) comprise the definitive statement on Elvis' life.

HARBINSON, W.A. *The Illustrated Elvis*. New York: Grosset and Dunlap, 1976. (OOP)
A superb fan's-eye view of Elvis' life and career, which captures the electricity of his personality.

MILLAR BILL. *The Drifters*. London: Studio Vista, 1971. (OOP)
A good portrayal of this group and the rhythm-and-blues scene of the 1950s.

A number of other books delve into the Black tradition from which rock 'n' roll sprang:

GROIA, PHILIP. *They All Sang on the Corner*. Sekauket, New York: Edmond Publishing Company, 1973.
A detailed account of doo-wop, which concentrates heavily upon New York.

SHAW, ARNOLD. *Honkers and Shouters*. New York: McMillan, 1978.
Covers the rhythm-and-blues scene from the record industry's perspective. Includes some good interviews.

HEILBUT, TONY. *The Gospel Sound*. New York: Simon and Schuster, 1971.
The definitive study on the development of this music. (OOP)

BROVEN, JOHN. *Rhythm and Blues in New Orleans*. Gretna, Louisiana: Pelican, 1978.
A well-written, well-researched account of rhythm-and-blues in the Crescent City. Includes discussions on Little Richard and Fats Domino.

ROWE, MICHAEL. *Chicago Breakdown*. New York: DaCapo, 1979.
A very thorough overview of the blues in the Windy City. Covers all major labels and stars.

GROOM, BOB. *The Blues Revival*. Hatboro, Pennsylvania: Legacy Books, 1971.

A discussion of the awakening of white interest in the blues, especially in England. Primarily deals with the Black influences on rock.

BENGT and OLSSON. *Memphis Blues*. London: Studio Vista, 1971. (OOP)
A fairly comprehensive survey of blues and early soul in Memphis up through the Stax record era.

Other published information on the music world of the 1950s includes:
ESCOTT, COLIN AND HAWKINS, MARTIN. *Sun Records*. New York: Music Sales, 1980.
A history of the company that produced Elvis Presley, Jerry Lee Lewis, Carl Perkins, Johnny Cash, and others.

PALMER, ROBERT. *Baby That Was Rock 'n' Roll: The Legendary Leiber & Stoller*. New York: Harcourt Brace Jovanovich, 1978.
Primarily a picture book of artists who recorded Leiber and Stoller songs, it also features a lively introduction by John Lahr which overemphasizes the sexual themes in the work of this songwriting team.

REDD, LAWRENCE. *Rock is Rhythm and Blues: The Impact of Mass Media*. East Lansing: University of Michigan Press, 1974.
Discusses the important role the mass media played in popularizing rhythm-and-blues, and in turn early rock 'n' roll.

MIDDLETON, RICHARD. *Pop Music and the Blues*. London: Victor Gollancz Ltd., 1972. (OOP)
Describes the relationship between pop music and the blues from the 1950s through the late 1960s.

Goldmine: A periodical primarily aimed at record collectors. It features many detailed articles on rock 'n' roll performers of the 1950s.

THE EARLY SIXTIES

No book by itself addresses the music of this period. The closest to do so is:
POLLACK, BRUCE. *When Rock Was Young*. New York: Holt, Rinehardt, and Winston, 1981.
Examines the period 1955–1964 on a yearly basis, with short autobiographical sketches by various artists, as well as interviews with such people as Neil Sedaka, Shirley Alston of the Shirelles, and Little Anthony.

Several books examine folk music:
BRAND, OSCAR. *The Ballad Mongers*. New York: Funk and Wagnalls, 1962.
A history of pre-Dylan folk music. A good introduction to the subject.

DENISOFF, R. SERGE. *Sing a Song of Social Significance*. Bowling Green: Popular Press, 1972.
Traces the protest song in America with an emphasis on the 1960s.

DETURK, D. AND POULIN, A. *The American Folk Scene*. New York: Dell, 1967. (OOP)
Presents an excellent collection of essays on the early 1960s folk revival. Captures the spirit of the period and the issues involved.

Other books delve into the rock and folk relationship:

VASSAL, JACQUES. *Electric Children: Roots and Branches of Modern Folk-Rock*. New York: Taplinger, 1976.

ELIOT, JARC. *Death of a Rebel*.

SCOPPA, BUD. *The Byrds*. New York: Scholastic Books, 1971. (OOP)
An excellent history of the group's career through 1970. The section on folk rock is very good, as is the coverage of the late 1960s-early 1970s country rock.

SANDER, ELLEN. *Trips: Rock Life in the Sixties*. New York: Scribner, 1973). (OOP)
This book covers more than just folk rock; however, it is one of the few books to address Greenwich Village's influence on rock.

The British arrival has been described in:

SCHAFFNER, NICHOLAS. *The British Invasion: First Wave to New Wave* New York: McGraw-Hill, 1982.
Covers the presence of British rock in America. Includes good overview, biographies, and discographies of major performers. All periods are covered well.

A number of biographies have appeared on the Beach Boys:

PREISS, BYRON. *The Beach Boys*. New York: Ballantine, 1979.

LEAF, DAVID. *The Beach Boys and the California Myth*. New York: Grosset and Dunlap, 1978. (OOP)

TOBLER, JOHN. *The Beach Boys*. Secaucus, New Jersey: Chartwell Books, 1978. (OOP)

BARNES, KEN. *The Beach Boys in Words and Pictures*. New York: Sire Books, 1976. (OOP)

THE LATE SIXTIES

An enormous amount of information has been produced on this period and the counterculture. Major works include a number of anthologies.

QUINN, EDWARD G., AND DOLAN, PAUL J. *Sense of the Sixties*. New York: Macmillan, 1968.

PERRUCCI ROBERT AND PILISUK, MARC. *The Triple Revolution Emerging*. Boston: Little Brown and Co., 1971.

Youth in Turmoil. New York: Time-Life, 1969. (OOP)
A paperback adaptation of a special issue of *Fortune*.

The Establishment and All That. Santa Barbara, California: Center for the Study of Democratic Institutions, 1970. (OOP)
A collection of articles from *Center Magazine*.

KORNBLUTH, JESSE. *Notes from the New Underground*. New York: Viking Press, 1968. (OOP)

HOROWITZ, DAVID, LERNER, MICHAEL, AND PYES, CHRIS. *Counterculture and Revolution*. New York: Random House, 1972. (OOP)

KOPKIND, ANDREW AND RIDGEWAY, JAMES. *Decade of Crisis*. New York: World Publisher, 1972. (OOP)
Collection of articles from *Hard Times*.

Other books related to the counterculture include:

OBST, LYNDA ROSEN. *The Sixties*. New York: Random House, 1977.
A profusely illustrated yearly account of the decade.

ROSZAK, THEODORE. *The Making of the Counter Culture*. New York: Doubleday, 1969.
Provides an in-depth consideration of the youth culture's philosophical base from an academic perspective. Most of the figures discussed in the book were at best vague shadows within the average young person's mind.

WOLFE, TOM. *Electric Kool-Aid Acid Test*. New York: Farrar, Straus, and Giroux, 1968.
Vividly captures the mood and spirit of psychedelia.

REICH, CHARLES A. *The Greening of America*. New York: Random House, 1970.
The first reevaluation of history in terms of the late 1960s experience.

THOMPSON, WILLIAM IRWIN. *At the Edge of History*. New York: Har-Row, 1972.

KENISTON, KENNETH. *Youth and Dissent*. New York: Harcourt, Brace, Jovanovich, 1971.

LINDEN, EUGENE. *Affluence and Discontent*. New York: Viking Press, 1979.
An appraisal of the consumer society.

DRANE, JAMES. *A New American Reformation*. New York: Philosophical Library, 1973.
An optimistic evaluation of the rock revolution which examines the spiritual

implications of the youth culture of the 1960s and looks into the "Jesus Freaks."

LESTER, JULIUS. *Search for the New Land*. New York: Dial, 1969. (OOP) A black viewpoint of the late 1960s. Great opening line.

WOLFE, BURTON H. *The Hippies*. New York: Signet Books, 1968. (OOP)

YABLONSKY, LEWIS. *The Hippie Trip*. New York: Western Publishing Company, 1968. (OOP)

CRAVEN, SHERRI. *Hippies of the Haight*. St. Louis: New Critics Press, 1972. (OOP)

FEIGELSON, NAOMI. *The Underground Revolution*. (New York: Funk and Wagnalls, 1970. (OOP)

DEL RENZIO, TONI. *The Flower Children*. London: Solstice Publications, 1968. (OOP)

SIMMONS, J. L. AND WINOGRAD, BARRY. *It's Happening, A Portrait of the Youth Scene Today*. Santa Barbara, California: McNally and Loftin, 1966. (OOP)

ATCHESON, RICHARD. *The Bearded Lady*. New York: John Day, 1971. A survey of the commune scene. (OOP)

ALD, RAY. *The Youth Communes*. New York: Tower Publications, 1970. (OOP)

MALCOLM, HENRY. *Generation of Narcissus*. Boston: Little Brown, 1971. A not very sympathetic view of the youth rebellion. (OOP)

ALDRIDGE, JOHN W. *In the Country of the Young*. New York: Harper and Rowe, 1969. (OOP) A critically sceptical view of the youth movement of the late 1960s.

LABIN, SUZANNE. *Hippies, Drugs and Promiscuity*. New Rochelle, New York: Arlington House, 1972. (OOP) The Mrs. Trollop of the 1960s reporting on the youth scene. She is not overjoyed by what she perceives.

A number of important articles also appeared which helped clarify the period:

DENNEY, REUEL. "American Youth Today, A Bigger Cast, A Wider Screen." *Daedalus* 91 (1962): 124–144.

DAVID, FRED. "Why All of Us May Be Hippies Someday." *Transaction* 5 (1967): 10–18.

HOWARD, JOHN ROBERT. "The Flowering of the Hippie Movement." *Annals of the American Academy of Political and Social Sciences* 382 (1969): 43–55.

DENISOFF, R. SERGE AND LEVINE, MARK H. "Generations and Counter-Culture." *Youth and Society* 2 (1970): 33–58.

SHEPHERD, WILLIAM C. "Religion and Counter-Culture—A New Religiosity."
Sociological Inquiry 42 (1972): 3–9.

Numerous publications concentrated upon the music of the era, including many
anthologies:

EISEN, JONATHAN. *The Age of Rock*. New York: Vintage Books, 1969.

WILLIS, ELLEN. *Beginning to See the Light*. New York: Alfred A. Knopf, 1981.
A collection of essays by the former rock critic for *New Yorker,* who has
also contributed to numerous other periodicals, including *The Village
Voice.* This anthology covers the 1970s as well as the 1960s and ranges
into many non-rock domains.

Rock Guitarists, Volume 1 and 2. New York: Guitar Player Books, 1975 & 1978.
A collection of articles and interviews from *Guitar Player* magazine.

LANDAU, JON. *It's Too Late to Stop Now*. San Francisco: Straight Arrow Books,
1972. (OOP)
A collection of *Rolling Stone,* Boston *Phoenix,* and *Crawdaddy* articles
and reviews written by one of the most perceptive commentators of the
period.

LYDON, MICHAEL. *Rock Folk: Portraits from the Rock 'n' Roll Pantheon,* New
York: Dial Press, 1971. (OOP)
A collection of biographical studies, many of which appeared in *Ramparts.*

MARCUS, GREIL. *Rock and Roll Will Stand*. Boston: Beacon Press, 1969. (OOP)
The introductory essay is an excellent articulation of the role of rock in
adolescent life.

PALMER, TONY. *Born Under a Bad Sign*. London: William Kimber, 1970. (OOP)
A collection of biographical essays written from a British perspective.

EISEN, JONATHAN. *The Age of Rock 2*. New York: Vintage Books, 1970. (OOP)
Together with the first volume it forms a comprehensive overview of the
rock scene of the late 1960s from a number of vantage points.

GOLDSTEIN RICHARD. *Goldstein's Greatest Hits*. Englewood Cliffs, New Jersey:
Prentice-Hall, 1970. (OOP)
Collection of this *New York Times* rock critic's work.

CHRISTGAU, ROBERT. *Any Old Way You Choose It*. Baltimore: Penguin Books,
1973. (OOP)
A collection of essays written by a *Village Voice* contributor.

DENISOFF, R. SERGE AND PETERSON, RICHARD A. *The Sounds of Social
Change*. Chicago: Rand McNally, 1972. (OOP)
Essays addressing the sociology of rock music.

Other publications which cover the music and its impact include:

PICHASKE, DAVID. *A Generation in Motion: Popular Music and Culture in the Sixties*. New York: Schirmer Books, 1979.
Concentrates more on the culture than the music, but does a good job of capturing the period. Uses many direct quotations.

PICHASKE, DAVID. *The Poetry of Rock, The Golden Years*. Peoria, Illinois: The Ellis Press, 1981.
Covers the music of the late 1960s by examining the albums of the major performers. A good literary analysis of the songs which takes into account the social scene.

ROSENSTONE, ROBERT. "'The Times They Are A-Changin,' The Music of Protest." *Annals of the American Academy of Political and Social Science* 382 (1969): 131–144.

HARMON, JAMES. "The New Music and Counter-Culture Values." *Youth and Society* 4 (1972): 61–85.

SEATON, S. LEE AND WATSON, KAREN ANN. "Counter Culture and Rock." *Youth and Society* (1972): 3–20.

DOUKAS, JAMES. *Electric Tibet*. Hollywood, California: Dominion Publishing Company, 1969. (OOP)
A view of the San Francisco scene.

JASPER, TONY. *Understanding Pop*. London: CCM Press Ltd., 1972. (OOP)
Primarily an examination of rock as a media form, which at times is superficial and at others informative.

A number of biographies have also been written, which further flesh out the rock world of the 1960s:

DAVIES, HUNTER. *The Beatles*. New York: McGraw-Hill, 1968.
Remains the definitive work on the group.

NORMAN, PHILIP. *Shout!* New York: Simon and Schuster, 1981.
The most recent Beatle biography. Adds a few new tidbits.

SCHAFFNER, NICHOLAS. *The Beatles Forever*. Harrisburg, Pennsylvania: Cameron House, 1977.
A well-written, well-illustrated, superb study of the group. Does a good job in capturing the immediacy of the Beatles and places the entire phenomenon within its social context.

MELLERS, WILFRID. *Twilight of the Gods*. London: Faber and Faber, 1973.
A good study of the Beatles from a musically technical point of view, but for the musically illiterate a total drag.

GABREE, JOHN. "The Beatles in Perspective." *Down Beat* 34 (November 16, 1967): 20–22 + .
Tempers the Beatle myth.
GREENFIELD, JEFF. "They Changed Rock, Which Changed the Culture, Which Changed Us." *New York Times Magazine* 16 February 1975, 12.
A concise statement on the impact of the Beatles.
SCADUTO, ANTHONY. *Bob Dylan.* New York: W.H. Allen, 1972.
The best biography on the Dylan of the 1960s.
GRAY, MICHAEL. *The Art of Bob Dylan.* New York: E.P. Dutton, 1972.
A stimulating analysis of Dylan's work through *New Morning*.
MCGREGOR. *Bob Dylan: A Retrospective.* New York: Doubleday, 1972.
An exceptionally good collection of essays on this performer.
RINZLER, ALAN. *Bob Dylan, The Illustrated Record.* New York: Crown Publishers, 1978.
Good coverage of Dylan's career through the mid-1970s.
WELCH, CHRIS. *Hendrix.* New York: Flash Books, 1973.
A very good account of Hendrix's life and career.
HENDERSON, DAVID. *Jimi Hendrix: Voodoo Child of the Aquarian Age.* New York: Doubleday, 1978.
Reputed to be the definitive work on this star.
HOPKINS, JERRY AND SUGARMAN, DANIEL. *No One Here Gets Out Alive.* New York: Warner Books, 1980.
A good biography of Jim Morrison.
HERMAN, GARY. *The Who.* New York: Macmillan, 1972.
Excellent discussion of the group in relationship to their time and place.
FRIEDMAN, MYRA. *Buried Alive: The Biography of Janis Joplin.* New York: William Morrow, 1973.
A very good account, written by Janis' former publicist.
DALTON, DAVID. *Janis.* New York: Simon and Schuster, 1971.
A collection of photographs, songs, and the like.
ROWES, BARBARA. *Grace Slick.* New York: Doubleday, 1980.
An unprovocative biography of a provocative woman and her times.
WALLEY, DAVID. *No Commercial Potential: The Saga of Frank Zappa.* New York: Outerbridge, 1972.
A very informative account on the leader of the Mothers of Invention.
MARSH, DAVID. *Paul Simon.* New York: Music Sales, 1978.
Good coverage of this singer-songwriter's career.
DALTON, DAVID. *Rolling Stones.* New York: Amsco Music Publishing, 1972.
The only worthwhile publication on this group.

JAHN, MIKE. *Jim Morrison and the Doors*. New York: Grune and Stratton, 1969. (OOP)
An excellent impression that delves deeply into the Doors' image.

GLEASON, RALPH. *The Jefferson Airplane and the San Fransico Sound*. New York: Ballatine, 1969. (OOP)
A first-hand study of the Airplane and the early San Francisco scene.

HARRISON, HANK. *The Dead Book*. New York: Links Books, 1973. (OOP)
Primarily a view of the lifestyle of the Grateful Dead.

LANDAU, DEBORAH. *Janis Joplin: Her Life and Times*. New York: Paperback Library, 1971. (OOP)
Places Janis within the context of her times.

THE SEVENTIES AND EIGHTIES

No overview of the music of this decade has as yet been compiled. However, a number of books have appeared which deal with certain aspects of the music.

REID, JAN. *The Improbable Rise of Redneck Rock*. Austin, Texas: Heidelberg Press, 1974.
Covers the advent of southern rock.

FAWCETT, ANTHONY. *California Rock, California Sound*. Los Angeles: Reed Books, 1978.
A superficial study of a deceptively unsuperficial subject.

COON, CAROLINE. *1988: The New Wave Punk Rock Explosion*. New York: E.P. Dutton, 1977.
An overview of the British punk scene as it was emerging.

HEBDIGE, DICK. *Subculture: The Meaning of Style*. London: Metheun, 1979.
An excellent analysis of the punk movement from a sociological perspective.

BURCHILL, JULIE AND PARSONS, TONY. *The Boy Looked at Johnny*. London: Pluto, 1980.
Considers the musical implications of punk.

DAVIS, STEPHEN, AND SIMON, PETER. *Reggae Bloodlines*. London: Anchor, 1977.
Best book on the subject, although not totally accurate.

PALMER, MYLES. *New Wave Explosion: How Punk Became New Wave Became the 80's*. New York: Proteus Publishers, 1981.

BAKER, GLENN A. AND COPE, STUART. *The New Music*. New York: Crown, 1981.

An extensively illustrated consideration of the music of the 1980s via biographical appraisals of numerous performers. A superficial vista which can serve mainly as an introduction to today's scene.

A number of biographies on various performers have also appeared:

DEFRECHOU, CAROL. *Neil Young*. New York: Music Sales, 1978.

FLEISCHER, LEONORE. *Joni Mitchell*. New York: Music Sales, 1976.

NOLAN, TOM. *The Allman Brothers Band, A Biography in Words and Pictures*. New York: Sire Books, 1976. (OOP)

COHEN, MITCHELL S., *Carole King, A Biography in Words and Pictures*. New York: Sire Books, 1976.

MARSH, DAVE. *Born to Run*. New York: Doubleday, 1979. A biography of Bruce Springsteen.

GAMBACCINI, PETER. *Bruce Springsteen*. New York: Quick Fox, 1979.

STEIN, CATHI. *Elton John*. New York: Popular Library, 1975.

GRAHAM, SAMUEL. *Fleetwood Mac*. New York: Warner Books, 1978.

SWENSON, JOHN. *Headliners: The Eagles*. New York: Tempo, 1981.

DEMOREST, STEVE. *Alice Cooper*. New York: Popular Library, 1974.

YORKE, RITCHIE. *The Led Zeppelin Biography*. Toronto: Metheun, 1976.

GROSS, MICHAEL. *Robert Plant*. New York: Popular Library, 1975.

NELSON, PAUL AND BANGS, LESTER. *Rod Stewart*. New York: Delilah Communications, 1981.

MILES, *Pink Floyd*. New York: Music Sales, 1981.

DAVIS, JUDITH. *Queen: An Illustrated Biography*. New York: Proteus Publishers, 1981.

CARR, ROY AND MURRAY, CHARLES SHARR. *Bowie, An Illustrated Record*. New York: Avon, 1981.

ROACH, DUSTY. *Patti Smith: Rock and Roll Madonna*. New York: And Books, 1979.

REESE, KRISTA. *Elvis Costello*. New York: Proteus Publishers, 1981.

SUTCLIFFE, PHIL AND FIELDER, HUGH. *The Police*. New York: Proteus Publishers, 1981.

PIDGEON, JOHN. *Eric Clapton*. London: Panther, 1975. (OOP)

WALTERS, CHARLEY. *Headliners: Fleetwood Mac*. New York: Tempo, 1979. (OOP)

SCHRUERS, FRED. *Headliners: Blondie*. New York: Tempo, 1980. (OOP)

BANGS, LESTER. *Blondie*. New York: Simon and Schuster, 1980. (OOP)

ADRIA BOOT AND VIVIEN GOLDMAN, *Bob Marley, Soul-Rebel-Natural Mystic*, New York: St. Martins Press, 1982.

Other books which also relate to the period and rock music in general include:

SPITZ, ROBERT. *The Making of Superstars*. New York: Doubleday, 1978.
An excellent look at the record industry from the inside, as it happens.

CHAPPLE, STEVE AND GAROFALO, REEBEE. *Rock 'n' Roll is Here to Pay*. Chicago: Nelson-Hall Inc., 1977.
An extremely informative view of rock as an economic entity. Good history of the industry.

BACON, TONY. *Rock Hardware*. New York: Crown Publishers, 1981.
An adequate examination of the various instruments and equipment used in creating rock. Includes some history, major figures, photographs.

HERMAN, GARY. *Rock 'n' Roll Babylon*. New York: G.P. Putnam's Sons, 1982.
A well-written, well-ilustrated consideration of the decadence wrought by affluence. Covers the entire history of rock.

EISEN, JONATHAN. *Altamont*. New York: Avon, 1970. (OOP)
A collection of essays covering the final rock festival of the 1960s. The book expresses the disillusionment which was beginning to set in at this time.

Discography

Compiled and Described by Manu "33/45/78" Junker

A music book without a discography is like a house without windows. Thus, the following is a list of important recordings either alluded to or mentioned in the text. It is intended to be not only a list, but also a short history lesson, as well as a practical shopping guide. I've tried to be brief yet thorough, objective yet lavish with my praise. When you dive into this sea of vinyl and discover the wonders waiting below the surface, don't let your prejudices and preconceptions weigh you down or fog your vision. As Raphael Levine would say, "have many opinions, but few convictions."

Those records marked with an asterisk (*) are especially significant releases. Also, many of these records might be a little hard to locate in places like that little record store in the shopping center on the main drag outside of town. Don't despair, you can always mail order. A reliable source for blues, vintage rock, country, folk and international music is:

Downhome Music
10341 San Pablo Avenue
El Cerrito, California 94530
[415-525-1494]

They publish newsletters and comprehensive catalogues. Good folks, good service, good stuff. Highly recommended.

Two reliable sources for reggae are:
V.P. Records
170–03 Jamaica Avenue
Queens, New York 11432
[212-291-7058]

and

Chin Randy's
1342 St. John's Place
Brooklyn, New York 11213
[212-778-9470]

Reggae records come and go like weather patterns, so you've got to grab while you can or they are gone . . . . . Rrrrright?

Rock and pop items should be a little easier to locate. Seek and you should find. This list reflects the current market of February 1982. Remember, records go in and out of print continuously.

ROCK ANTECEDENTS

Before rock there was music, believe it or not. In fact, there were many forms of music, just as there are today. Rock 'n' roll, of course, grew out of what had gone before. The three styles which played most critical roles in the development of this seemingly radical departure from taste and decorum were blues/gospel, country and western, and pop.

Pop

Short for popular. Short for popular with whites. As the sound of the majority, pop upheld certain standards of taste and decorum that many persons had come to think of as the only standards. It had settled into a formula, taking the smooth road of least resistance: music as tranquilizer. Music performed by entertainers, written by writers, produced by producers, engineered by engineers, arranged by arrangers, and so on. The work of major labels, giant ant colonies.

Because this type of music is outside the scope of this book, records by such well-known stars as Bing Crosby, Dean Martin, Nat "King" Cole, Patti Page, the Mills Brothers and many others will not be included. However, in a rash moment you might wish to seek out the following:

This is the Big Band Era (RCA Victor VPM 6043)

Musical components of swing survived into rock, especially in arranged rock (e.g. Bobby Darin's rendition of "Mack the Knife") and may even be heard in combination with gospel music in such songs as Ray Charles' "Hallelujah I Just Love Her So."

Frank Sinatra: *This Is* (Capitol M-11883); *In the Wee Small Hours* (Capitol SM-581)

Such diverse singing stars as Jim Morrison and Van Morrison have listed as an influence this crooning teen idol of the 1940s, whose audience has never deserted him. If you don't believe such claims, Jim's "Riders on the Storm" and Van's "(It Ain't Easy Being) Green" and "Autumn Song" should sway you.

Lambert, Hendricks, and Ross: *Best of . . .* Columbia C-32911)*

More jazz than pop, this band was a big influence on such later performers as Joni Mitchell, Dan Hicks and His Hot Licks, and Maria Muldaur.

Les Paul and Mary Ford: *The World is Still Waiting for the Sunrise* (Capitol SM 113078)

Les Paul was one of the early experimenters with overdubbing and other studio wizardry. His guitar work, which such guitar luminaries as Jeff Beck and Jimi Hendrix admired, further enhanced his reputation.

Perez Prado: *This Is . . .* (RCA VPS-6066)

Kitsch Latin music. None other than the B-52's have listed this sort of thing among their all-time favorites.

Blues

Because so much of rock 'n' roll has been blues based, this section is fairly extensive. Along with mentioning various records, I have tried to flesh out the major performers in order to help the listener see the men and women who made this kind of music as living, vital beings and not just names.

Note: Many of these recordings are reissues of old, scratchy seventy-eights. Sound quality varies, but at least we have something. How many records of Bach playing organ have you heard?

PRE-WAR OR COUNTRY BLUES

Acoustic music. The sound of unamplified instruments, small groups, solo performers, wandering minstrals. Many people, including fanatics, have forgotten that most of these songs served as dance music. These early singer-songwriters established forms still in use today.

Roots of Rock (Yazoo 1063)
Good introduction. Fourteen early blues numbers that were later revived by rock personages. The jacket is all solid liner notes.

Robert Johnson: *King of the Delta Blues Singers* (Columbia CL1654)*; *King of the Delta Blues Singers, vol 2* (Columbia 30034)*; *Delta Blues* (Roots RL 339) Austrian import
Robert Johnson is probably the most famous early blues artist. He is also one of the best. Many of his compositions, "Love in Vain," "Crossroads," "Sweet Home Chicago," and others have been revived countless times. It's almost scary how good his own renditions are.

Speaking of scary, if we are to believe certain sources, Johnson may have sold his soul, not to some record company, but to the forces of darkness. This association between the blues and Beelzebub, between revelry and deviltry, did not begin with the fundamentalist reactionaries of the 1950s. It probably started back in the days when voodo was still a force in the South. (For further discussion turn to the Gospel section of the discography.)

By the way, *Delta Blues* contains alternate takes of the same songs on the other albums. Before the age of mixing, editing and overdubbing everything was recorded directly. Consequently artists often did the same song several times. Sometimes the versions are radically different.

Bessie Smith: *World's Greatest Blues Singer*/includes booklet (Columbia C633)*; *Any Woman's Blues* (Columbia 30126); *Empty Bed Blues* (Columbia 30450); *The Empress* (Columbia 30818); *Nobody's Blues But Mine* (Columbia 31093)
Supposedly a big influence on many female rock singers, especially Janis Joplin. Inspiration, certainly, but influence? Well, Ms. Smith, the Empress of Classic Blues, sounds very controlled in her moaning. I don't see much connection, but judge for yourself. All her recorded output is available on these Grammy-winning double record sets.

—*The Great Jugs Bands* (Origin Jazz Library 4)
Jug Band music certainly helps put to rest the tired notion that blues are always sad. Most blues are about life in all its aspects. Some are happy, some aren't. Certainly they dwell on misery more than your usual pop fare, but at least they do so in a realistic manner. This may be one reason why these old records seem to age like fine wine.

Jug Band music experienced a revival during the urban folk boom. In Great Britain it helped launch the "skiffle" movement, from which, of course, emerged the Beatles and many of their moptop friends.

Mississippi John Hurt: *The Best of Mississippi John Hurt* (Vanguard VSD 19/20)*; *Monday Morning Blues* (Flyright 443) U.K. import

Hurt's gentle blues conquered the Newport Folk Festival of 1963. Certainly his songs possess a winning charm. If Robert Johnson is the "devil," Hurt proves there must be a power for good somewhere. *Best of* . . . was recorded live at a college concert, a most appropriate setting since most of his fans were college students. *Monday* is Library of Congress material. The Library of Congress Archive of Folk Song does much valuable work documenting and researching the varied American cultural traditions.

Reverend Gary Davis: *The Guitar and Banjo of* . . . (instrumentals) (Prestige 7725); *Pure Religion and Bad Company* (lyrics) (77 LA-12/14)* U.K. import

A self-taught Segovia, this blind virtuoso showed many students, including Jorma Kaukonen, how to make the blues sound like more than three chords and a cat fight. Yes, he really was a reverend. For most of his career he sang only religious lyrics. This is not so unusual; many blues musicians convert to the church. (Another famous example is Robert Wilkins, whose "Prodigal Son" can be heard redone by the Rolling Stones on *Beggar's Banquet*.)

Sonny Terry and Brownie McGhee: *Best of* . . . (Prestige 7715)

Brownie's brother, Sticks, had an early rock 'n' roll hit with "Drinkin' Wine Spo-Dee-O-Dee." However, this McGhee, with his long-time partner, harmonica wizard Sonny Terry, sticks to more traditional approaches. These two make a decent living . . . for blues musicians.

Leadbelly: *Leadbelly* (Capitol SM 1821); *Leadbelly* (Columbia C30035)*

Leadbelly was the first "authentic" bluesman to travel and perform extensively in white circles. Working with, some say for, John Lomax, early curator of the Library of Congress' Folk Song Archives, he gained notoriety for both himself and his music in such diverse places as Paris, London, and New York. In my list he represents early Texas-Louisiana blues. Some claim that the blues first developed in this large, often boastful state.

Jesse Fuller: *The Lone Cat* (Good Time Jazz 10039)

Originally from Georgia, Fuller settled in the Bay Area (Oakland), and composed such songs as "San Francisco Bay," "Beat It on Down the Line," and "Monkey and the Engineer." He influenced many folksingers, such as Ramblin' Jack Eliott, and such rock groups as the Grateful Dead. His one-man band routine, complete with twelve-string guitar, harmonica or kazoo, big bass drum, hi-hat cymbal, fodella (a pedal-operated bass instrument), and occasional tambourine always brought a smile. By the way, it is widely reported that Fuller ate a quart of ice cream every day for breakfast.

Boogie Woogie (French RCA PM 42395) French import

This three-LP box set is mostly jazz but then, this style of jazz is mostly blues. Boogie woogie was very popular in the 1930s, 1940s, and 1950s, and a lot of it can be found in rock 'n' roll.

Blue Roots: Chicago/the 30's (Folkways RBF 16)

Folkways was one of the first labels to begin systematically reissuing old records and releasing new ones without much concern for commerciality. This particular anthology includes the original "Key to the Highway," "Going Down Slow," and other early urban blues.

POST-WAR OR URBAN BLUES

I could list two hundred records in this section and still fail to cover the subject! This music is the backbone of rock 'n' roll. Without it there would be no rock 'n' roll, or at least no rock 'n' roll as we know it. Instead there would be only the pop music discussed earlier. Just think, . . . no, I can't, it's too horrible a thought!

For convenience I have divided modern blues into general geographic regions.

Chicago

When most people think of the blues they think of the Windy City. Some important figures in Chicago blues who have influenced rock include:

Muddy Waters: *Muddy Waters* (Chess 427-005)* French Import; *Back in the Early Days* (Syndicate Chapter 001/2) U.K. Import; *Good News* (Syndicate Chapter 003) U.K. Import Almost avuncular in 1982, Waters (nee McKinley Morganfield) is the "father" of the tough Chicago sound. His earliest records are the most historically significant. Listening to them you hear a real blues preacher at the height of his powers.

Howlin' Wolf: *Howlin' Wolf* (Chess 427-016)* French Import; *Real Folk Blues* (Chess 515-011) French Import; *Howlin' Wolf* (Charly 30134) U.K. Import; *Heart Like Railroad Steel* (Bluesball 2001) Chess outtakes
If Muddy Waters is a blues preacher, then Wolf (nee Chester Burnett) was an eloquent spokesman for the other side. Magnificently menacing in person, Wolf on his records projects an equally sinister image. That voice! That voice! Also note Hubert Sumlin's excellent guitar work.

Sonny Boy Williamson #2 (Chess 427-004) French Import
Harmonicist/singer Williamson toured the "mother" country accompanied by such later famous Anglos as Jimmy Page, Eric Clapton, and others. His records feature fine Windy City session men such as Robert "Jr." Lockwood and Willie Dixon.

Elmore James: *One Way Out* (Charly CRB 1008)* U.K. import; *Got to Move* (Charly CRB 1017) U.K. import; *Whose Muddy Shoes?* (Chess 515-006) French import; *Original Folk Blues* (United 7743); *Legend of Elmore James* (United 7778)
James was the master of electric slide guitar. His followers are legion. His hero was Robert Johnson.

J.B. Lenior: *J.B. Lenior* (Chess/Vogue 427003) French import; *Mojo Boogie* (Flyright 564)* U.K. import; *Down in Mississippi* (L & R 42-012)* German import; *Alabama Blues* (L & R 42-001)* German import
They say that a prophet is without honor in his hometown. Lenoir was the first major figure in blues to begin writing songs directly protesting social and political conditions. He also abandoned the popular electric sound for the acoustic and played more for listening than dancing. He had to go to Europe to do these things!

Jimmy Reed: *Upside Your Head* (Charly CRB 1003)* U.K. import
Laid back blues. Reed enjoyed a large, mixed audience, and many of his songs, "Big Boss Man," "Honest I Do," "Baby, What Do You Want Me to Do?" have become standards. His unique lazy shuffle style and guitar-harmonica blend have influenced a number of rock performers.

Fenton Robinson: *I Hear Some Blues Downstairs* (Alligator 4710); *Somebody Loan Me a Dime* (Alligator 4703)*
Hound Dog Taylor: *Beware of the Dog* (Alligator 4707)
Buddy Guy: *Buddy Guy* (Chess 427-006) French import
Otis Rush: *Right Place, Wrong Time* (Bullfrog 301)
Koko Taylor: *The Earthshaker* (Alligator 4711)
Five contemporary artists who should be of interest to rock fans.

Anthologies: *On the Road Again* (Muskadine 100)* *Blues is Killing Me* (Juke Joint 1501); *Chicago Slickers* (Nighthawk 102); *Chicago Ain't Nothin But a Blues Band* (Delmark 624); *Blues in D Natural* (Red Lightin' 005) U.K. import; *Okeh Chicago Blues* (Epic EG 37318)* Late 40's includes Muddy Waters' first commercial recordings; *Chicago/The Blues Today vol 1–3* (VSD 79216-79218); *Living Chicago vol. 1–6* (Alligator 7701-7706)

Memphis

Memphis, down the river from Chicago, is another important blues center. It has seen essentially six eras of blues: 1) the jug band period of Gus Cannon, the Memphis Jug Band, Memphis Minnie, and others; 2) the Beale Streeters period of B.B. King, Bobby Bland, and Johnny Ace; 3) the Black Sun Records days of Howlin' Wolf, Junior Parker, Rufus Thomas; 4) the white Sun rockabilly madness of Elvis, Jerry Lee Lewis, Carl Perkins, and many others; 5) the Stax Soul sound of Sam and Dave, Booker T. and the M.G.'s, Carla Thomas, and others; 6) the Hi times with Al Green, Willie Mitchell, O.V. Wright, and their contemporaries.

B.B. King: *Live at the Regal* (ABC 724)*; *Best of B.B. King* (Ace CH 30)* U.K. import; *B.B. King 1949–1950* (United 7788); *The Jungle* (United 7742); *Best of B.B. King* (ABC 767); *Live and Well* (ABC 819); *The Earliest King* (Blues Boy 301)

The ambassador of the blues, King is king of the dominant postwar style. A marvellous guitarist (his style is much imitated), an amazing singer (blues is primarily a vocal art), a polished performer, and an eloquent spokesman for the whole genre, Reilly "Blues Boy" King deserves his success.

Ike Turner: *I'm Tore Up* (Red Lightnin' 0016) U.K. import; *The Great Album of Ike and Tina Turner* (Festival 148) French import

Since his late teens Turner has been producing, playing, and promoting his own brand of hard rocking Southern Soul blues. His most famous work has been in collaboration with Tina, a dynamic performer.

Albert King: *Travelling to California* (King 1060); *I'll Play the Blues* (Stax 8513)

King (no relation to B.B.) became an important figure in blues just as it was becoming popular with audiences outside the Black community. Accordingly, he has been around the world several times. No wonder he plays a "Flying V" guitar!

Bobby "Blue" Bland: *Here's the Man* (Duke 75); *Best of Bobby Bland* (Duke 84)

Though he doesn't record there, Bland got his start in Memphis. Like his colleague, B.B. King, this soulful singer has managed to acquire a sizeable white audience without alienating his Black constituency.

Junior Parker: *Junior Parker and Billy Love* (Charly 30135) U.K. import; *The ABC Collection* (ABC 30010)*; *Driving Wheel* (Duke 76)*

Herman "Junior" Parker was a pioneer in smooth soul/blues singing. He is most famous, however, for "Mystery Train," a song he recorded for Mr. Sam Phillips' Sun label in 1953, a year many recall with fondness for another reason.

Anthologies: *Blues Came Down from Memphis* (Charly 30125); *Memphis Blues* (United 7779); *Walking the Back Streets Crying* (Stax 7004); *Blues Consolidated: Parker and Bland* (MCA DLPX 73)*

New Orleans and Louisiana

New Orleans has always been known for its music. Its music is unique, and the best way I can explain this to you is by recommending some fine records.

Professor Longhair: *Mardi Gras in New Orleans* (Nighthawk 108)*; *New Orleans Piano* (Atlantic SD 7225)

"Fess" (nee Roy Byrd) was described by no less an authority than Alan Toussaint as "the Bach of Rock." Why, without him there would be no Huey Smith, no Fats Domino, no fun. Well, they may have been without him, but they wouldn't have been the same!

Champion Jack Dupree: *Blues from the Gutter* (Atlantic 40526) French import

Dupree represents the blues expatriates. Other blues musicians who prefer Europe to America include Willie Mabon and Peter "Memphis Slim" Chatman.

Guitar Slim: *The Things That I Used to Do* (Specialty 2120)

Eddie "Guitar Slim" Jones, an intense blues preacher, was famous as much for his uninhibited stage act and strident guitar sound as for his few recording sessions. Incidentally, Ray Charles leads the band on this disc.

Slim Harpo: *Best of* . . . (Excello EX 8010)
"King Bee," and "Hipshake," were hits for Slim Harpo, and hits for the Rolling Stones. Operating in the Jimmy Reed set up—guitar and harmonica holder—Slim (nee James Moore) made a name for himself as far away from the bayou country as the United Kingdom.
The Excello Story (Excello 28025)
Excello anthology. Located in Nashville, the label relied on the studios of Jay Miller from Crowley, Louisiana for many of its blues releases.

Texas and the West Coast

Texas, a big place; some say the blues originated here. Others say Mississippi. Wherever the blues first came from a good deal settled in the Lone Star State. Many of the best post-war Texas blues artists spent a lot of time on the west coast.
T-Bone Walker: *T-Bone Jumps Again* (Charly CRB 1019)* U.K. import
T-Bone is a thrilling guitarist in the southwestern style made famous by Charlie Christian. He is also a fine singer in the west coast style that Nat "King" Cole popularized. He is superb on this compilation of late forties Capitol material.
Freddy King: *17 Original Greatest Hits* (King 5012)* *Best of* . . . (MCA 690)
King's King/Federal materials are his most influential, although his more recent MCA sides are better known to the rock audience.
Lightnin' Hopkins: *Early Recordings* (Arhoolie 2007); *Original Folk Blues* (United 7744)
Prolific, yet consistent, Hopkins is a blues poet. Never less than solid, he is the rock of Gibraltar (without the monkeys). Note: On January 30, 1982, the day after I wrote this, Sam "Lightnin'" Hopkins passed on. One of the greatest is gone.
Big Mama Thornton: *In Europe* (Arhoolie 1028) *She's Back* MCA 68)
Willie Mae "Big Mama" Thornton used to complain about how Elvis stole "Hound Dog" from her. Actually the two versions are markedly different. Leiber and Stoller have the copyright. Still, I can see where she may be bitter; a fine singer, she deserves a wider audience.
Clarence "Gatemouth" Brown: *San Antonio Ballbuster* (Charly CR 30169) U.K. import
Like many Texas bluesmen (T-Bone Walker, for instance) this man has a wild stage act. Although Brown often fiddles and picks a kind of country rock (he even cut an album with Roy Clark), this reissue from the 1950s is strictly blues.
Johnny "Guitar" Watson: *The Gangster is Back* (Red Lightnin' 0013) U.K. import
Watson, now a popular funk performer, got his start playing solid Texas/west coast blues. This crucial release contains the original "Gangster of Love."
Jimmy McCracklin: *My Rockin' Soul* (United 7719); *Let's Get Together* (Imperial 24011)*
Ex-boxer turned singer, McCracklin, like ladies' fashions, changes with the times. *Let's Get Together* gives a good picture of west coast blues in the 1960s.
Pee Wee Crayton: *Pee Wee Crayton* (Crown 5157)
Somewhat T-Bone Walkerish, Crayton, like Thornton, has spent a lot of time touring with Johnny Otis.
Anthology: *Central Avenue Blues* (Ace of Spades 1001)

Detroit

John Lee Hooker: *This is Hip* (Charly CRB 1004) U.K. import; *Moanin' and Stompin' the Blues* (King 1085)*; *Live and Well* (Ornament CH 7-104) German import
One word describes the music of John Lee Hooker: boogie. His hypnotic intensity has profoundly influenced white bands such as Canned Heat, with whom the great man has recorded.
General Blues Anthologies: *The Story of the Blues* (Columbia 30008); *Guitar Star* (Red Lightnin' 0017) U.K. import; *America's Music Roots* (Festival 1008) French import; *Great*

Blues Men (Vanguard VSD 25/26)*; *20 Greatest Blues Hits* (United 7748); *Black Music Sampler* (Charly CRM 2018)* U.K. import

Gospel

Anyone who likes the blues should have no problem enjoying gospel. They are very similar. Before the Second World War many gospel records were made by blues singers or former blues singers, and after the war many gospel singers switched over to blues! Although any blues fan might enjoy gospel, most gospel followers want nothing to do with the blues. One reason for this, of course, is the frank "worldliness" of the blues. Another is its reputation of being associated with not only the bar and brothel scene but also the occult. For an interesting discussion of this subject consult, J.L. Dillard, *Lexicon of Black English* (New York: Seabury Press, 1977), Chapter 4.

Gospel music is sanctified music, music of the spirit. It is participative music; expressive music. Its range of emotion is wide, moving from great sadness to great gladness, from abject humility to exuberant pride. Designed to attract; developed to involve, Gospel music has influenced rock 'n' roll more than sales charts would seem to indicate. It has trained a generation of Black Soul singers and inspired many songwriters of all hues.

The Gospel Sound, vol. 1 & 2 (Columbia, G-31086 & KG 31595)*

Unfortunately, these two albums are out of print, but they are like ten thousand lions and tigers. The most comprehensive and well-balanced anthologies around, they deserve wider circulation. They were compiled by Tony Heilbut, whose name is a watchword for quality in the field. Should you see his name on any album, whether it be as producer, compiler, or liner note writer you know the record is worth buying.

EARLY GOSPEL

Blind Willie Johnson: *Blind Willie Johnson* (Yazoo 1058)*

Antiphonal guitar, growling mock bass voice, driving rhythm, down-to-earth lyrics. Tempered in fire, light wrapped in shadows. Raw power. Johnson's hauntingly beautiful "Dark was the Night, Cold the Ground" went out on the Voyager II Space Probe. There's an old story that he once was arrested for singing his version of the Samson and Delilah tale on a county courthouse's steps. "If I Had My Way, I'd Tear this Building Down," indeed.

Rosetta Tharpe: *Gospel Train* (MCA 1317)*

Swinging, jazzy, sanctified shouting from the most popular soloist of her day. The duets with Marie Knight, later a rhythm-and-blues singer, are especially fine. The band features Tharpe on guitar, Sammy Price on piano, Pops Foster on bass, and a young Kenny Clarke on drums. Need I say more?

Golden Gate Quartet: (RCA CL 42111) German Import

The polished, practiced precision of this a capella foursome won them worldwide fame. This two LP set includes both sacred and secular material. Professional jubilee singing at its finest.

All My Appointed Time (Stash 114)*

More a capella singing. One side is all-male groups, the other is all-female groups and soloists. Nothing but the best. Good notes. Heilbut again!

In the Spirit, vol. 1 & 2 (Origin Jazz Library 12 & 13)

Two anthologies on a blues label. Very interesting gospel material mostly done by famous country blues artists.

Negro Religious Music, vol. 1 & 2 (Blues Classics BCLP 17 & 18)
Gospel at Its Best (MCA 28083)

MODERN GOSPEL

The so-called, "Golden Era," this is the period between 1945 and 1960 when gospel groups could fill stadiums everytime they came to town. Every town had its own groups, every group had its own sound. The competition was fierce, the music was getting harder, more intense, electrified, electrifying.

Alex Bradford: *Abyssinian Baptist Gospel Choir* (Columbia ACS 8348)*
A choir behind soloists singing up a storm. Sounds like fifty Little Richards all at once!

Shirley Caesar: *He Heard My Cry* (Thunderbird TDR-301); *From the Heart* (Road Show RS/H 866H)
He Heard My Cry includes a song/testimony about being approached to sing the rock 'n' roll. The jackpot goes up, but the singer yields not.

Dorothy Love Coates: *The Best of . . ., vol. 1* (Specialty SPS 2134)*
Another one who never sold out. A major talent, "Dot" puts them in the aisles everytime with her firey, honest singing and writing.

Dixie Hummingbirds: *Best of . . .* (Peacock PLP 138); *Live* (Peacock 28105)*
A premier quartet, their leads, Ira Tucker and James Walker, can do it all. Their backup singers are smooth as silk or rough as sandpaper, depending on what is required.

Five Blind Boys of Mississippi (Peacock PLP 139)*
Archie Brownlee, the man who gave Ray Charles his call to renounce his Nat "King" Coleish ways. It doesn't take a genius to hear the similarity between these two giants, one known internationally, the other a forgotten man.

Mahalia Jackson: *World's Greatest Gospel Singer* (Kenwood 505)*; *How I Got Over* (Columbia C 34073)*
Mahalia, no last name necessary. Her phrasing, her feeling, her timing. She's got it. Soul. She's got it. The Queen of Gospel. There are many great female singers; each is unique, each is first rate. Mahalia is certainly in that number. Her later work tends to be tepid; I suggest her early and live recordings.

Roberta Martin Singers: *Old Ship of Zion* (Kenwood 507)
Early pop/gospel.

Pilgrim Travellers: *Best of . . .* vol. 1 (Specialty 2121)
Texas a capella—very bluesy. Lou Rawls later sang with this popular quartet

Sensational Nightengales: *Best of . . .* (Peacock PLP 137)*
The lead singer here sounds just like Wilson Pickett. That's because it's June Cheeks, Pickett's idol. Soul roots!

Soul Stirrers: *Sam Cooke and the Soul Stirrers* (Vee Jay VJS 18013); *The Original Soul Stirrers* (Specialty SPS 2137); *Two Sides of Sam Cooke* (Specialty 2119); *Gospel Soul of Sam Cooke, vol. 1* (Specialty 2116), vol. 2 (Specialty 2128)
Sam Cooke, often called the father of Soul music, started in gospel. He owes much of his style to his hero, R.H. Harris, often called, "Pops," the father of quartet-style gospel. Some of Cooke's best recordings are gospel numbers, "Hem of His Garment," for instance. Some of his best secular numbers are based on gospel songs, "Soothe Me," "That's Where It's At," "Good News." Harris, incidentally, is one of the greatest singers around. That more of his fine music is not available is a crime; that he doesn't get more opportunity to record is our loss, even more than his.

Staple Singers: *The Best of . . .* (Vee Jay 5019)
Popular now as a kind of message Soul group, the Staples started in gospel. Mavis Staple is a fine singer, Roebuck "Pops" Staple is a fine, funky guitarist.

Swan Silvertones: *Love Lifted Me* (Specialty 2122)*
Claude Jeter! Jeter's smooth, high falsetto is a finely chiseled diamond. Without it there would have been no role model for young Al Green, young Smokey Robinson. All hail to Jeter, although the whole group is excellent.

Swanee Quintet: *20 All Time Greatest Hits* (Creed 23092)
Downhome Augusta gospel. This group toured with James Brown. They taught him how to scream?

Clara Ward Singers: *Very Greatest 21 Original Hits* (Nash 7222); *Packin' Up* (Savoy M6 14020)*
A very good all-female group, featuring the stupendous Marion Williams.

Marion Williams: *Blessed Assurance* (Atlantic 7302)*; *This Too Shall Pass* (Nashboro 7204)
Long a force in the Clara Ward Singers, Ms. Williams is among that number mentioned with Mahalia Jackson.

Greatest Gospel Gems, vol. 1 & 2(Specialty SPS 2144 & 2145)*
Excellent anthologies of the early 1950s.

Ladies and Gentlemen of Gospel (Nashboro 7157)
Strong survey of Nashboro soloists.

CONTEMPORARY GOSPEL

This generally means bigger choirs, fuller musical accompaniment, and either more intense screaming or, in the case of some "crossover" acts, less emotional display.

Rance Allen Group: *I Feel Like Goin' On* (Stax 4136)
Gospel Soul from Stax, vintage 1977.

Andrae Crouch: *Best of . . .* (Light 5678); *Live in London* (Light 5717)
Grammy Award-winning group blends (some say dilutes) gospel with contemporary Christian music and pop. Crouch probably gets happy at the bank.

Aretha Franklin: *Amazing Grace* (Atc. 2-906); *Songs of Faith* (Chess 515-007)
I like *Amazing Grace*. The version of "Mary, Don't You Weep" is equal to anything the First Lady of Soul has blessed us with. *Songs of Faith* predates her Atlantic soul period.

Edwin Hawkins: *Best of . . .* (Buddah 5708)
Ironic perhaps that the first gospel song to sell a million ("Oh Happy Day") should be available on a label named after another sage, but that's the record business for you. Choir of the late 1960s. Hip!

Troy Ramey: *Great Change* (Nashboro, 7201)

Supreme Angeles: *Supreme* (Nashboro 7110)*; *People Get Ready* (Nash 7226)
An abundance of screaming and shouting. These are two younger groups following in the fancy footsteps of Tucker, Cheeks, Brownlee, et al.

Mighty Clouds of Joy: *Changing Times* (Epic JE 35971)
Almost disco gospel from this popular twenty-year-old quartet.

B.C. and M. Choir (Savoy 14475)*
Good contemporary choir. I have emphasized quartets and female shouters in this list, as they had the greatest influence on rock, but choir is the big thing now.

Al Green: *Belle* (Hi HLP 6004)
Al Green's first full-on, or nearly full-on, sacred album. A good example of gospel pop. See the section on Soul for other more secular releases by this excellent singer.

Country Music

Country and western is a deep well from which rock 'n' roll has frequently drawn. Being largely Southern—at least originally—country grew up with the blues. The easy way out is to say country is white, at least "poor white," while blues is Black, at least "poor Black." But that would be missing some important features the two musical styles share. Both place importance on the "ragged but right" idea. Both are folk musics and stress sincerity, performer/audience rapport, relatively simple structure, down-to-earth (occasionally even "dirty") subject matter, and a danceable rhythm.

Although I mention with a great deal of bipartisan pride that there has been cultural/musical interchange (Bill Malone in *Southern Music* is on the right track here), differences also exist. Country is conservative while blues has been "upwardly mobile." Country exhibits a greater rigidity in terms of obvious morality, musical time, and historical tradition. It emphasizes the straightforward narrative and upholds the social, religious, and political standards of the lower-class white majority.

Country has an often cherished (and expurgated) tradition to uphold. Artists are practically compelled to invoke the names of psat stars at every show. They are also encouraged to express religious sentiment, with most major country singers have at least one album of religious material. Furthermore, although many country songs are gritty, many others are sentimental, almost maudlin. Mothers, the old home town, ex-es, even favorite pets get the treatment. (Jenks "Tex" Carmen went so far as to record the deeply moving "My Dog, My Everything," wherein he goes so far as to beg his dear, trusted pal to forgive him for various failings and shortcomings. Tears still fall like rain whenever the needle hits this platter at our home because, yes friends, I too once had a . . . oh, never mind . . .) Anyway, you get the idea. Country music can be terrifically a maudlin.

Also, such virtues as patriotism, hard work, self-sacrifice, and productivity are implied in much country music. Much country music is also downright depressing. The so-called "white man's blues" lacks much of the ironic humor found in much Black blues. Early death, death by car wreck, death by freezing, death by heartbreak, death by proxy! Country music had a strong thanatostic side in the good old days.

However, there is another side to this story, some country music has been affirmative, healthy, and positive. This can be said of much of the instrumental music, for instance. Instrumental virtuosi, borrowing heavily from jazz rather than blues, avoided much of the Sisyphean. They kept the fire. And honky tonk music, while not always cheerful, tended to dwell more on the dance floor than on the beer mug full of misery.

Country music has influenced rock as profoundly as any style of music has. No one growing up in the South or Southwest could avoid the stuff. It travels extensively and transplants easily (Tex Appleseed?). It also has learned to adapt. In the past twenty-five years it has given and taken much.

Jimmy Rodgers: *This Is . . .* (RCA VPS-6091)*; *My Rough and Rowdy Ways* (RCA Victor ANLI-1209); *Best of . . .* (RCA AHLI-3315)
The father of modern country music. Also its first crossover artist. Rodgers, a charismatic performer, despite an eventually terminal case of tuberculosis, had no reservations about performing Black blues, Victorian parlor songs, Tin Pan Alley concoctions, novelty tunes, sentimental weepers, yodels, anything and everything (except sacred material).

The Carter Family: *Mid the Green Fields of Virginia* (RCA Victor ANLI-1107)*; *Lonesome Pine Special* (RCA-Camden 2473)
Stars the magnitude or Rodgers, their music is much more traditional, solemn, even mournful. An abundance of sacred songs.

Bob Wills: *Anthology* (Columbia RG-32416); *24 Great Hits* (MGM MG-2-5303); *Best of . . .* (MCA 153)

Wills, like Rodgers from Texas, helped put the "western" in country music. He also helped put the beat in the music. One of the first bands to mix swing (drums and horns) with western (guitars and fiddles), Bob Wills and the Texas Playboys were very big in the southwest and California from the late 1930s to the early 1950s. Wills' ebullent sound and extroverted stage show reflects the diversity of the musical styles crossing paths throughout the southwest. Note: Charlie Christian, the father of electric jazz guitar, plays much the same style as Wills' guitarist of the same era, Eldon Shamblin.

Hank Williams: *The Immortal Hank Williams* (MGM MM 9097/106) Japanese import; *24 of Hank Williams' Greatest Hits* (MGM SE 4755-2); *Memorial Album* (MGM E3-272)*; *40 Greatest Hits* (MGM 2683-071)* U.K. import

Divorced from his wife at twenty-seven, dismissed from the Grand Ole Opry at twenty-eight, dead at twenty-nine, Hank Williams was one of America's outstanding songwriters. Like the old television ad says, "Hank's gone now but his songs live on." Many of his compositions, "I'm So Lonesome I Could Cry," "Your Cheatin' Heart," "I Saw the Light," and many others, are standards in both pop and country. Besides being a phenomenal "folk poet," Williams was a very soulful singer. A monumental, though tragic, figure.

The Delmore Brothers: *Best of* . . . (Starday 962)

Late 1940s white boogie.

Sons of the Pioneers: *Country and Western Jamboree* (Camden ADL 2-0579); *Cool Water* (RCA ANLI 1092).

Very Hollywood but very good. Their early sides swing hot country (*Jamboree*). Their later work (*Cool Water*) approaches easy listening. (But this is not necessarily pejorative . . . Bob Nolan's mini-epics and tone poems, such as "Cool Water" and "Tumbling Tumblewoods," clearly influenced later Californians such as Brian Wilson of the Beach Boys.)

Kitty Wells: *Country Hall of Fame* (MCA Coral CDL 8504) U.K. import

Female honkytonk music.

Hank Thompson: *Best of* . . . (Capitol DT 1878)

Texas honkytonk music. Kind of a combination of small band western swing and Hank Williams. Incidently, it seems just about everything in the 1950s and 1960s is a combination of something and Hank Williams. His presence is still discernible in country music.

Merle Travis: *Best of* . . . (Capitol SM 2662) reprocessed for stereo

Includes "Dark as a Dungeon" and "16 Tons." Great guitar. The "Travis style" of playing was a big influence, especially on folk musicians such as Doc Watson and E.C. Ball.

Eddy Arnold: *Cattle Call* (RCA AYLI 3754)

Postwar crossover. Country with strings, all crooning and moon, June, spooning. This was known then as the "Nashville Sound."

Hank Snow: *Best of* . . . *vol. 1 & 2* (RCA LSP-3478 & 4798)

Includes "I'm Movin' On," and "The Golden Rocket." Country boogie, very big in the 1950s.

Marty Robbins: *Gunfighter Ballads and Trail Songs* (Columbia CG-33630)

A million-selling country album. Robbins started about the same time as rock 'n' roll (he even cut a few rockabilly titles). Songs like "El Paso" and "Big Iron" influenced his peers on both sides of the fence.

Bill Monroe: *16 Greatest Hits* (Columbia CS 1065)*

The father of bluegrass. Group here includes Flatt and Scruggs, who later introduced this infectious music to northern college students.

Johnny Cash: *I Walk the Line* (Columbia PC 8990)*; *At Folsom and at San Quinton* (Columbia C6-33639)

Originally in the Sun stable, Cash made such a smooth transition to country no one ever really identified him with rockabilly.

George Jones: *White Lightnin'* (Chiswick 13) U.K. import
Bluesy Alabama-born writer and singer. A real original, his superb style at turns tongue-in-cheek then tragic, Jones has become well known to rock audiences since his cause was picked up by New Waver Elvis Costello.
Patsy Cline: *Country Hall of Fame* (MCA 8077) U.K. import
From the late 1950s, early 1960s—the Nashville Sound (country muzak). Includes "I Fall to Pieces," and "Crazy," with an occasional scorcher like "Walkin' After Midnight."
Anthologies: *Country Hits of the Forties* (Capitol SM 884); *Country Hits of the Fifties* (Capitol ST 885); *Stars of the Grand Ole Opry* (RCA CPL2-0466); *Mister Charley's Blues* (Yazoo 1024); *Dance with the Devil* (Rambler 102)*; Hot as I Am (Rambler 105)

Rhythm and Blues

Some, Lawrence Redd for one, say that rock 'n' roll is rhythm and blues. Maybe. The music, more a cross between jazz, jump, and gospel than generic blues, is very similar. The lyrics, though, are much too "adult." When Wynonie Harris sings about the joys of his fifteen-year-old flame, Little Lucy Brown, he's telling it to the judge, not the malt shop crowd.
Lionel Hampton: *Historical Recording Sessions (1939–1941)* (RCA PM 42417) French import; *Hampton* (Contemporary 3502)
Lionel Hampton, the king of rock 'n' roll? This early swing pioneer, just a little younger than Count Basie, was once billed as such. Just goes to show, I guess that rhythm and blues may be rock 'n' roll. It's certainly extroverted and dance crazy, all thundering drums, honking saxophones, and shouting singers. But rock 'n' roll? The high level of musicianship, attributable to the jazz background of most of the performers, made it hard for the kids to imitate. still the incessant beat and sing-along choruses were a snap. Just snap your fingers!
Louis Jordan: *Best of . . .* (MCA 2-4079)*
Crucial "jump" bandleader with broad crossover appeal. This altoist, singer, and upbeat entertainer with his heavily boogie-based novelty songs warmed the throne for such later stalwarts as Chuck Berry and Bill Haley. Check "Saturday Night Fishfry." Is this 1947?
Wynonie Harris: *Good Rockin' Blues* (King 5040)*
Roy Brown: *Hard Luck Blues* (King 5036)*; *Good Rockin' Tonight* (Route 66 KIK-6) Swedish import
Mentioned together, both are associated with the song "Good Rockin' Tonight." Brown wrote and sang it, Harris just sang it, usually in a big hall over a blaring band without a microphone!
Percy Mayfield: *Best of . . .* (Specialty SPS 2126)
Curtis's father. Includes "Please Send Me Someone to Love," "Strange Things Happening," and "River's Invitation." Important writer and singer of the 1950s. Still active.
Little Willie John: *Free at Last* (King 5034)*
Includes "Fever," "Talk to Me," and "Let Them Talk." Ballads and big band blast-outs. John was a big influence on James Brown, who later recorded on this same label, one of the giant "indies" of the era.
Eddie "Cleanhead" Vinson: *Cherry Red Blues* (King 5035)
More from the King label. Excellent, hard saxophoning and singing from this Texas-born jazz man.
Ruth Brown: *Sweet Baby Mine* (Route 66 KIK 16) Swedish import; *Ruth Brown* (Atlantic 4585)* Japanese import
LaVern Baker: *LaVern Baker* (Atlantic 8007-P-4581A)* U.K. import; *Ladies Sing the Blues* (Savoy SJL 2233)

Dinah Washington: *What a Difference a Day Makes* (Mercury ML 8006)
Female vocalists. Mostly shouters, since a shouter's voice carried the furthest into rock.
Dominoes with Clyde McPhatter: *18 Original Greatest Hits* (King 5006)*
The Five Keys: *14 Original Greatest Hits* (King 5013)
The Ravens: *The Greatest Group of Them All* (Savoy 2227)
Male vocal group. Early doo-wop and/or jump.
Paul Williams: *The Hucklebuck* (Saxophonograph 500)
Jimmy Liggins: *I Can't Stop It* (Route 66 KIK 18) Swedish import
Noble Watts: *Blast Off* (Flyright 547) U.K. import
Earl Bostic: *14 Hits* (King 5099)
Bill Doggett: *14 Hits* (King 5010)
Instrumental rhythm and blues.
Anthologies: *The Original Johnny Otis Show, vol. 1 & 2* (Savoy 2230* & 2252); *Honkers and Screamers* (Savoy 2234)*; *The Shouters* (Savoy 2244); *This is How It All Began* (Specialty 2117)*; *New York Rhythm and Blues* (Flyright 552) U.K. import; *Old King Gold vol. 2* (King KS 16002–498); *Gabe's Dirty Blues* (Gusto GTS 110); *Original Rhythm and Blues 1948-1952* (Sunbeam 401); *Okeh Rhythm and Blues* (Epic EG 37649)*; *Singin' the Blues* (MCA 2-4064)*

ROCK PIONEERS

Figures who began to garner big sales in the blossoming "teen market" without radically altering their early styles.
Fats Domino: *Legendary Masters* (United Artists LWB 9958)*; *Fats Domino Story vols. 1–5* (United Artists UA 30067-30071)* U.K. import
A big man in the emerging big beat style. Fats could rock without sounding like he was disrobing. This made him acceptable to most (most!) parents. He's sold even more records than Pat Boone (see Homogenized Rock).
Bill Haley: *Golden Hits* (MCA 2-4010)*
The first international rock star. "Rock Around the Clock" rocked around the world. Haley mixed country and Louis Jordan-style jump blues. Rock 'n' roll accordian?
Johnny Ace: *Memorial* (MCA X-71)
Equally assured with a ballad or a boomer.
Joe Turner: *Joe Turner* (Atlantic 8005)
Blues shouter turned rock 'n' roll star at forty! Stranger things happen, but not everyday.
Chuck Willis: *King of the Stroll* (Atlantic P-4587)* Japanese import
The king of the stroll (a popular dance) Willis performed wearing a turban instead of a crown. Rock 'n' roll with marimbas!
Huey Smith and the Clowns: *Rockin' Pneumonia and Boogie Woogie Flu* (Chiswick CH9)* U.K. import
Great New Orleans party music with Professor Longhair style piano (see New Orleans Urban Blues), and intentionally sloppy group vocals.
Little Richard: *Grooviest 17 Original Hits* (Specialty 2113)****** *The Fabulous . . .* (Specialty 2104)
The flamboyant, in fact flaming, self-promoted prettiest man in show business. A wild performer, his piano pounding and falsetto "wooing" sound like a 45 r.p.m. single of gospel star Alex Bradford (also on the Specialty label) speeded up to 78!

Hank Ballard and the Midnighters: *20 Hits* (King 5003)
Many of their earliest cuts (e.g. "Work with Me Annie") were emasculated and covered by more wholesome artists. They hit the rhythm-and-blues charts with "The Twist," a largely borrowed melody.
Etta James: *Good Rockin' Mama* (Chiswick 33) U.K. import; *Etta James* (Chess 2000) U.K. import
Hard voice. *Good Rockin' Mama* includes her cover of "Work with Me Annie," "Dance With Me Henry."
The Original Drifters with Clyde McPhatter: *The Early Years* (Atco 33-375)*
First major "gospel-like" Soul vocal group. Their early hits included "Money Honey" and "Whatcha Gonna Do," the tune of which Ballard borrowed for "The Twist."
Ray Charles: *Ray Charles* (Atlantic 8006)* Japanese import
Essential Soul.
Chuck Berry: *Best of . . .* (Gusto 0004)*; *Golden Decade* (Chess 427-008)***** French import; *Golden Decade vol. 2* (Chess 427-009)* French import
Chuck Berry songs are vintage rock 'n' roll at its best. Both visceral and poetic, commercial yet uncompromised.
Bo Diddley: *Bag of Tricks* (Chess 427-011) French import; *I'm a Man* (MF 2042)
Like Berry, Mr. Diddley recorded for Chess. Bo (nee Ellis McDaniels) never found the success of Berry, but at least he has continued to grow as an artist. *I'm a Man* is from the mid-1970s, the "Shave and a Haircut" beat, but somewhat expanded.
Clovers: *The Clovers* (Atlantic P-4588-A) Japanese import
Important bridge between rhythm and blues and rock 'n' roll.
Anthologies: *This is How it All Began vol. 2* (Specialty 2118); *Rock 'n' Roll Dance Party* (Sonet 5022) Dutch import; *The Ace Story vol. 1* (Chiswick CH 11); *Rock 'n' Roll Embers* (Ember 2002)* U.K. import; *Shake Rattle and Roll* (New World 249)*

Rockabilly

Rockabilly caused a stir; panic among parents, panting among participants. It was a music aimed squarely at teenagers, music that advocated "getting wild," getting "Dixie fried," and "ripping it up." This is revolutionary music. People had sung about tearing off the roof before; never had they sounded so serious! And now, not only were they tearing off the roof, they were knocking down the walls as well. Everybody talks about rockabilly being "white boys singing Negro." Certainly that's a major part of it. Rockabilly, though, is really jived-up country music borrowing blues but not appropriating it. Notice how smoothly all the major rockabilly figures made the transition back to solid citizen, country "sanger": Elvis Presley, Johnny Cash, Jerry Lee Lewis, Carl Perkins, Harold Jenkins (Conway Twitty).
Elvis Presley: *The Sun Sessions* (RCA AFM1-1675)*; *Gold Records vol. 1 & 2* (RCA AFLI-1707 & 2075)*; *His Hand in Mine* (RCA ANLI-1319)*; *Legendary Performer vol. 1* (RCA CPL-1-0341); *40 Greatest Hits* (RCA PL-42691)* U.K. Import
Presley's career is the history of the art form in microcosm: the slow gestation, education, percolation, catalyst, big bang, explosive force, propulsion, zenith, coast, gradual attrition, general stagnation, occasional flashes of brilliance, slow fade, dust to dust. Of course, the King must die, the myth is greater than the individual, the Golden Bough as microphone stand.
Otis Blackwell: *These are My Songs* (Inner City 1032)
A collection of songs which Blackwell wrote and performed for Elvis and others. Includes "All Shook Up," and "Whole Lotta Shakin' Goin' On."

Jerry Lee Lewis: *The Essential* (Charly 2001)* U.K. import
Jerry Lee Lewis sounds like he plays piano with his fists! Talk about pounding piano! Lewis can be a genuine wild man. And yet he is capable of great subtlety. Listen, for example, to "Whole Lotta Shakin' Goin' On." This is very controlled hysteria.

Carl Perkins: *Rocking Guitarman* (Charly CR-30003) U.K. import; *Dance Album* (Charly CRM 2012)* U.K. import
A solid singer, composer and guitarist, Perkins may come across as too placid for your average rockabilly rebel. But "Blue Suede Shoes," "Boppin' the Blues," "Honey Don't," and "Matchbox" make him top flight all the way.

Buddy Holly: *The Complete Buddy Holly* (Coral CDM-SP-807) U.K. import; *20 Golden Greats* (MCA 3040)*
Holly, the first near-sighted rock star, was very far-sighted in his intelligent attempts to appeal to as wide an audience as possible. His rave-ups are honest and his ballads are sincere. A very strong writer, his songs are standards, his records classics. Essential.

The Rock 'n' Roll Trio: *Tear It Up* (Solid Smoke 8001)
Johnny and Dorsey Burnette with Paul Burlison. Non-Sun label Memphis rockabilly, a little more country, a little more primitive. Very good.

Gene Vincent: *The Bop That Just Won't Stop* (Capitol SM 11826); *Memorial Album* (Capitol 25156-81001/2)* French import
Capitol record's answer to Elvis, Vincent was even more abandoned in his attack. Attack is the right word. In "Be Bop A Lula" Brother Gene definitely gets wild toward the virginal, some might say frumpy, cartoon character Little Lulu.

Wanda Jackson: *Rockin' with Wanda* (Capitol 1007)* U.K. import
Capitol's female answer to Elvis, Jackson is one of the few truly exuberant rockabilly-ettes. Excellent!

Ritchie Valens: *Best of . . .* (Rhino/Delfi RNDF 200)
Early Latin rocker. Along with Holly and J.R. "Big Bopper" Richards one of the "three stars."

Ronnie Hawkins: *Rockin'* (Pye NSPL 28238) U.K. import
Arkansas rock. Early expatriate (rockabilly missionary?) Moved to Canada, hired the Band for his back-up group, taught them a thing or two.

Billy Lee Reilly: *Legendary Sun Performer* (Charly CR 30131) U.K. import
One of the better "obscure" artists. Why he never made it I'll never know.

The Everly Brothers: *Living Legends* (Warwick WW 5027)*
Their Cadence label material. All their hits, including "Wake Up Little Susie."

Anthologies: *The Sun Box* (Sun Box 100)* U.K. import 3 record set covering blues, country, and rockabilly; *Best of Sun Rockabilly vol. 1* (Charly CR 30123) U.K. import; *Victor Rock 'n' Rollers* (RCA PL 42809)* U.K. import; *Imperial Rockabilly* (United Artists 30103)* U.K. import; *The Million Dollar Quartet* (Sun 1006)* U.K. import; *Rave from the Grave* (Union Pacific UP 004) U.K. import; *Rockabilly Stars vol 1 and 2* (Epic EG-37620 & 37621); *Wild, Wild Young Women* (Rounder 1031)

Doo Wop: Streetcorner Soul

Doo Wop is essentially a capella or mostly vocal harmonizing. It was very popular in the 1950s and early 1960s, especially among urban teenagers. Black groups outnumbered white groups, but the style appealed to both races. There were even a few mixed groups! Much of the sound came out of gospel quartets (the Soul Stirrers, Swan Silvertones, Dixie Hummingbirds) and/or pop singing groups (the Ink Spots and the Mills Brothers). Collectors of the music are extremely fanatical. I risk their ire by including only a few important records.

Chess Doo Wop (Chess 2004)* French import
Moonglows, Flamingos, among others.
Frankie Lymon and the Teenagers (Gee 701)
The Spaniels: *Great Goodley Moo!* (Charly CRM-1021) U.K. import
The El Dorados: *Bim Bam Boom* (Charly CRM-1025) U.K. import
Doo Wop Special (Atlantic 4590) Japan import
Penguins, Crescendos, and others.
Olympics: *Golden Greats* (Everest 4109)
Lee Andrews and the Hearts (Lost-Nite 1)
The Jesters (Lost-Nite 3)*
The Five Satins (Lost-Nite 8)*
Dion and the Belmonts: *Greatest* (Columbia C-31942)
The Persuasions: *Street Corner Symphony* (Capitol 872)*; *Comin' at Ya* (Flying Fish 93); *Stardust* (Catamount 905)

The last group is a contemporary a capella quintet. Not merely a revivalist group, they are perpetuators. Jerry Lawson is an excellent lead singer. The whole group is fine, with heavy gospel and Temptations influence.

Homogenized Rock:
Rock for the Whole Family

Wherein the middle-of-the-road moguls wrest control of the "music industry" out of the hands of the mavericks. Not the nadir some think, but not all that important to the theme of this book either. Thus the list is relatively short.

Elvis Presley: *Gold Records vol. 3 & 4* (RCA LSP-2765 & 3921)
The new Elvis! Many of the principal musical insurrectionists of the late 1950s were by 1960 dead, detained, or delivered. Elvis got drafted. Did the Army make a man out of him? It certainly helped make him seem like a nice boy.

Pat Boone: *16 Great Performances* (MCA DP-4006)
Pat Boone has sold more than fifty million records. That's a lot of saddleshoes, hoss.

Ricky Nelson: *Legendary Masters* (United Artists UAS-9960)
West coast rockabilly. Perhaps because it was recorded so near the ocean, this music sounds a little watered down. Fine lead guitar though (James Burton).

Sam Cooke: *This Is* (RCA UPS-6027)*; *You Send Me* (Camden ACLI-0445)
Cooke is regarded as the father of Soul music, but he was also a major crossover artist. Though many of his productions are overproductions (with strings and inane choruses), many are miracles of simplicity. In both cases this great voice shines through. Essential.

TEEN IDOLS
Bobby Vee: *Singles Album* (United Artists 30253) U.K. import
Frankie Avalon:*Venus* (De-Lite DLT 2020)
Connie Francis: *Very Best* (MGM 4167)
Neil Sedaka: *Pure Gold* (RCA Victor ANLI 1314)

Chubby Checker: *Greatest Hits* (Abkco 4219)
"The twist" and other dance sensations.
  Roy Orbison: *All Time Greatest Hits* (Monument 8600); *More Greatest Hits* (Monument 6621)
"Operatic rock" from former Sun rockabilly.
  Platters: *19 Original Greatest Hits* (King 5002); *Double Gold* (Mercury X-4601)*
Smooth vocal group sounds.
  Coasters: *20 Great Originals* (Atlantic 30057)* U.K. import; *Early Years* (Atco 33-111)*
Humorous little mini-dramas. Mostly written and recorded by Leiber and Stoller.
  Drifters: *Golden Hits* (Atco 8153)*
Specialists in Latin Soul with strings and castanets.

"GIRL" GROUPS

Shangri-Las: *Golden Hits* (Phillips 6336-215) U.K. import
Ronettes: *Greatest Hits* (Phil Spector International 2307-003)* U.K. import
Chiffons: *Everything You Wanted to Hear* (Laurie LRSIP-1001)
Dixie Cups: *Will Live Forever* (Charly CRM 2004) U.K. import
Anthology: *Charly's Angels* (Charly 30143)* U.K. import

Instrumental Rock

While the airwaves were being jammed by the likes of Johnny Tiltson and so on, some hard sounds
were getting through. Rhythm and blues was changing its look and name (see Soul) and instrumentals
were keeping the beat. This instrumental tradition, heavily grounded in r & b and physical jazz,
came out of a need for lounge acts, bands, or records suitable for dancing.
  Duane Eddy: *Legend of Rock* (London 5003/4)* U.K. import; *16 Greatest Hits* (Jamie 3026)
The king of "twang." Heavy reverb guitar.
  The Champs: *Go Champs Go* (Line 6-24598) German import
Including "Tequila."
  Ventures: *Golden Greats* (Liberty LRP 2053)*
The ultimate instrumental rock "combo" (a popular term for these groups).
  Link Wray: *Early Recordings* (Chiswick CH 9) U.K. import
  King Curtis: *Best of* (Atco 33-266)*
  Joe Houston: *All Night Long* (United 7774)
  Wailers: *The Fabulous Wailers* (Allied CR-3075)
The Wailers are an important Pacific Northwest group. This section of the country kept the spirit
of early rock alive well into the 1960s. Its accomplishments are anthologized on *The History of
Northwest Rock vol 1 and 2* (Great Northwest Music Co. GNW 4007 & 4008), which include the
Kingsmen, Dave Lewis, Don and the Goodtimes, Paul Revere and the Raiders, and others.
  Dick Dale and the Deltones: *Greatest Hits* (GNP Crescendo 2095)*
The original Fender guitar surfing sound.
  Anthology: *Rock 'n' Roll Instrumentals vol 1 & 2* (Guitar 76/100 & 76/200)

ROCK 'N' ROLL ANTHOLOGIES
FROM ROCK PIONEERS
THROUGH HOMOGENIZED ROCK
Age of Rock 'n' Roll (MCA 3096) U.K. import

American Graffiti Soundtrack (MCA 2–8007)*
More American Graffiti (MCA 8007)*
Echoes of the Rock (Roulette 113)
Oldies But Goodies
Multi-volume series: cheap pressings, bad sound, low price.
Leiber and Stoller: Only in America (Atlantic K 99098)* U.K. import

THE FOLK BOOM

While sit-ins to protest blatant, intolerable racial injustice were going on at lunch counters throughout the South, similar things were occurring in some of the smokey little clubs where rock 'n' roll first was played. All of a sudden people were sitting down instead of dancing. And they were listening to the words! They were nodding their heads in agreement as often as to the beat.

Roots

Anthology of American Folk Music vol. 3 (Folkways 2953)
The Bible of the revival movement. Excellent anthology and interesting artifact. Covers all aspects of folk, including the blues.
    Folk Revialists/Folk Socialists:
Most of the first folk enthusiasts were political liberals and aesthetic conservatives.
    Woody Guthrie: *Library of Congress Recordings* (Electra EKL 271/2)*; *This Land is Your Land* (Folkways FTS 31001)*; *Dust Bowl Ballads* (RCA CPLI-2099)
Guthrie actually worked harder than he liked to admit. He wrote a thousand songs, many of them American classics. He is generally considered the father of the urban folk movement. If not the father, then at least the first father figure to such important folkies as Bob Dylan, Joan Baez, and Donovan Leitch. To Arlo Guthrie Woody was more than a father figure, of course.
    The Almanac Singers: *Talking Union* (Folkways 35285)
Guthrie, Seeger, and others. The first important "folk group."
    The Weavers: *Greatest Hits* (Vanguard VSD 15/16); *Best of . . .* (MCA 2-4052)
More commercial version of the Almanacs. The first popular "folk group." They even had a hit single, "Goodnight Irene."
    Pete Seeger: *World of . . .* (Columbia C6-31949); *Rainbow Quest* (Folkways 2454)
Alumnus of the above, Seeger comes from a musical family. A tireless traveller, his singing has won him many admirers throughout the world. His talking, heavily political, has often gotten him into trouble.
    Burl Ives: Best of . . . (MCA 24034)
While most of the other folk singers (Seeger, Guthrie, etc.) were blacklisted or intimidated into silence during the McCarthy era, Ives popularized a less militant folk music.

Popular Folk

After the first wave, a second more accessible wave of "professional" folk musicians set in.
    Kingston Trio: *The Folk Era* (Capitol ST 2180); *Greatest Hits vol. 1* (Capitol SM-1705)*

Peter, Paul and Mary: *Best* (Warner Brothers 2552)*
New Christy Minstrels: *Greatest Hits* (Columbia CS 9279)
Brothers Four *Brothers Four* (Columbia CS-8603)
Limelighters: *Pure Gold* (RCA ANLI 2336)

Professional Folk

Joan Baez: *Hits/Greatest and Others* (Vanguard 79332)*; *First Ten Years* (Vanguard 4668); *Ballad Book* (Vanguard 41/42)*
It's hard to believe this woman was once considered a threat to our nation's security. She was so infamous that even Al Capp created a cartoon character around her, Joanie Phoney. She influenced countless teenage sopranos and gave Bob Dylan's career a big boost.

Bob Dylan: *Bob Dylan* (Columbia JC 8579)*; *Freewheelin'* (Columbia JC 8786)*; *Times They Are A-Changin'* (Columbia PC 8905)

Doc Watson: *Essential* (Vanguard VSD 45/46); *On Stage* (Vanguard VSD 9/10)*
A real musician! Excellent guitarist and father of another excellent guitarist. A man for all seasons, adopted by the folk audience, has adapted his approach to their needs. Folk usually means city folk. Most of the participants are urban(e). Watson is country and he played country, until he moved to the city.

Odetta: *Essential* (Vanguard VSD 43/44)
Black folk singer combining elements of blues, gospel, and ballad singing. A very strong voice.

Ian and Sylvia: *Greatest Hits vol. 1 & 2* (Vanguard VSD 5/6 & 23/24)
Early and successful folk/country blend. Ian Tyson's writing is especially strong.

Jim Kweskin Jug Band: *Greatest Hits* (Vanguard VSD 13/14)
Influential Boston-area band. Members included Geof and Maria Muldaur, Bill Keith, and Richard Green.

Richie Havens: *Mixed Bag* (MGM 4598)
Black folk singer/poet. Very popular at Woodstock and for awhile afterward.

Holy Modal Rounders: *Holy Modal Rounders* (Prestige 7720)*
"Psychedelic" folk music. Off beat, humorous, early hippie prototypes.

New Lost City Ramblers: *New Lost City Ramblers* (Folkways FA 2491)
First major "city grass" band featuring Mike Seeger (Pete's half brother).

Judy Collins: *In My Life* (Electra 74027)*; *Wild Flowers* (Electra 74012); *Who Knows Where the Time Goes?* (Electra 74033)
The first truly "pop" folkess, famous for popularizing the work of such writers as Joni Mitchell, Leonard Cohen, and Bob Dylan before the big singer/songwriter boom. She also "covered" rock songs, such as "In My Life," in the folk style.

Buffy Sainte-Marie: *Best of . . .* (Vanguard VSD 3/4)
Native-American folk.

We Shall Overcome (Columbia CS-8901)
The theme song of the civil rights movement.

Anthologies: *Greatest Folk Singers of the 60's* (Vanguard VSD 17/18); *Bread and Roses* (Fantasy 79009)*

An Interesting Offshoot:
Guitar Eccentrics

Solo guitar music has become a kind of "new age easy listening." You hear it on television documentaries, at supermarkets, and in natural food restaurants. It is influencing many young plectarists, especially in the West and Midwest.

John Fahey: *Best of* (Takoma 7058)†; *Essential* (Vanguard 55/56)
Fahey is the father of both this music and the first big label for it (Takoma). His liner notes read as easily as "Finnegin's Wake."

Leo Kottke: *Greenhouse* (Capitol SN-16065); *6/12 String Guitar* (Takoma 7024)*; *Leo Kottke 71–76* (Capitol ST-11576)
Most famous Fahey "student", Kottke has gone on to great fame through his humor, goose-like singing, and dazzling finger pick or slide work.

William Ackerman: *Childhood/Memory* (Windham Hill 1006)*
The father of the new "minimalist" variant and its amazingly popular label (Windham Hill). These records carry no liner notes. They kind of look like ECM jazz label covers, in fact.

Alex DeGrassi: *Slow Circle* (Windham Hill WHS-C-1003)*; *Clockwork* (Windham Hill WHS-C-1018)

Robbie Basho: *Art of the Acoustic Steel String Guitar* (Windham Hill WHS-C-1010)
Other Windham Hill stars. Basho started in the Fahey camp.

Another Offshoot:
Dawg Music

Very hot licks-oriented swing, bluegrass fusion. This modern acoustic music is especially popular with the adroit.

David Grisman Quintet: *David Grisman Quintet* (Kaleidoscope F-5)*; *Rounder Album* (Rounder 0069); *Quintet '80* (Warner Brothers BSK 3469)
Popular enough to be on a major label, Grisman is the force behind this style.

Tony Rice Unit: *Acoustics* (Kaleidoscope F-10)
Guitarist with the above quintet.

Mark O'Connor: *Pickin' in the Wind* (Rounder 68)
The kind of guy that makes music teachers feel ten feet tall! At twelve, O'Connor began blowing people's minds with his musical olympics.

EARLY CALIFORNIA

Developing concomitantly with folk was another mostly middle-class music, the California sound. By this point (the point of no return?) rock 'n' roll musicians were influencing young aspirants. A second generation of rock was evolving. So much for the passing fad theory. If anything was passing it was the baton from hand to hand.

Eddy Cochran: *Legendary Masters* (United Artists LWB 9959)*
Crucial early rock figure. Includes "Summertime Blues," "Cut Across, Shorty," "Come On, Everybody." Cochran was especially popular in the United Kingdom, where he was killed in a traffic accident.

Phil Spector: *Greatest Hits* (Warner/Spector 2SP-9104)******
Twenty-seven Top Ten "mini-operas for kids." Spector is not only the father, but also the mother of the go for broke (baroque?) rock 'n' roll production job. Though most revered for his work in the early 1960s, this enigmatic figure is still a relatively young man in 1982.

The Beach Boys: *Surfer Girl* (Capitol SN-16014); *Surfin' Safari* (Capitol N-16012); *Endless Summer* (Capitol 11307)*; *Good Vibrations: Best of the Beach Boys* (Reprise 6484)*; *Pet Sounds* (Capitol 2458)*
This immensely popular group inherited and combined the legacies left by the previously named two figures. Brian Wilson, a genius, mixed Spector, Cochran, the Four Seasons, the Four Lads, the Students, the Lettermen, Chuck Berry, and just about everything else out at the time with his own unique engineering, musical, and sociological ideas, and came up with the ultimate formula for pop success. It still works for performers like Captain and Tennille and 10 cc. but, sadly, not for the Wilson brothers.

Jan and Dean: *Legendary Masters* (United Artists LWB 9961)
Second-level surf group often produced by Brian Wilson. Similar to the Beach boys, but more informal.

Association: *Greatest Hits* (Warner Brothers 1707)
Vintage non-surfing California rock. Heavy Beach Boys influence.

Anthologies: *Golden Summer* (United Artists LI 627-H2); *California Rock* (Columbia C2-37412)

FIRST BRITISH INVASION

American musical heritage coming back refracted to the United States, and coming back with a vengence. Suddenly, it was the big thing. In fact, almost everything was British, from rock 'n' roll to fashions and accents. The Empire strikes back!

The Beatles: *All lps, but especially: Meet the Beatles* (Capitol ST 2047); *Sergeant Pepper's Lonely Hearts Club Band* (Capitol SMAS 2653)*; *The Beatles;1962–1966* (Apple 3403)*; *The Beatles/1967–1970* (Apple 3404)*

John Lennon: *Plastic Ono Band* (Apple 3372)*; *Mind Games* (Apple 3414)*; *Walls and Bridges* (Apple 3416)

Paul McCartney: *McCartney* (Apple 3363); *Band on the Run* (Apple 3415)*

George Harrison: *All Things Must Pass* (Apple 639); *Living in the Material World* (Apple 3410)

Ringo Starr: *Sentimental Journey* (Apple 3365).

The Rolling Stones: *Big Hits: High Tide and Green Grass* (London NPS-1)*; *Through the Past Darkly* (London NPS-3); *England's Newest Hit Makers* (London PS-375)*; *Aftermath* (London PS-539); *Between the Buttons* (London PS-499); *Beggar's Banquet* (London PS-539)*; *Let It Bleed* (London NPS-4)*; *Hot Rocks* 64-712 (London 2PS-606/607); *Out of Our*

Heads (London PS-429); *Sticky Fingers* (Rolling Stones RLS-39105)*; *Tatoo You* (Rolling Stones 16052)

The Who: *Magic Bus/My Generation* (MCA 2-4068)*; *Sell Out/Happy Jack* (MCA 2-4067), *Tommy* (MCA 2-1005)*; *Live at Leeds* (MCA 37000)*; *Who's Next* (MCA 3024); *By Numbers* (MCA 2161); *Who Are You?* (MCA 37003)
First "power trio."

Kinks: *Greatest Hits* (Reprise 6217)

Animals: *Best of* . . . (Abkco AKO 42260)*; *Greatest Hits* (MGM 4602)

John Mayall and the Bluesbreakers: *John Mayall and the Bluesbreakers* (London LC-50009); *Hard Road* (London PS-502)

Them: *Story of Them* (London LC 50001); *featuring Van Morrison* (Parrot PRR-BP-71053/4)*
Includes, "Here Comes the Night" and that teenage anthem to end all teenage anthems, "Gloria." Though another group had the hit, Them's lead singer, Van Morrison, wrote it.

Manfred Mann: *Best of* (Capitol N-16073); *Roaring Silence* (WBR BK-3-55)
Came back as the Earth Band with a Springsteen cover, "Blinded by the Light," thus proving to some that Bruce was the new Dylan after all.

Yardbirds: *Greatest Hits* (Epic 26246)
Early psychedelic experimenters, spotlighting great lead guitarists such as Jeff Beck, Eric Clapton, and Jimmy Page.

Zombies: *Early Days* (London PS-557)

The Hollies: *Greatest Hits* (Epic PE-32061); *Greatest* (Capitol N-16056)

Mop Top Groups

Gerry and the Pacemakers: *Best of* (Capitol SM-11898)

Herman's Hermits: *Herman's Hermits* (ABKCO AKO 4227)

The Seekers: *Best of* . . . (Capitol SN-16104)

American Mop Tops

The Young Rascals: *Greatest Hits* (Atco 8190)*
Excellent New York area "blue-eyed soul" band. Dropped the "young" from their name as their style matured.

Sir Douglas Quintet: *Best of* . . . (Takoma 7086)*
Their name was designed to confuse the anglophilic public into thinking they came from across the sea.

Gary Lewis and the Playboys: *Golden Greats* (Liberty 7468) Produced by Leon Russell.

Jay and the Americans: *Greatest 'Hits* (United Artists LM 1010)

Paul Revere and the Raiders: *Greatest Hits* (Columbia C-35593)

Tommy James and the Shondells: *Best of* . . . (Roulette 42040)

Bobby Fuller Four: *Best of* . . . (Rhino/Delfi RNDF-201)

Left Bank: *Walk Away, Renee* (Smash Single 1416)*

Mitch Rider and the Detroit Wheels: *Mitch Rider !* . . . (Roulette 200634.270) German import
Beau Brummels: *Best of* . . . (Rhino RNLP 101)
First major "San Francisco Band." Produced by Sylvester Stewart.
Monkees: *Greatest Hits* (Arista 4089)
Television's answer to the Beatles. Unbelievably popular.

FOLK ROCK

Add the impact of the Beatles to the background of the folk movement and you get folk rock. Very popular in the mid-1960s.

Bob Dylan: *Another Side of* (Columbia PC 8993)*; *Bringing It All Back Home* (Columbia JC 9128)*; *Highway 61 Revisited* (Columbia JC 9189)*; *Blonde on Blonde* (Columbia)*
Bob Dylan is the "father" of folk rock and possibly the most important songwriter of his generation. It is impossible to overestimate his influence both lyrically and musically. He tends to write anthems more than songs and "speaks" whether consciously or coincidently for his generation.

Byrds: *Best of* . . . (Columbia C-31795)*; *Mr. Tambourine Man* (Columbia 9172); *5-D* (Columbia CS-9349); *Sweetheart of the Rodeo* (Columbia CS-9670)*
Like Dylan, the Byrds were important trend setters of the 1960s. They were the first major post-Beatle American band, one of the first "Dylan cover bands" (*Mr. Tambourine Man* for instance), one of the first psychedelic bands (*5-D* album), and one of the first country rock bands (*Sweetheart of the Rodeo*).

The Lovin' Spoonful: *Best of* . . . (Buddah BDS 5706)*
Important "Top 40" group. John Sebastian was their leader. They had a big influence on the emergent "hippie" sound.

Simon and Garfunkel: *The Sounds of Silence* (Columbia 9269); *Parsley, Sage, Rosemary, and Thyme* (Columbia 9363)*; *Bridge Over Troubled Water* (Columbia 9914)*; *Greatest Hits* (Columbia 31350)*
"Librarian Rock!" Outsold Dylan, but never got the highbrow or hippie acceptance. Important "pop rock."

The Mamas and Papas: *20 Golden Hits* (Dunhill DXS 50145)*
Very popular group. Broad crossover appeal. Their leader, John Phillips, helped organize the Monterey Pop Music Festival.

Donovan: *Greatest Hits* (Epic BXN 26439)
Began as the "British Dylan" (acoustic guitar, harmonica, Greek fisherman's cap), his first hit even made reference to the wind! However, when he went electric and leaned more towards jazz than blues, Donovan finally shook the shadow.

Sonny and Cher: *Best of* . . . (Atco 219)
Spector protegé Sonny Bono and wife. First famous for their "wild costumes," later for their Las Vegas act and television show.

The Turtles: *1968* (Rhino 901)
Tom Rush: *The Circle Game* (Elektra 74018)*
Paul Butterfield Blues Band: *East/West* (Elektra 7315)* *Golden Butter* (Elektra ELK-7E-2005)*

The Blues Project: *The Blues Project* (Elektra ELK 7264)
Two important American "white blues bands" who traveled the folk circuit. Butterfield's group included Mike Bloomfield, an early guitar idol, and the Blues Project included Al Kooper, an important keyboard player and producer.

EARLY SOUL

Soul, like rock, is a convenience term. Most often it is used to mean teen-oriented Black music of the 1960s and 1970s. Soul and rock have frequently dovetailed, especially during the "British Invasion" and the disco boom, but I list it separately since the tradition is distinct. This list is hardly comprehensive. I stick mostly to rock-influenced records.
    James Brown: *Solid Gold* (Polydor 2679.044)***** U.K. import; *Live at the Apollo, vol. 1* (Solid Smoke 8006)*; *Best of* (Polydor PD-1-6340); *Can Your Heart Stand It!!!* (Solid Smoke 8013)
Mister dynamite, mister outta sight. The king of showbusiness, the king of rhythm and blues. . . . James Brown is not modest, though his beginnings were. Still, much of what soul brother number one boasts has basis. Certainly he was the single most important figure in the music for almost twenty years. Socially he has been a respected voice. Musically he has either helped invent or popularized screaming, intense "hard soul," funk, rapping, long jams, bad jams, and disco.
    Jackie Wilson: *Solid Gold* (Brunswick G-111)*
Brilliant hard-driving singer. A dynamic performer with operatic strength and range. Pre-Motown Barry Gordy production. From here it would be not only easy, but sensible to divide our list according to label, as each tended to have its own sound, its own producers and its own stars.

MOTOWN
In some ways ahead of, in other ways right behind James Brown in importance. More important because the deliberately designed "sound of young America" crossed over more often and more dramatically; less important because the family at Motown did not "speak for the people" nor originate as many innovations as the "godfather of soul" did.
    Marvin Gaye: *Anthology* (M9-79431)*; *What's Goin' On* (Tamla T6-31051)*
    Four Tops: *Greatest Hits* (M7-662); *Anthology* (M9809 s3)
    Supremes: *The Supremes* (M 9794)*
    Martha and the Vandellas: *Martha and the Vandellas* (M5-111)*
    Temptations: *Anthology* (M7-8243)*
    Miracles: *Anthology* (M7-93R3)*
    Junior Walker and the Allstars: *Anthology* (M7-796R2)
    Jackson 5: *Anthology* (M7-868)
    Stevie Wonder: *Looking Back* (Anthology) (M-804 LP 3)*; *Motown Revue vol. 2* (M5-20641)*

STAX/VOLT/ATLANTIC
Otis Reading: *Best of* (Atco 25A-301)
Aretha Franklin: *Greatest Hits* (Atco 8295)*; *Gold* (Atlantic SD-8227)*

Wilson Pickett: *Greatest Hits* (Atlantic SD-2-501)*
Sam and Dave: *Best* (Atlantic SD-8218)
Solomon Burke: *Best of* . . . (Atco 8109)
Percy Sledge: *Best of* . . . (Atlantic 8210)
Anthologies: *Soul Years* (Atco 2-504)*; *Stax 15 Original Big Hits, vol. 2*
(Stax 8502)

VEE JAY

An important Chicago blues and rhythm and blues label. Most albums are out of print domestically.
The Impressions: *The Vintage Years* (Sire SASH 3717-2)*
Jerry Butler: *Up on Love* (Charly CRB 1005)* U.K. import
Betty Everett: *Hot to Hold* (Charly CRB 1006) U.K. import

SOUL FROM NEW ORLEANS

Lee Dorsey: *Gonna Be Funky* (Charly CRB 1001)*
A highly recommended New Orleans soul record.
All of These Things (Bandy 7007)
We Sing the Blues (Bandy 70010)*
Both are recommended anthologies.

THE HIPPIE, HIPPIE SHAKE

Hippie music was not dance music; it was more mental than physical. The imagination danced.

Bay Area

Generally speaking, the Bay Area bands were very ecclectic, blending folk, rock, soul, blues, a misunderstanding of classical Indian methods, cheap electronic gimmicry. John Coltrane's kind of jazz without the chops and on guitar instead of saxophone.
Grateful Dead: *Grateful Dead* (Warner Brothers WS-1689); *Anthem of the Sun* (Warner Brothers WS 1749); *Live/Dead* (Warner Brothers WB 1830); *Bear's Choice* (Warner Brothers BS-2721)
Jefferson Airplane: *Surrealistic Pillow* (RCA AYLI-3738)*; *After Bathing at Baxter's* (RCA AFLI- 4545); *Crown of Creation* (RCA AYLI-3797); *Volunteers* (RCA AYLI-3867); *Worst of* . . . (RCA AYLI-3661)*
Jefferson Starship: *Blows Against the Empire* (RCA AYLI-3868)*; *Red Octopus* (Grunt 0999); *Gold* (Grunt BZLI-3247)*
Hot Tuna: *Hot Tuna* (RCA AYLI-3864)
Janis Joplin: *Cheap Thrills* (Columbia 9700)*; *Pearl* (Columbia 30322)*; *Greatest Hits* (Columbia 32168)*
Electric Flag: *A Long Time Comin'* (Columbia 9597)*

Steve Miller Band: *Sailor* (Capitol 2984); *Children of the Future* (Capitol SKAO 2920)
Quicksilver Messanger Service: *Quicksilver Messanger Service* (Capital 2904)*
Santana: *Santana* (Columbia PC 9781); *Borboletta* (Columbia PC 33135); *Greatest Hits* (Columbia PC 33050); *Welcome* (Columbia 32445); *Abraxis* (Columbia HC 40130)
Country Joe and the Fish: *Electric Music for Mind and Body* (Vanguard 79224); *From Haight Ashbury to Woodstock* (Vanguard VSD 6545)
Creedence Cleerwater Reival: *1969* (Fantasy FSY-CCR 69); *1970* (Fantasy FSY-CCR 70); *More Creedence Gold* (Fantasy FSY-9430)*
Moby Grape: *Moby Grape* (Columbia 9498)
Youngbloods: *This is . . .* (RCA VPS-6051)
East coast emigrees, most famous for "Let's Get Together," a hippie anthem of sorts.
It's a Beautiful Day: *It's a Beautiful Day* (Columbia 11790-5)
Rock violin, early "jazz rock."
Dan Hicks and His Hot Licks: *Striking It Rich* (MCA 670)
More recent group for Hicks, an original member of the "first" hippie group, the Charlatans. Very swing/hot jazz-oriented acoustic group. Excellent guitar (Jon Girtin) and violin (Sid Page).
Blue Cheer: *Vincebus Eruptum* (Phillips: PL 9001)
Sly and the Family Stone: *Greatest Hits* (Epic PE-30325)*
Very important Soul/rock band. Sly Stewart laid much of the groundwork for funk style.

Los Angeles

L.A. always has been a musical capital, so the bold adventuring three hundred miles to the north altered consciousness more than music here.
The Doors: All lps, but especially: *The Doors* (Elektra 74007)*; *Greatest Hits* (Elektra 5E-515)*
Buffalo Springfield: *Buffalo Springfield* (Atco 200); *Again* (Atco 226); *Retrospective* (Atco 38-105)*
Gained widespread popularity only after breaking up. The members included Steve Stills, Neil Young, Richie Furay, and Jim Messina.
Steppenwolf: *16 Greatest Hits* (MCA 37049)
Iron Butterfly: *In-a-Gadda-da-Vida* (Atco 250)
From the fall of 1968 to the summer of 1969 this record remained on the charts longer than the Beatles, Airplane, Dead, Stones, Smokey Robinson, James Brown, anybody!
Canned Head: *Boogie with . . .* (Liberty LN 10105)
Spirit: *Best of . . .* (Epic 32271)
Captain Beefheart and His Magic Band: *Trout Mask Replica* (Reprise 2027)
Taj Mahal: *Taj Mahal* (Columbia CS 9579); *Natch'l Blues* (Columbia CS-9698)*

East Coast

Can you imagine Tuli Kupferberg with flowers in his hair? This is soot-covered, urban hippie music. More cynical and/or bombastic than the others.
The Velvet Underground: *. . . and Nico* (Verve 5008)*; *White Light/White Heat* (Verve 5046); *Loaded* (Cotillion 9034); *Rock and Roll Diary* (Arista A2L 8603)*

The Fugs: *The Fugs* (ESP 1028)

Vanilla Fudge: *Vanilla Fudge* (Atco 224)

Blood, Sweat and Tears: *Child is Father to the Man* (Columbia 9720); *Greatest Hits* (Columbia 31170)*

British

Much louder, more obviously blues-based, more structured than the American sound. This might be called the second British invasion.

Jimi Hendrix: *Are You Experienced?* (Reprise 6261)*; *Axis: Bold as Love* (Reprise 6281)*; *Electric Ladyland* (Reprise 6307); *Cry of Love* (Reprise 2034)*; *Rainbow Bridge* (Reprise 2040); *Band of Gypsies* (Capitol 472); *Smash Hits* (Reprise 2276); *Soundtrack* (Reprise 2RS 6481)

Cream: *Disraeli Gears* (RSO-1-3010)*; *Goodbye* (RSO-1-3013); *Best of Cream* (Atco 291)

Jeff Beck: *Truth* (Epic 26413); *Beck-Ola* (Epic 33779); *Early* (ACD SN-7141)*

Procul Harum: *Best of . . .* (A&M 4401)*; *A Salty Dog* (A&M SP 4179)

Moody Blues: *Days of Future Passed* (Deram 18012)*; *In Search of the Lost Chord* (Deram 18017); *A Question of Balance* (Threshold 3); *Seventh Sojourn* (Threshold 7)

Symphonic rock.

Joe Cocker: *With a Little Help From My Friends* (A&M D-4182); *Mad Dogs and Englishmen* (A&M 6002)*

Ten Years After: *Sssh* (Chrysalis CH 1083); *Classic Performances* (Columbia 34366)

Savoy Brown: *Raw Sienna* (Parrot PAS 71036); *Best of . . .* (London LC 50000)

Led Zeppelin: *Led Zeppelin* (Atlantic 8216)*; *II* (Atlantic 8236); *III* (Atlantic 7201); *IV* (Atlantic 7208); *House of the Holy* (Atlantic 9255)*; *Physical Graffiti* (Swan Song 2-200); *Presence* (Swan Song 8415); *The Song Remains the Same* (Swan Song 2-201)

Bonzo Dog: *History of the . . .* (United Artists LWB 321); *Best of . . .* (United Artists LKAO 5517)

Pentangle: *Sweet Child* (Reprise 6334)*

Excellent U.K. folk/jazz rock group.

Rod Stewart: *Every Picture Tells a Story* (Mercury 609); *Gasoline Alley* (Mercury 61264); *Blondes Have More Fun* (Mercury 3261)

Elton John: *Greatest, vol. 1 & 2* (MCA 5224 & 5225)

Pink Floyd: *Ummagumma* (Harvest 388)*

Jethro Tull: *Stand Up* (Chrysalis CHR-1042); *Aqualung* (Chrysalis CH4 1044)*; *M.U. (Best of)* (Chrysalis CYS 1078); *Thick as a Brick* (Chrysalis CHR 1003)

Early "theatrical rock."

Fairport Convention: *Leige and Lief* (A&M 4257)*

Traffic: *Mr. Fantasy* (United Artists LO-6651); *Low Spark of High Heeled Boys* (Island ILPS 9180)*; *Shootout at a Fantasy Factory* (Island ILPS 9224); *Best of* (United Artists 5500)

COUNTRY (NATURAL) ROCK

A major post-psychedelic trend toward softer and simpler sounds. Emphasis on the positive, the upbeat and the pollution-free. Idyllic rock/rustic rock.

Dillard and Clark: *Through the Morning/Through the Night* (A&M SP-4203)
The Flying Burrito Brothers: *Gilded Palace of Sin* (A&M 4175); *Burrito Deluxe* (A&M 4258)
Graham Parsons: *GP* (Reprise MS-2123); *Grievous Angel* (Reprise 2171)
Emmylou Harris: *Quarter Moon in a Ten-Cent Town* (Warner Brothers WB-BSK-3141)*; *Profile* (Best of) (Warner Brothers 3258); *Luxury Liner* (Warner Brothers BSK-3115); *Pieces of the Sky* (Reprise 2284); *Elite Hotel* (Reprise MSK 2286)
The Band: *The Band* (Capitol STAO 132)*; *Rock of Ages, vol. 1* (Capitol SN 16008)
The Grateful Dead: *Workingman's Dead* (Warner Brothers 1869); *American Beauty* (Warner Brothers 1893); *Europe '72* (Warner Brothers SWX 2668); *Dead Reckoning* (Arista A2L-8604)
New Riders of the Purple Sage: *New Riders of the Purple Sage* (Columbia PC 30888)
Nitty Gritty Dirt Band: *Will the Circle Be Unbroken* (United Artists UAS 9801)
Commander Cody and His Lost Planet Airmen: *Lost in the Ozone* (MCA 37107); *Live From Deep in the Heart of Texas* (MCA 659)
Poco: *Deliverin'* (Epic 30209); *A Good Feelin' to Know* (Epic 31601); *Very Best of . . .* (Epic PE6-33537)
Crosby, Stills and Nash: *Crosby Stills and Nash* (Atco 19117)*
Crosby, Stills, Nash and Young: *Deja Vu* (Atco 19118)*
Neil Young: *Decade* (Warner Brothers 3RS-2257); *Everybody Knows This is Nowhere* (Warner Brothers MSR-2282)*; *Rust Never Sleeps* (Warner Brothers HS 2295)
Steven Stills: *Steve Stills* (Atlantic JP 7202)
Graham Nash: *Songs for Beginners* (Atco 7204)
David Crosby: *If I Could Only Remember My Name* (Atco 7203)*
Dan Fogelberg: *Home Free* (Epic 31751); *Netherlands* (Epic 34185); *Captured Angel* (Epic 33499); *Souvineers* (Epic PE 33137)*
Fire Fall: *Fire Fall* (Atlantic SD 19125); *Best of . .* (Atlantic 19316)
Asleep at the Wheel: *Texas Gold* (Capitol ST-11441); *Collision Course* (Capitol SW 11726)
Joe Ely: *Hard Country* (Epic SE 37367); *Live Shots* (MCA 5262)
Doctor Hook and the Medicine Show: *Best of . . .* (Columbia 34147)
Bob Dylan: *John Wesley Harding* (Columbia PC 9604)*; *Nashville Skyline (Columbia PC 9825); New Morning* Columbia PC 30290)

Oklahoma Rock

Sooner rock! For a brief period in the mid-1970s, Oklahoma, of all places, became an important rock area. The sound is a cross between L.A. rock (many of the musicians have spent time there) and Southern rock.

Leon Russell: *Leon Russell* (Shelter SRL 52007); *. . . and the Shelter People* (Shelter SRL 52008)
J.J. Cale: *Naturally* (MCA 37104); *Troubadour* (MCA 37103)*
Delaney and Bonnie: *On Tour* (Atco 326)*
Eric Clapton: *Layla* (RSO 2-3801)*; *Just One Night* (RSO RS-2-4202)*; *Slow Hand* (RSO RS-1-3030)*; *461 Ocean Boulevard* (RSO 1-3023)
Clapton is actually British, but was profoundly influenced by time spent in and around Tulsa.

SOUTHERN ROCK

The Allman Brothers Band: *Live at the Filmore* (Capricorn CPN-2-0131); *Eat a Peach* (Capricorn CPN-2-0102)*; *Brothers and Sisters* (Capricorn CPN 0111)*

Lynryd Skynyrd: *Pronounced* (MCA 5221)*; *2nd Helping* (MCA 5222); *One More for the Road* (MCA 2-10014)

Marshall Tucker: *Marshall Tucker Band* (Warner Brothers WB 3608); *Where We All Belong* (Warner Brothers WB 3608); *Greatest Hits* (Warner Brothers BSK 3611)

Charlie Daniels Band: *Night Rider* (Epic PE 34402); *Fire on the Mountain* (Epic PE 34365)*

Amazing Rhythm Aces: *Amazing Rhythm Aces* (Columbia CPN-2-0131)

Atlanta Rhythm Section: *Are You Ready?* (Polydor 2-6236)

Elvin Bishop: *Struttin' My Stuff* (Capricorn CPN 0165)*

Dixie Dregs: *Night of the Living Dregs* (Capricorn 0216)*

Molly Hatchet: *Molly Hatchet* (Epic JE 35347)

Outlaws: (Arista AB 4042)

Ozark Mountain Daredevils: *The Best of . . .* (A&M SP 3202)

Pure Prairie League: *Collection* (RCA Int 5101)* U.K. import

Jimmy Buffett: *White Sport Coat and Pink Crustacean* (MCA 37026); *Changes in Latitudes, Changes in Attitudes* (MCA 37150)

Anthologies: *South's Greatest Hits, vol. 1 & 2* (Capricorn CPN 0187 & 0209)*; *Volunteer Jam* (Capricorn 0172)

FOLK POP AND POP ROCK

Folk with pop overtones (such as, heavy production, "contemporary" lyrics, commercial success).

America: *Greatest Hits* (Warner Brothers WBR K 3110)*

Arlo Guthrie: *Best of . . .* (Warner Brothers K 3117); *Alice's Restaurant* (Reprise 6267)

Carly Simon *Best of . . .* (Elektra 6E-109)*

Cat Stevens: *Teaser and the Firecat* (A&M 4313); *Tea for the Tillerman* (A&M 4280); *Catch Bull at Four* (A&M 4365); *Greatest Hits* (A&M SP 4519)*

Don McLean: *American Pie* (United Artist UAS 5535)*

Neil Diamond: *Gold* (MCA 2007); *12 Greatest* (MCA 5219)

Seals and Crofts: *Summer Breeze* (Warner Brothers BS 2629); *Greatest Hits* (Warner Brothers BSK 3109)

Morris Albert: *Feelings* (RCA Victor AYLI 3876)

The Roches: *The Roches* (Warner Brothers WB 3298)

Melanie: *Best of . . .* (Buddha 5705)

SINGER/SONGWRITERS

People known or critically acclaimed for their songs. Many of their songs have been recorded by others.

Tim Hardin: *Memorial* (Polydor PD-1-6333)*

Talented, but self-destructive New York folkie. Songs include "Misty Roses," "Reason to Believe," "If I Were a Carpenter."

Fred Neil: *Everybody's Talkin'* (Capitol St-294)*
Talented, but reclusive, New York folkie who retired to the Florida Keys in the late 1960s.
Gordon Lightfoot: *Very Best* (United Artists UALA 243-6)
First major Canadian singer to succeed in America since Hank Snow.
Leonard Cohen: *Leonard Cohen* (Columbia 2733); *Best of . . .* (Columbia JC 34077)
Van Morrison: *Astral Weeks* (Warner Brothers 1768)*; *Moondance* (Warner Brothers 1835)*;
Tupelo Honey (Warner Brothers 1950); *St. Dominic's Preview* (Warner Brothers 2633)*;
Beautiful Vision (Warner Brothers 3652); *This is Where I Came In* (Bang 6467-625)* U.K.
import
Randy Newman: *12 Songs* (Reprise 6373)*; *Sail Away (Reprise 2064)*
Joni Mitchell: *Clouds* (Reprise 6341); *Joni Mitchell* (Reprise 6293); *Blue* (Reprise 2038)*;
Ladies of the Canyon (Reprise 6376); *For the Roses* (Asylum 5057)*; *Court and Spark*
(Asylum 1001); *Miles of Aisles* (Asylum 202)
Laura Nyro: *New York Tendaberry* (Columbia 9737); *Christmas and the Beads of Sweat*
(Columbia 30259)
Phil Ochs: *I Ain't Marching Anymore* (Elektra 7287)
James Taylor: *Sweet Baby James* (Warner Brothers 1843); *Mudslide Slim and the Blue
Horizon* (Warner Brothers 2561); *Greatest Hits* (Warner Brothers BSK 3113)*
Carole King: *Tapestry* (Ode 77009)*; *Music* (Ode 77013); *Wrap Around Joy* (Ode 77024)
Paul Simon: *There Goes Rhymin' Simon* (Columbia 32280)*; *Still Crazy After All These
Years* (Columbia 33540)
John Prine: *John Prine* (Atlantic SD 8296); *Prime Prine* (Best of . . .) (Atlantic SD 18202)
John Sebastian: *John Sebastian* (Reprise 6379)*
John Denver: *Greatest Hits* (RCA CPLI 0374)
Jackson Browne: *Jackson Browne* (Asylum 5051); *Late for the Sky* (Asylum 7E-1017);
Running on Empty (Asylum 6E-113A)*
Janis Ian: *Stars* (Columbia 32857); *Between the Lines* (Columbia 33394)
Garland Jefferies: *Ghost Writer* (A&M 4629); *American Boy and Girl* (A&M 4778)
Joan Armatrading: *Show Some Emotion* (A&M 4663); *Me, Myself, I* (A&M 4809)
Bruce Cockburn: *Dancing in the Dragon's Jaw* (Millenium BXLI 7747)*
Tom Waits: *Closing Time* (Asylum SD 5061)*; *Heart of a Saturday* (Asylum 7E 1015)*;
Blue Valentine (Asylum 6E 162); *Nighthawks at the Diner* (Asylum 7E 2008)*
Excellent L.A. "lowlife" poet and barroom pianist. Smokey voice, whiskey stained throat.
Michael Franks: *The Art of Tea* (Reprise 2230)*
Harry Chapin: *Greatest Stories Live* (Elektra 8E 6003)
Bob Dylan: *Blood on the Tracks* (Columbia PS 33235); *Planet Waves* (Asylum 7E 1003);
Slow Train Comin' (Columbia DC 36120)*

L.A. INTERNATIONAL

Ry Cooder: *Into the Purple Valley* (Reprise 2052)*; *Chicken Skin Music* (Reprise 2254)*;
Showtime (Warner Brothers 3059)*; *Bop Until You Drop* (Warner Brothers 3358)*
War: *Greatest Hits* (United Artists LA 648-6)*; *The World is a Ghetto* (United Artists S 652)*
Chicago: *Greatest Hits* (Columbia JC 33900); *Transit Authority* (Columbia JC 33)
Alice Cooper: *Greatest Hits* (Warner Brothers BSK 3107)

Bonnie Raitt: *Bonnie Raitt* (Warner Brothers WS 1953); *Give It Up* (Warner Brothers 2643); *Green Light* (Warner Brothers 3630)*

Little Feat: *Sailin' Shoes* (Warner Brothers 2600)*; *Dixie Chicken* (Warner Brothers 2686); *Waiting for Columbus* (Warner Brothers 2BS 3140)*

Loggins and Messina: *Sittin' In* (Columbia PC 31044); *Full Sail* (Columbia PC 32540)

Linda Ronstadt: *Different Drum* (Capital ST 11269); *Greatest Hits, vol. 1 & 2* (Asylum 6E-106 & 5E-516)

Fleetwood Mac: *In Chicago* (Sire 2XS 6009); *Future Games* (Reprise 6465); *Bare Trees* (Reprise 2278); *Fleetwood Mac* (Reprise K 2281)*; *Rumours* (Warner Brothers BSK 3010)*

Eagles: *Greatest Hits* (Asylum 6E 105)*; *Desperado* (Asylum 5068); *Hotel California* (Asylum 6E 103)

Steely Dan: *Can't Buy a Thrill* (ABC 758); *Pretzel Logic* (ABC 808); *Aja* (ABC 1006); *Greatest Hits* (ABC 1107/2)

Doobie Brothers: *Best of . . .* (Warner Brothers L 3112)*; *Takin' It to the Street* (Warner Brothers 3899); *Minute by Minute* (Warner Brothers K-3193)*

Christopher Cross: *Christopher Cross* (Warner Brothers L 3383)

Dire Straits: *Dire Straits* (Warner Brothers K 3266)

The Knack: *Get the* (EMI 11948)

Rickie Lee Jones: *Rickie Lee Jones* (Warner Brothers 3296); *Pirates* (Warner Brothers 3432)

Toto: *Toto* (Columbia JC 35317)

Maria Muldaur: *Maria Muldaur* (Warner Brothers 2148)*

Nicolette Larson: *Nicolette* (Warner Brothers BSK 3243)

Warren Zevon: *Excitable Boy* (Asylum 6E 118)*

Cheech and Chong: *Greatest Hits* (Warner Brothers BSK 3614)

THROWBACK ROCK

Contemporary, but they follow earlier forms.

Bruce Springsteen: All lp's but especially: *Born to Run* (Columbia 33798)*

Tom Petty and the Heartbreakers: *Damn the Torpedoes* (Backstreet MCA 5105)*; *You're Gonna Get It (MCA 37116); Hard Promises* (Backstreet MCA 5160)

Boz Scaggs: *Silk Degrees* (Columbia 33920); *Hits* (Columbia FC 36841); *Boz Scaggs* (Atlantic SD 19166)

Steve Miller: *The Joker* (Capitol 11235); *Fly Like an Eagle* (Capitol SW 11497); *Greatest Hits 74–78* (Capitol 11872)*

Hall and Oates: *Abandoned Luncheonette* (Atco 19139)*; *Private Eyes* (RCA AFLI 4028); *Bigger Than Both of Us* (RCA AYLI 3866)

Average White Band: *Average White Band* (Atlantic 19116)*

Mink Deville: *Le Chat Bleu* (Capitol ST 11955); *Cabretta* (Capitol ST 11631)*

Steve Winwood: *Arc of the Diver* (Island ILPS 9576)

Doctor John: *His Best . . .* (Pickwick 263)

Bob Seger: *Against the Wind* (Capitol 500-12041); *Night Moves* (Capitol ST 11557)*; *Tonight at Nine* (Capitol STBK 12182)

Roy Buchanan: *Live Stock* (Polydor 6048)*; *Loading Zone* (Atco 19138)

Peter Frampton: *Comes Alive* (A&M PR 3703)*

Fabulous Thunderbirds: *Fabulous Thunderbirds* (Takoma 7068)

Steeleye Span: *Below the Salt* (Chrysalis CHR 1008)*; *Parcel of Rogues* (Chrysalis CHR 1040)
George Thorogood and the Destroyers: *George Thorogood and . . .* (Rounder 3013); *More* (Rounder 3024)

HARD ROCK/HEAVY METAL

Carnivorous rock! Dual carberator guitars. Largely white, male audience.

British

Black Sabbath: *Black Sabbath* (Warner Brothers 1871); *Bloody Sabbath* (Warner Brothers 2695)
Deep Purple: *Deep Purple in Rock* (Warner Brothers 1877)
Uriah Heep: *Best of . . .* (Mercury SRM-1-1070)
Queen: *Greatest Hits* (Elektra 5E 564); *A Night at the Opera* (Elektra 7E 1053); *The Game* (Elektra 5E 513)
Mott the Hoople: *All the Young Dudes* (Columbia PC 31750); *Greatest Hits* (Columbia PC 34368)
Supertramp: *Breakfast in America* (A&M SP 3708)*; *Crime of the Century* (A&M 3647); *Paris* (A&M 6702)
Judas Priest: *Hell Bent for Leather* (Columbia JC 35706)
Robin Trower: *Live* (Chrysalis CHR 1089); *Bridge of Sighs* (Chrysalis CHR 1057)
Foreigner: *4* (Atlantic 16999); *Double Vision* (Atlantic 19999)
Bad Company: *Bad Company* (Swan Song 8507); *Burnin' Sky* (Swan Song 8500)*
Genesis: *ABACAB* (Atlantic 19313); *Duke* (Atlantic SD 16014); *Selling England by the Pound* (Atlantic 19277); *Your Own Special Way* (Atlantic SP 38-100)
ELO: *Box of Their Best* (Jet Z4X 36966); *El Dorado* (Jet JZ 35526); *Ole Elo* (Jet JZ 35538)
Free: *Free* (A&M 4204); *Best of . . .* (A&M 3663)
Ozzy Osbourne: *Diary of a Madman* (Jet F2 37492)
Wishbone Ash: *Wishbone Ash* (MCA 2343); *Argus* (MCA 2344)
UFO: *Lights Out* (Chrysalis 1127); *Phenomenon* (Chrysalis 1059); *Strangers in the Night* (Chrysalis 1209)
Def Leppard: *On Through the Night* (Mercury SRM 1-3828)
Motorhead: *Ace of Spades* (SRM 1 4011); *No Sleep 'Til Hammersmith* (Mercury SRM 1-4023)
Humble Pie: *Smokin'* (A&M SP 3132); *Eat It* (A&M SP 3701)
Styx: *Best of . . .* (RCA AQLI 3597)*; *The Grand Illusion* (A&M 4637)
Nazareth: *Hot Tracks* (A&M 4643)

American

Mountain: *Best of* (Columbia PC 32079)*
Z.Z. Top: *Best of . . .* (Warner Brothers 3273); *El Loco* (Warner Brothers BSK 3593)

Grand Funk Railroad: *On Time* (Capitol SN 16178); *Survival* (Capitol SW 764); *We're an American Band* (Capitol 91207)

Heart: *Babele Strange* (Epic FE 36371); *Dog and Butterfly* (Portrait FE 35553); *Dreamboat Annie* (Mushroom MRS 5005) Canadian import; *Little Queen* (Portrait 34799)

Ted Nugent: *Best of* (Epic 37667)*

Aerosmith: *Greatest Hits* (Columbia FC 36865)

Journey: *Escape* (Columbia TC 37408); *Infinity* (Columbia JC 34912); *Departure* (Columbia FC 36339)

Boston: *Boston* (Epic HE 44188)

Blue Oyster Cult: *Agents of Fortune* (Columbia PC 34164); *Cultosaurus Erectus* (Columbia JC 36550)

Pet Benatar: *Precious Time* (Chrysalis CYS 1346); *Crimes of Passion* (Chrysalis CYS 2175); *Heat of the Night* (Chrysalis 1236)

Van Halen: *Van Halen:* (Warner Brothers BSK 3075); *II* (Warner Brothers HS 3312)*; *Women and Children First* (Warner Brothers HS 3415)

REO Speedwagon: *Nine Lives* (Epic 35988); *Hi Infidelity* (Epic 36844); *A Decade of Rock and Roll* (Epic 36444)

Pat Travers: *Go for What You Know* (Polydor PD 1.6202)

Black Oak Arkansas: *Best of* (ACO 36-150)

Iron Maiden: *Maiden Japan* (Harvest MLP 15000)

Kansas: *Left Overture* (Kirschner HZ 34224); *Two for the Show* (PZ 2 35660)

Johnny Winter: *Johnny Winter* (Columbia CS 9826); *Second Winter* (Columbia KCS 9947)

J. Geils Band: *Best of* (Atco 19234); *Freeze Frame* (Atlantic EMI 500-17062)*; *Love Stinks* (Atlantic EIA 500-17016)

Sammy Hagar: *Live* (Capitol SMAS 11812)

Rick Derringer: *All American Boy* (Warner Brothers BSK PZ 32481)

Cheap Trick: *At Budokan* (Epic JE 35795)*

Kiss: *Dynasty* (Casa Blanca NBLP 7152)

Todd Rundgren: *Something/Anything?* (Warner Brother 2BX 2066)*; *Utopia* (Bearsville BR 6965); *Back to the Bars* (Bearsville 2BRX 6986)

Others

Hemispheres: *Hemispheres* (Mercury SRM 1-3743); *Exit Stage Left* (Mercury SRM 2-7001)

Rush: *2112 (Mercury SRM 1-1079); Moving Pictures* (Mercury SRM 1-4013); *All the World's a Stage* (SRM 2-7508)

AC/DC: *High Voltage* (Atco 36-142); *Highway to Hell* (Atco 19244)*

Scorpians: *Best of* (RCA AFLI 3516)

Bachman Turner Overdrive: *Best of* (Mercury SRM 696)

Angel City: *Face to Face* (Epic NJE 36344)

Anthology: *Heavy Metal* (Asylum DP 90004)

GLAM OR GLITTER ROCK

Theatrical and/or affected, often music of the "sexual underground." Sequins, face paint, and the like. Very important in the United Kingdom and Japan. Largely a "singles" market. Some lp's:

David Bowie (nee Jones): *Rise and Fall of Ziggy Stardust* (RCA AYLI 3843)*; *Diamond Dogs* (RCA AYLI 3889); *Aladdin Sane* (RCA AYLI 3890); *Young Americans* (RCA AFLI 099); *Station to Station* (RCA AFLI 1327)

Lou Reed: *Transformer* (RCA AYLI 3806); *Rock 'n' Roll Animal* (RCA AYLI 3664); *Walk on the Wild Side* (Best of) (RCA AYLI 3753)*

T-Rex: *Electric Warrior* (Reprise 6466)*; *Shider* (Reprise 2095)

The Stooges: *The Stooges* (Elektra 6E 7095) Canadian import

Bebop Delux: *Singles Album* (EMI SHSM 2034)

ART ROCK

Yaas . . . the music for "serious" rock afficianados.

King Crimson: *In the Court of the Crimson King* (Atlantic SD 19155)*; *In the Wake of Poseidon* (Atlantic SD 8266); *Larks' Tongues in Aspic* (Atlantic SD 7263)

Fripp and Eno: *No Pussyfooting* (EGS 102)

Robert Fripp: *Exposure* (Polydor PD-1-6201); *God Save the Queen* (Polydor PD-1-6266); *League of Gentlemen* (Polydor PD-1-6317)

Brian Eno: *Another Green World* (Islan 9351); *Here Come the Warm Jets* (Island 9268)*; *Music for Airports*

Gentle Giant: *Three Friends* (Columbia 31649); *Octopus* (Columbia 32022)

Jade Warrior: *Waves* (Island ILPS 9318)*

Pink Floyd: *Dark Side of the Moon* (Harvest 11163)*; *The Wall* (Columbia PC 2 36183); *Wish You Were Here* (Columbia 33453)

Roxy Music: *Roxy Music* (Atco 36–133); *For Your Pleasure* (Atco 36-134)*; *Country Life* (Atco 36-106A); *Stranded* (Atco 7045); *Greatest Hits* (Atco 36-103); *Siren* (Atco 36-127); *Manifesto* (Atco 38-114)

Emerson: Lake and Palmer: *Best of* (Atco 19283); *Pictures at an Exhibition* (Atco 19122); *Tarkus* (Atco 19123); *Trilogy* (Atco 19123)

Mike Oldfield: *Tubular Bells* (Epic 34116)*

Yes: *Classic* (Atlantic SD 19320)*; *The Yes Album* (Atlantic SD-19131)

Rick Wakeman: *The Six Wives of Henry VIII* (A&M 4361)

Jean Michel Jarre: *Oxygene* (Polydor PD-1-6112)

JAZZ/FUSION

Rock music influencing jazz, rather than the other way around.

Miles Davis: *In a Silent Way* (Columbia PC-9857); *Bitches Brew* (Columbia P6 26)

Deodato: *2001* (CTI 7081)

Stanley Clarke: *School Days* (Epic 36975)

Spyrogyra: *Morning Dance* (MCA 37148)

Herbie Hancock: *Headhunters* (Columbia PC 32731)*; *Mr. Hands* (Columbia JC 36578); *Thrust* (Columbia PC 32965)*; *Feets Don't Fail Me Now* (Columbia JC 35764)

Mahavishnu Orchestra: *Best of . . .* (Columbia JC 36394); *Birds of Fire* (Columbia PC 31996); *Between Nothingness and Eternity* (Columbia 32766); *Inner Mounting Flame* (Columbia PC 31067)*

Jan Hammer: *Live with Jeff Beck* (Epic PE 34433)
Jeff Beck: *Blow by Blow* (Epic 43409)
Weather Report: *Weather Report* (Columbia PC 30661); *Mysterious Traveler* (Columbia 32494)*; *Sweetnighter* (Columbia 32210); *Heavy Weather* Columbia 34418); untitled (Columbia 37616)*
Chick Corea and/or Return Forever: *Hymn of the 7th Galaxy* (Polygram 5536)
Crusaders: *Street Life* (MCA 3094)*
"Disco" jazz!
Jeff Lorber Fusion: *Fusion* (Inner City 1026)*
Larry Coryell: *11th House* (Vanguard 79342)
Jean-Luc Ponty: *Upon the Wings of Music* (Atlanta SD 18138); *Imaginary Voyage* (Atlanta 19136)
Defunkt: *Defunkt* (Hannibal HNBL 1301); *Razor's Edge* (Hannibal HNS 31201)
James "Blood" Ulmer: *Tales of Captain Black* (Artists House AH 9407); *Are You Glad to Be in America?* (Rough Trade 16); *Free Lancing* (CBS ARC 37493)*
Non-tempered funk. All instruments carry melody and rhythm. Key relatively unimportant. Very vital sounds, especially live.

LATER SOUL, DISCO, AND FUNK

Later Soul

Similar to Soul of the 1960s. These are the sons and daughters of the "blues preachers."
O.V. Wright: *Into Something* (Hi HLP 6001)*
Johnny Taylor: *Chronicle* (Stax STX 88901)*
Shirley Brown: *Woman to Woman* (Stax 1000)
Staple Singers: *Chronicle* (Stax 4119)*
Al Green: *Let's Stay Together* (Hi 8007)*; *Greatest Hits, vol. 1 & 2* (Hi 32089 & 32105)*
Neville Brothers: *Fiyo on the Bayou* (A&M SP 4866)
Johnny Nash: *I Can See Clearly Now* (Epic KE 31607)
Earth, Wind and Fire: *Best of . . .* (Columbia FC 35647)*; *Gratitude* (Columbia PG 33694)
Emotions: *Flowers* (Columbia PC 34163)
Gladys Knight and the Pips: *Greatest Hits* (Buddah 5653)
Raydio: *(Arista AB 4163)*
Ohio Players: *Fire* (Mercury SRM-1-1013); *Gold* (Mercury SRM-1-1122)
Kool and the Gang: *Greatest Hits* (Delite DEP 2015); *Ladies' Night* (Delite DSR 9513)
Rose Royce: *Greatest Hits* (Warner Brothers WHK 3457)
Post-Motown Norman Whitfield production.
Chaka Khan: *Whatcha Gonna Do* (Warner Brothers HS 3526)*
Labelle: *Nightbirds* (Epic 33075)

The Sound of Philadelphia

O'Jays: *Live in London* (Philadelphia International KZ 32953)
Harold Melvin and the Blue Notes: *Wake Up Everybody* (Phil. Int. PZ 33808)*; *Greatest Hits* (Phil. Int. 34232)
Lou Rauls: *Unmistakeably Lou* (Philadelphia International PZ 34488)

Later Motown

Commodores: *Greatest Hits* (Motown 7-912R1)*
Smokey Robinson: *A Quiet Storm* (Motown M5-19741); *Love Breeze* (Motown M5-23041); *Being With You* (Tamala T8-375M1)
Stevie Wonder: all lp's, but especially: *Talking Book* (Sire T7-319-R1)*; *Inner Visions* (Tamala T326V1); *Songs in the Key of Life* (Tamala 13-34062)*; *Hotter Than July* (Tamala T8-373M1)*
Four Tops: *Tonight* (Casblanca NBLP 7258))
Marvin Gaye: *Let's Get It On* (Motown M5-19241)
Diana Ross: *Diana* (Motown M8-936M1)

Others

Doctor Buzzard's Original Savannah Band: *Doctor Buzzard's . . .* (RCA AYLI 3767)*; *Goes to Washington* (Elektra 6E 218)*
Kid Creole: *Fresh Fruit in Foreign Places* (Sire 3534)
Pointer Sisters: *Their Fabulous Recordings* (MCA 3275)
Teddy Prendergrass: *TP* (Phil. Int. 36745)
Chic: *Greatest Hits* (Atlantic SD 16011)*
T.S. Monk: *House of Music* (Mirage 19291)
Luther Vandeross: *Never Too Much* (Epic 37451)*
Bill Withers: *Best of . . .* (Columbia JC 36877)*
Isley Brothers: *3 + 3* (Columbia PZ 32453); *Forever Gold* (T-Neck PZ 34452)*
Anthologies: *20/20* (Motown M9-937)*; *Motown Story* (Motown M9-726)*; *Seize the Beat* (Island IL 9667)*

Rapping

Rapping started a thousand years ago. Very popular these days, especially around the "Sugar Hill" area in Harlem.
Millie Jackson: *Live and Uncensored* (Spring/Polydor SP-2-6725); *Feelin' Bitchy* (Spring/Polydor SP-1-6715)*
Kurtis Blow: *The Breaks* (Mercury diso 12" 4010)*
Sugarhill Gang: *Sugarhill Gang* (Sugarhill 245)
Grandmaster Flash: *Freedom* (Sugarhill disco 12" 549)*
Greatest Rap Hits, vol. 1 & 2 (Sugarhill 240 & 262)

Disco

Disco was the rage of the late 1970s, signaling a return to dance.
Bee Gees: *Greatest* (RSO 2-4200)
Donna Summer: *On the Radio* (Casablanca NBLP-2-7191)
Barry White: *Greatest Hits* (20th Century T-493)
Odyssey: *Hang Together* (RCA Victor AFLO 3526)

Sylvester: *Step II* (Fantasy F-9556); *Too Hot to Sleep* (Fantasy/Honey Bee F 9607)
Gloria Gaynor: *Love Tracks* (Polydor PD-1-6184)
Thelma Houston: *Thelma Houston* (Motown M5-120); *Any Way You Like It* (Motown M5 22641)
Jacksons: *Destiny* (Epic JE 35552)*
Michael Jackson: *Off the Wall* (Epic FE 35745)
Village People: *Village People* (Casablanca NBLP 7064); *Cruisin'* (Casablanca NBLP 7118)
Anthologies: *Saturday Night Fever* (RSO 2-4001)*; *Steppin' Out* (Midsong BKLI 2423)

Funk

Funk is the sound of the sidewalk. It's as hot as the sunlight hitting the sidewalk and as hard as the pavement. Thick and rich with bubbling synthesizers and popping bass, it's, you know, funky.

James Brown: *Revolution of the Mind* (Polydor 25-3003)*; *Hot Pants* (Polydor PD 4054)*
Graham Central Station: *My Radio Sure Sounds Good to Me* (Warner Brothers K-3175)
All their early lp's are out of print. Come on Warner Brothers! Leader Larry Graham, ex-member of Sly and the Family Stone, is father of the "popping bass."
Funkadelic: *One Nation Under a Groove* (Warner Brothers K 3209)*; *Uncle Jam* (Warner Brothers K 3371; *The Electric Spanking of War Babies* (Warner Brothers BSK 3482)*
"Concept funk." Leader George Clinton a very important figure, inventor of the bop gun.
Bootsy's Rubber Band: *Player of the Year* (Warner Brothers K 3093); *Aah . . . The Name is Bootsy, Baby* (Warner Brothers B 2972)*
Brothers Johnson: *Look Out for #1* (A&M 4567)*; *Right on Time* (A&M 4644)
Stanley Clarke: *I Wanna Play for You* (Nemporer K22-35680)*
Johnny "Guitar" Watson: *Funk Beyond the Call of Duty* (DJM 714)
Lakeside: *Fantastic Voyage* (RCA/Solar BXLI 3720)*
Roger: *The Many Facets of Roger* (Warner Brothers 3594)
Godmomma: *Here* (Elektra SE 552)

Punk/Funk

Rock meets Soul, and that's not so common these days.
Rick James: *Garden of Love* (Gordy 68-995); *Street Songs* (Gordy 8-1002)*
Prince: *Controversy* (Warner Brothers 3601)
Was/Not Was: *Was/Not Was* (Island ILPS 9666)*

PUNK

Razor-blade rock. Very aggressive, unfettered, iconoclastic, intense. Misanthropic, but fun.

United Kingdom:

Sex Pistols: *Never Mind the Bullocks Here's the . . .* (Warner Brothers 3147)
Public Image Limited: *The Flowers of Romance* (Warner Brothers BSK 3536); *2nd Edition* (Warner Brothers/Island 2WX 3288)*

Clash: *The Clash* (Epic 36060)*; *Black Market* (Epic 4E 36846)*; *London Calling* (Epic E 36328)* *Sandinista* (Epic E3X 37037)
Damned: *Black Album* (IRS 70012)
Joy Division: *Still* (Factory 40)* U.K. import; *Closer* (Factory 6) U.K. import
Vibrators: *Permanent Wave* (Epic JE 36136)
Stiff Little Fingers: *Go for It* (Chrysalis CHR 1339)
Buzzcocks: *Different Kind of Tension* (IRS 009)
Slits: *Return of the Giant* (CBS 85269) U.K. import

U.S.A.

Patti Smith: *Horse* (Arista 4066); *Wave* (Arista AB4221); *Easter* (Arista AB 4171)
Ramones: *The Ramones* (Sire SR 6020); *Rocket to Russia* (Sire SR 6042)*; *Leave Home* (Sire 6031)
Dead Kennedys: *Fresh Fruit for Rotting Vegetables* (IRS 70014)
Plasmatics: *Metal Priestess* (Stiff WOW 666)
DMZ: *DMZ* (Bomp VOXX 200.004)
Wipers: *The Youth of America* (Park Avenue 82802)
Shaggs: *Philosophy of the World* (Rounder 3032)
Anthologies: *IRS Greatest Hits* vol 1 & 2/3 (IRS 501 & 70800)

NEW WAVE

British

Squeeze: *Argybargy* (A&M SP 4802)*; *East Side Story* (A&M 4854)*
Joe Jackson: *I'm the Man* (A&M SP 4794); *Look Sharp* (A&M 4743)
The Police: *Zenyatta Mondatta* (A&M 3720)*; *Ghost in the Machine* (A&M 3730); *Outlindos D'Mour* (A&M 4753); *Reggatta DeBlac* (A&M 4792)*
XTC: *Drums and Wires* (Virgin 13134)*
Siouxsie and the Banshees: *Siouxsie and the Banshees* (PVC PVC 8906)
Elvis Costello (nee Declan McManus): *My Aim is True* (Columbia JC 35037)*; *This Year's Model* (Columbis JC 35331)*; *Armed Forces* (Columbia 35709)*; *Almost Blue* (Columbia FC 37562)
Adam and the Ants: *Kings of the Wild Frontier* (Epic JE 37033); *Prince Charming* (Epic ARE 37615)
Jam: *All Mod Cons* (Polydor 1-6188)
Dave Edmunds: *Get It!* (Swan Song 8418)*
Nick Lowe: *Pure Pop for Now People* (Columbia 35329)
Pretenders: *The Pretenders* (Sire SRK 6083)*; *II* (Sire SRK 3572)
Peter Gabriel: *Peter Gabriel* (Mercury SRM 1-3848)*

American

Talking Heads: *77* (Sire 6036)*; *More Songs About Buildings and Food* (Sire 6058); *Remain in Light* (Sire SRK 6095)*

Pearl Harbor and the Explosions: *Pearl Harbor and . . .* (Warner Brothers 3404)
Joan Jett: *I Love Rock 'n' Roll* (Boardwalk NBI 33243)
Gang of Four: *Entertainment* (Warner Brothers 3446)
Television: *Marquee Moon* (Elektra 7E 1098)
Johnathan Richman: *The Original Modern Lovers* (Bomp 4021)
The Lounge Lizards: *The Lounge Lizards* (EG Records EGS 108)
The Tubes: *The Tubes* (A&M 4534); *Remote Control* (A&M 4751); *What Do You Want from . . .* (A&M 6003)*
Blondie: *Blondie* (Chrysalis CHR 1165); *Best of . . .* (Chrysalis 1337); *Parallel Lines* (Chrysalis CHE 1192)
Debbie Harry: *Koo Koo* (Chrysalis C4S 1347)
Devo: *Q: Are We Not Men?* (Warner Brothers K 3239); *Freedom of Choice* (Warner Brothers BSR 3435)
Grace Jones: *Warm Leatherette* (Island ISL 9592); *Nightclubbing* (Island ISL 9624); *Portfolio* (Island ILPS 9470)
Lydia Lunch: *Queen of Siam* (Celluloid 6561)*
Cars: *The Cars* (Elektra 6E-135)
Go-Go's: *Beauty and the Beat* (IRS 70021)
B-52's: *B-52's* (Warner Brothers BSK 3355); *Wild Planet* (Warner Brothers BSK 3471)
Rachel Sweet: *Fool Around* (Columbia JC 36101); *Protect the Innocent* (Stiff JC 36337); *And Then He Kissed Me* (Columbia ARC 37077)
Pere Ubu: *Art of Walking* (Rough Trade 4); *Modern Dance* (Rough Trade 7)
Magazine: *Play* (IRS 70015)
Residents: *Mask of the Mole* (Ralph 81527); *Fingerprince* (Ralph 1276)
Anthologies: *Live at CBGB's* (Atlantic SD 2 508)

REGGAE

There's no more to Reggae than meets the I. Toasts, shanks, versions, riddims, ska, sound systems, blues dances, rockers, rub a dub, one drop, rock steady, sufferers style, NYAHBINGHI. . . . It's hard enough for a natty dread to keep up much less a baldhead!

Since the early 1960s—remember "My Boy Lolipop" by Millie Small?—Jamaican music has played an enormous role in the internationalization of rock. It has profoundly influenced and been influenced by American, British, even African music. Reggae was always going to be the next big thing in rock.. In 1970, "Israelites" by Desmond Decker sparked speculation; in the mid-1970s Bob Marley inspired many imitators who may or may not have known they were playing rebel music. Now in the early 1980s New York and London are becoming reggae capitals. Dennis Brown and Black Uhuru are touring abroad, producers such as Lee Perry and Mickey Dread are working with rock bands and everybody's talking again. Jah Appleseed strikes again!

This list is only a springboard. Reggae is largely a singles market, and singles are usually pressed in very small quantity. I rely almost exclusively on albums; they're hard enough to find! Reggae changes like the weather. In order to keep current read:

Black Music
153 Praed Street
London W2, England
which covers contemporary soul, reggae and popular jazz.

Reggae Roots

SKA

The off-beat, jazz-imbued Caribbean dance music of the early 1960s. Though derivative of New Orleans rhythm and blues, it is very unique. Currently "the Bluebeat" is being revived in the U.K.
Intensified vol. 2. (Island MLPS 9597)*
Excellent anthology, includes most of the stars and such songs as the phenomenal "6 and 7 Books" by a very young Toots and the Maytals.
The Skatalites: *Best of* (Studio One—no number)
All instrumental. A very popular combo featuring guitarist Ernest Ranglin.
Don Drummond: *In Memory of* (Studio One—no number)*; *100 Years After* (Studio One SOL 1114)*
Legendary trombonist, highly regarded by world jazz community..
Prince Buster: *Fabulous Greatest Hits* (Melodisc MS-1)*
Early "talk over" artist. A major force in the mid-1960s.

ROCK STEADY

Where ska tended to be frantic and very jazzy with a full horn section predominating, rock steady was slow and soulful. The bass began to stand out instead of up, and for the first time singers were more important than bands.
Hottest Hits vol. 1 (Front Line 1034)*
Late 1960s hits from the Treasure Isle label. Includes the original "Tide is Hide" by the Paragons and "Cry Tough" by Alton Ellis.
From Bam Bam to Cherry Oh Baby (Trojan TRLS 51)*
Excellent rock steady and early reggae collection. Includes the original "Cherry Oh Baby" by Eric Donaldson and other Jamaican song festival winners.

REGGAE

Emphasis on rock-related material. Although this list may seem long, it is actually an abridged version. It's unbelievable how many records come out of Jamaica every year. And the F.D.A. says ganja makes you lazy!
Bob Marley and/or the Wailers: all lp's except most posthumorous "R.I.P. offs" Most important lps: *African Herbsman* (Trojan TRLS 62)*; *Burnin'* (Island ILPS 9256)*; *Natty Dread* (Island 9281)*; *Rastaman Vibration* (Island 9383)*; *Exodus* (Island 9498)*; *Survival* (Island 9542)*
Peter Tosh: *Equal Rights* (Columbia PC 34670)*
Militant original Wailer.
Bunny Wailer: *Blackheart Man* (Island MLPS 9415)*; *Sings the Wailer* (Mango MLPS 9629)
Mystical, original Wailer. Bunny (nee Neville Livington) is a consistent singer, writer, and producer. These two albums represent his stylistic extremes.
Toots and the Maytals: *Best of* (Trojan 171)
For twenty years the undisputed kings of hard gospel-flavored reggae.
Jimmy Cliff: *Wonderful World, Beautiful People* (A&M 4251)
A gifted singer, writer, and producer, Cliff's international following is huge.

Gregory Isaacs: *Cool Ruler* (Virgin Front Line FL 1020); *Mister Isaacs* (Micron 009) Canadian import

Smooth one-octave crooning. Best on the planet. Warning to feminists: lyrics occasionally sexist, even for reggae, which is extremely "old fashioned" about that kind of thing.

Burning Spear: *Marcus Garvey* (Island ILSP 9377)****; *Studio One Presents* (Studio One SOLP 0150)

Spear (nee Winston Rodney) is proudly assertive of his Black roots. One of the earliest people to sing about Marcus Garvey and write songs about Africa as if he were there instead of merely wanting to go.

Linton Kwesi Johnson: *Forces of Victory* (Mango MLPS 9566)

Social minded poet who chants in a not quite singing, not quite toasting manner. Very political.

Aswad: *Showcase* (Grove/Island ASWAD-1)

Reggae spawned in the United Kingdom, as is Johnson.

Yabby You: *Ramadam* (D.L. International—no number)* U.K. import; *Deliver Me from My Enemies* (Grove GMLP 001) U.K. import Much "Jah music" is Biblical in tone and lyrical allusion. Vivian Jackson (a.k.a. Yabby You) sings with the power of an Old Testament prophet. Superb.

Dennis Brown: *Wolf and Leopard* (D.E.B. MOLP 01)

Very popular and influential. Started at age twelve! One of Bob Marley's favorites.

The Mighty Diamonds: *Right Time* (Virgin V-2052)*

Very militant. An important early "rockers style" lp.

The Congos: *Heart of the Congos* (Black Art—no number) Jamaican import also available on the U.K. Go Feet! label.

Dense atmospheric Rasta record produced by Lee Perry. Features the brilliant falsetto singing of Cedric Myton. A great record to get red with.

Horace Andy: *Skylarkin'* (Studio One SOL 1116)

Andy has been a major influence on later high-voiced singers such as Barrington Levy, Hugh Mundell, Madoo, Tristan Palmer, Ranking Scroo, Badoo.

Black Uhuru: *Vital Selection* (Virgin VX 1004)*; *Red* (Island ILPS 9625)*

Remember Lt. Uhuru in *Star Trek*? No relation. Uhuru means freedom in Swahili. Very militant, modern, and popular vocal trio. Includes female singer Puma Jones, a rarity, as not too much reggae on the distaff side.

Rita Marley: *Who Feels It?* (Shanachie 43003)

The Abysinnians: *SATTA* (Azul 2000)* Canadian import

Essential listening. Uncompromising Rasta trio responsible for the marvelous "Satta a Masagana," practically the "anthem" of the whole movement.

Shaggs: *Philosophy of the World* (Rounder)

Vibrators: *Permanent Wave* (Epic JE 36136)

Stiff Little Fingers: *Go for It* (Chrysalis CHR 1339)

Buzzcocks: *Different Kind of Tension* (IRS 009)

Slits: *Return of the Giant* (CBS 85269) U.K. import

Anthologies

The Harder they Come (Mango MLPS 9202))*****

Both the film and its soundtrack are cult classics.

Rockers (Mango MLOPS 9587)*
Another excellent soundtrack. Unfortunately it does not contain all the music from this entertaining film.

Creation Rockers, vol. 1–6 (Trojan TRLS 180-185)* U.K. import
Six-lp collection, each volume starts with ska and ends in rockers style.

Monkey Business (Trojan TRLS 188)*****
If you want to buy only one reggae anthology, get this one (and *The Harder The Come*, and *Rockers*, and *Pirates Choice*.)

Pirates Choice (Studio One SOLP 0666)*
Marvelous Studio One anthology. Includes some great rare material.

DEE-JAY

Talking over music is a refined art in Jam Down. Many "dee jays" are big stars. Since the early 1960s most, if not all, singles have featured instrumental versions on the flip side. This way the dee jays, many of whom work for the sound systems, can take any song and turn it into a toast. In fact, anyone who buys the single can! Many Jamacian songs are made using the same instrumental backing track, now called a "riddim."

Big Youth: *Everyday Skank/the Best of Big Youth* (Trojan TRLS 189)*
For a while in the late 1970s Jah Youth (nee Marley Bucchan) was the biggest thing in reggae. But toasting is like boxing, no one stays on the top forever. A very competitive field.

Mickey Dread: *Dread at the Controls* (Trojan TRLS 178)
Very popular in the U.K. Mr. Campbell has worked extensively with the Clash.

Poppa Michigan and General Smilie: *Rub-a-Dub Style* (Studio One-no number)*
The first, and some say the best, "tag team" toaster unit. Big in the early 1980s. The Studio One riddims, although often quite old, always sound fresh.

Client Eastwood and General Saint: *Two Bad D.J.* (Greensleeves DREL 24)
Most popular duo on the toasting circuit. Excellent record, often hilarious.. Infectuous riddims.

Lone Ranger: *On the Other Side of Dub* (Studio One SOL 5454)*; *Rose Marie* (Techniques-no number)*
Most popular 1980s style dee jay. Very original. Combines toasting and singing. Rrright?

General Echo: *Rocking and Swing* (DRS LP-001)*
Superb young toaster brutally murdered by the police. Revolutionized the style with this lp.

P.S. (PERSONAL STATEMENT)

This being the age of one-quarter truth, I expect that I have made some errors, omissions, and outrageous distortions for which I apologize. However, if a writer's enthusiasm really can inspire a reader's interest, then maybe you will pick up where I put my pencil down. Feel free. In a field like this there is always room for another party.

Speaking of parties, I'm sure we'll have one to celebrate the long-awaited publication of this might tome. To it I will be sure to personally invite the following friends who helped yours truly keep on pushing:

Beth Murphy and various other Murphies, Daniel the Lion, Jah Henry Lee, George Bigley, Jack Cook, the old folks at Downtown, Tower Records (HRS-97 QARS-85), Mom and Pops, Kailas Hanatani, Prince Asaf, Frank Beach, Devika Follasco, my typist, Archie the cockroach, Mehitebel, El Stimler and Lew Rothstein, the new king of Western Bop.

To all my friends both met and unmet, I offer a warm Maholo and Aloha Yer Pal Manu

Index

SONG/ALBUM TITLE INDEX